"We are moving into a new era of urban life, an era in which the poor and rich alike live in both the city and the suburbs. To meet the new challenges, God is calling us back to biblical community to serve and to testify. *Linking Arms, Linking Lives* is the cutting edge of this movement. Taken seriously, this book will redefine ministry. This work, with sensitivity and insight, exposes what nearly always lies beneath the surface of urban-suburban partnership attempts. The authors, all experienced and field-tested leaders, not only show us why we need biblical community, but *how*. This is a field guide like none other, a book for Christians everywhere to read and carry with them."

Michael O. Emerson, Allyn & Gladys Cline Professor of Sociology; founding director, Center on Race, Religion, and Urban Life, Rice University; author, *Divided by Faith*, *United by Faith*, *Against All Odds*, and *People of the Dream*

"This book has teeth on it—not just vision but the tools to build the vision. *Linking Arms, Linking Lives* is a beautiful invitation to bust out of the ghettos of wealth and poverty and reimagine the world together. The voices that created this book are contemporary heroes of the faith whose experiences bring their words to life. May it move us closer to God's dream for our neighborhoods and world."

Shane Claiborne, author, activist, and recovering sinner, www.thesimpleway.org

"*Linking Arms, Linking Lives* informs the Christian church on why and how we should speak to each other. It is a biblically based, practical approach to how we can unite urban and suburban Christians under Christ's lordship to do ministry."

Luis Cortés Jr., president, Esperanza

"The geography and demography of America's urban-suburban world is changing rapidly. The suburban better-off are living closer geographically to the urban poor than ever before but are also more completely separated from their poor neighbors. This separation is affecting the church, as it tends to be the church of one group or the other, but seldom of both at the same time. Being separated impoverishes both sides and undermines the ability of local churches to deal with issues of poverty, racism, and injustice.

"This book is a call to partnership, to seeking out and becoming neighbors across the urban-suburban divide. Written by four giants in the evangelical engagement with the poor in the city over the last forty years, this book provides the biblical insights and practical wisdom any congregation can use to become living witnesses to the whole gospel of Jesus Christ."

Bryant L. Myers, professor of international development,
School of Intercultural Studies, Fuller Theological Seminary

"*Linking Arms, Linking Lives* offers compelling reasons, comprehensive guidance, and relevant practices for implementing urban-suburban partnerships in the twenty-first century. The experience and wisdom of these veterans of community ministry combined with a treasure trove of contemporary examples makes this book a resource-rich gift. I highly recommend it!"

Curtiss Paul DeYoung, professor of reconciliation studies,
Bethel University

"The vast changes taking place in the city require that the church discover new ways of seeing urban mission and develop new strategies, new partnerships, and a host of new leaders to carry it out. This book has its finger on the pulse of the new global city, and every practitioner committed to God's work there will love it."

Randy White, national coordinator for urban projects,
InterVarsity Christian Fellowship

Linking Arms,
Linking Lives

Linking Arms, Linking Lives

How Urban-Suburban Partnerships
Can Transform Communities

RONALD J. SIDER • JOHN M. PERKINS
WAYNE L. GORDON • F. ALBERT TIZON

BakerBooks

a division of Baker Publishing Group
Grand Rapids, Michigan

© 2008 by Ronald J. Sider, John M. Perkins, Wayne L. Gordon, and F. Albert Tizon

Published by Baker Books
a division of Baker Publishing Group
P.O. Box 6287, Grand Rapids, MI 49516-6287
www.bakerbooks.com

Printed in the United States of America

Library of Congress Cataloging-in-Publication Data
Linking arms, linking lives : how urban-suburban partnerships can transform communities / Ronald J. Sider . . . [et al.].
    p. cm.
    Includes bibliographical references (p.   ).
    ISBN 978-0-8010-7083-9 (pbk.)
    1. Church work. 2. Church and social problems. 3. City churches. 4. Suburban churches. I. Sider, Ronald J.
    BV4400.L56 2008
    253.09173—dc22
                                                  2008024302

In keeping with biblical principles of creation stewardship, Baker Publishing Group advocates the responsible use of our natural resources. As a member of the Green Press Initiative, our company uses recycled paper when possible. The text paper of this book is comprised of 30% post-consumer waste.

Contents

Acknowledgments

This book testifies to its very subject—partnership. It could not have been written without the many partners who made it possible, the most obvious being the partnership between the four authors. What you have in your hands is a book that took several years of face-to-face meetings, conference calls, and email correspondence between Wayne Gordon, John Perkins, Ron Sider, and Al Tizon, sharing their experiences and stories of partnership with one another. The fact that one of us pastors an active growing church (Wayne), and the others teach seminary courses (Ron and Al), run non-profit organizations (John and Ron), and fly about the country speaking here and there (all of us), this project could have easily been relegated to the back burner. But the importance of understanding effective ministry partnership for the twenty-first century compelled us to press on.

John, Ron, and Wayne agreed on the approach, outline, and basic content via emails and conference calls. Al then spent considerable time talking face-to-face with each of the three as well as doing other research for the book. He then wrote the first draft of the book and carefully incorporated the others' suggested edits. John, Ron, and Wayne gratefully acknowledge Al's central role as the person who wrote this book. But Al acknowledges in turn that he could not have done it without the other three, because they provided much of the raw data for the book from their vast and varied ministry experiences.

So if any oversights, gaping holes, or glaring mistakes exist, blame should go to all four!

As the authors of this book, we want to thank the many practitioners, churches, organizations, and businesses that were willing to share their experiences of ministry partnerships across the urban-suburban divide. They are the ultimate heroes in this story. If this book manages to inspire others to serve the poor via urban-suburban partnership, the credit goes collectively to those who go before them. Thanks also to Perry Bigelow, who not only encouraged us to write this book but also gave the necessary financial resources to make it possible. Many thanks go to Helen Davis, a student at Palmer Theological Seminary, who served as special assistant to the project, doing much of the nitty-gritty administrative work, as well as making important editorial suggestions. Bob Hosack at Baker Books demonstrated much patience with us in seeing this project to completion, and for this we also extend our appreciation.

A partnership with which this book does not deal directly, but which certainly underscores all other partnerships, is the one we enjoy with our wives. John and Vera Mae have been married for fifty-seven years, Ron and Arbutus for forty-seven, Wayne and Anne for thirty-one, and Al and Janice for twenty-seven. Together, we represent 162 years of marital and ministry partnership! We dedicate this book to these, our life partners; for without them by our sides, we simply cannot do what we do, preach what we preach, and write what we write.

John M. Perkins, Jackson, MS
Ronald J. Sider, Philadelphia, PA
Wayne Gordon, Chicago, IL
Al Tizon, Upper Darby, PA
February 2008

Foreword

When I arrived in Chicago from San Jose, California, in 1990 to establish a church in the Mexican community of La Villita, the inner city was *the* place to minister. In fact, twenty years ago when most of us thought about ministry to the poor, we thought immediately of the urban centers of our nation. But the winds of change are blowing.

A few years ago at a Christian Community Development Association conference, a well-respected Latino sociologist shared the results of a comprehensive demographic study that he and his colleagues had just conducted with Latinos in the Chicagoland area. I was shocked and admittedly even a bit skeptical when he shared that over 50 percent of all Latinos in Chicago, many of which would be classified as "poor," now live in the suburbs.

I would still be skeptical if I had not been witnessing this shift myself ever since. The *suburbanization of poverty*, as urbanologist Bob Lupton calls it, is real. I never thought the day would come when the poor would be as prevalent in suburbia as they are in urban neighborhoods. But this is reality in the twenty-first century as many poor Latino-Americans, African-Americans, and others are being displaced and pushed out by gentrification and all that comes with that phenomenon.

Such a shift has compelled urban practitioners to rethink some things. For example, we have to redefine *urban ministry*. It is no longer serving in the physical city; instead it is serving the underclass, regardless of where they live. This shift in the distribution of poverty on the urban-suburban landscape has forced us to go not only to the city with the gospel but also to the suburbs.

This shift also affects our view of *partnership* with suburban churches and ministries. Because suburbanites were once *over there*, it was easier to stereotype them as those rich, white folks who were so removed from the "hood" that the only thing they were really good for with regard to urban ministry was their money. "We can tolerate their insensitivity and general ignorance about urban life as long we get that van they promised, get our gym painted, or get their financial support!" Relationships between us were shallow at best. "But that's okay," we reasoned, "because they're so far away." The shift of the poor to the suburbs and of the wealthy to the city has changed all of this. Now we are forced to face each other, get to know each other, and learn to live and work together.

Which brings me closer to the topic of this book on urban-suburban partnerships. It cannot be any more timely because of what's happening on the scene today. Urban and suburban Christians may live closer to each other than ever before, but we still have much to learn about loving each other and working together for the kingdom. This book embodies what seems to be a new wind of the Spirit blowing all around us.

It comes after many years of hurt and frustration on both sides. For years, those of us working on the front lines of ministry among the poor in the city longed for the day when our suburban brothers and sisters would finally *get it*—the day when they would be able to put aside paternalistic tendencies and truly partner with us in serving the poor. Conversely, I have heard the frustrations of suburban workers and volunteers who have taken a leap of faith to get involved with inner-city ministries, offering their time, talent, and money, only to feel pushed away, rejected, and treated with mistrust and suspicion. I am certain that both sides have imagined and prayed for a different kind of relationship in which they experience kingdom partnership— the kind that reflects justice and reconciliation, transforms lives and communities, and glorifies God.

I feel this fresh wind of the Spirit, for example, when well-known pastors with large national followings realize that growing large churches in all-white, middle-class suburban communities is not the final frontier of mission. Some of these pastors of megachurches are talking openly about their own conversions to a more holistic understanding of the gospel, and they have been mobilizing their members to get engaged in hands-on ministries of poverty alleviation and reconciliation.

I also feel this fresh new wind when I am among emerging young leaders who can see past tired old divisions and are more committed to pursuing authentic dialogue with brothers and sisters of every culture and race. Many committed suburban Christians are becoming the new gentry of transitioning urban neighborhoods, bringing with them strong convictions of compassion and justice, and thus forging a different kind of gentrification—gentrification with justice.

From pastors of megachurches to *suburban revolutionaries*, what is needed today is a message of hope that we can truly come together as urban and suburban believers. Is it possible to forge strong relationships across this great divide—relationships that serve and empower the poor in the name of Jesus? The authors of this book think so.

We need guidance from seasoned leaders who can give us biblical and practical insights regarding how to cross the urban-suburban divide for the sake of the kingdom. John Perkins, Ron Sider, Wayne "Coach" Gordon, and Al Tizon are trusted friends who love the Lord, love the poor, love the church, and have invested their lives to being agents of community, justice, and reconciliation. I believe the principles, reflections, and wise counsel contained in this book will provide great encouragement for all of us who recognize that we are living in a new day with new realities and new opportunities.

Noel Castellanos, Chief Executive Officer
Christian Community Development Association
February 2008

Introduction

Personal Words from the Authors

In 1983 at an urban ministry conference in Washington, DC, well-known Pastor E. V. Hill performed a marriage ceremony between urban and suburban churches. The story goes that after Hill finished his presentation on partnership,

> a man [from Richmond, Virginia] raised his hand and said, "I'd like to apply what I've learned here back in my own city. But I don't know anyone there to get started with who is in the inner city" [he represented a suburban group]. Pastor Hill responded by saying, "Well, is anyone else here from Richmond?" And lo and behold, on the other side of the room was a bunch of people from an urban church. And they said, "We're from a city church." So Pastor Hill said, "Well, I'm going to marry you. By the powers vested in me I now pronounce you partners. Go back to your city and minister together."[1]

This "ceremony" is the way the leaders of Strategies to Elevate People (STEP) of Richmond, Virginia, tell their *creation narrative*. As a testimony to the power of this story to inspire Richmond Christians to work together, at the time of this writing STEP enters its twenty fifth year of existence as a facilitator of urban and suburban churches working together to provide spiritual and social services with and for the poor.

This book celebrates this kind of partnership. It features churches, organizations, businesses, and individuals doing holistic ministry together across the *urban-suburban divide*—that great cultural gulf that distances Christians who live, work, and minister in the city from Christians who live, work, and minister in suburbia. We have written this book in order to address this divide partly because we have grown weary of using words like *urban* and *suburban* (which we use quite frequently in our respective vocations) without knowing what they mean anymore! The sociocultural landscape has changed dramatically enough in the last thirty years that these terms have taken on new meanings. So we felt it was time to understand these words afresh in order to keep the ministry of the gospel relevant in the world.

Others use *urban* and *suburban* as well, but unfortunately, these words often draw yet another divisive line between people. Among the lines drawn between male and female, young and old, black and white, rich and poor, conservative and liberal, and so on, there is a thickening line drawn between urban and suburban. On one side of the divide, so the stereotype goes, stand the *urban Christians*: the edgy, socially active, multicultural, radical types who don't think twice about rocking the boat for the sake of change. On the other side stand the *suburban Christians*: the resourced, comfortable, monocultural (read, all-white), upwardly mobile, conservative types who are content to maintain the status quo. But like all stereotypes, such descriptions mix truth with fiction. This book attempts to look beyond these stereotypes and make a case for ministry partnerships that cross the urban-suburban divide for the sake of God's transformational work in the world.

Such a book needed to be written, for the plight of the poor continues to plague our land. In response, many Christian workers have linked arms and lives to minister together, and they have done it by freely crossing the urban-suburban line. From all indications, many more Christians want to do the same. This book seeks to affirm the people already involved in this type of partnership as well as to provide the practical catalyst for those who want to become involved.

It would have been ironic, bordering comical, for a lone author to write a book on partnership. So we decided to collaborate on this project, integrating our own unique perspectives into a shared vision of urban-suburban partnership. Since we will be speaking as a united voice throughout, we thought personal introductory words from each of us would give insight into the personalities that have informed this book.

From Ron Sider, Theologian

I am a farm boy whom God called to the city. For the last forty years my wife, Arbutus, and I have lived in lower-income, interracial sections of Philadelphia—for seven years at Broad and Diamond in North Philadelphia and since 1975 in lower Germantown. For much of that time we have been active in urban churches seeking to develop and expand holistic programs that empower poor, urban people with the help of suburban, small town, and rural partners.

Sometimes the partnerships have been significant and fruitful; sometimes they have been frustrating. I remember dedicated folk from outside the city who donated time, skills, and money in costly, generous ways. I also remember times when our city programs and leaders failed, wasted resources, and discouraged noncity partners. And again and again, I recall the frustration of trying unsuccessfully to find adequate resources for good, urgent urban programs.

I must confess that I sometimes became angry as I thought about the enormous wealth and other resources in suburban congregations and realized that only a small fraction of that abundance could make possible greatly expanded holistic ministries in the city. I know I sometimes succumbed to self-righteous anger at what I felt was *hard-hearted selfishness* on the part of my wealthy suburban brothers and sisters.

But I also know they were sometimes frustrated with mistakes and failures in city programs. I know that all of us deserve some of the blame for the failures. I also know that lots of urban and suburban people want to do it better. I am convinced that effective urban-suburban partnerships are essential for both communities. Good urban programs urgently need outside resources. And rural and suburban congregations desperately need to learn what only inner-city churches can teach.

It is not, however, only our mutual need for each other that moves me. I believe a biblical theology of the church demands such partnership. At the heart of the gospel is the claim that the messianic kingdom long predicted by the prophets has broken decisively into history in the person and work of Jesus. Jesus's new community, the body of Christ, is called to be the visible expression of that new social order in which all the sinful dividing walls between Jew and Gentile, black and white, rich and poor, male and female are now being overcome by the power of the Spirit. Again and again the New Testament makes it clear that economic sharing within the one body of Christ is an essential mark of the church (Acts 2:42–47; 4:32–35; 6:1–7; 1 Cor. 11:20–34; 2 Cor. 8–9). This economic sharing is not an extra that we can ignore or embrace as we choose. It is a nonnegotiable, central theological demand upon anyone who longs to live out a biblical understanding of the church.

For all these reasons, I am enthusiastic about this book.

From John Perkins, Community Organizer and Reconciler

What is going on in the American scene today reminds me of the early days of my seventy-seven years of life and the historic events that occurred in the 1960s and 1970s. I first witnessed the movement from the rural areas to the cities. Then there was a period during which city people moved to the suburbs. Now we are seeing the movement from suburbia back to the city. It is this current movement to the urban context that provides a great opportunity for whole-life discipleship and evangelism. The way urban and suburban Christians interact with each other potentially can be a great example of God's light shining—a city set upon a hill.

The roots of the Christian Community Development Association (CCDA) go back to the time when my wife and I returned to Simpson County, Mississippi, in 1960, around the time the civil rights movement was starting. The civil rights movement and a Christian-based community development movement (which later became CCDA in 1989) ushered in a revolution of change that sparked nationwide interest.

But long before then, we suffered hardships and prejudices in Simpson County, the place I called home. The sharecropping system was in full strength when I was growing up. We worked hard to raise crops, only to give most of it away to farm owners so we could have a place to live. World War II began to bring that period of sharecropping to an end, because the young men, including myself, returned from the war wanting freedom. We sought a better way of life in other communities, other cities. My family joined that search for something better by moving to California.

Some families who had grown up in Christian homes looked to the church for assistance and guidance, but I saw the church as a place of useless emotional release; worse, as an expression of white oppression. I saw the black church as a place established by white folks for us to do what they wanted us to do: to be peaceful and quiet and accept our oppression. I felt that people went to church out of emotion and then went back into their communities and accepted the oppression of whites. But then something remarkable happened: at the age of twenty-seven I became a Christian. My conversion was in a fundamentalist, suburban Bible church movement in the San Gabriel Valley, and there I heard basic biblical teaching.

When I left Mississippi I said I would never go back, but my growing faith in Christ changed my heart and mind. I returned to Mississippi in 1960, and by the following year I found myself in the midst of the civil rights movement. Then Medgar Evers, one of the movement's most outspoken leaders, was killed in 1963, along with three civil rights workers in Philadelphia, Mississippi, who were killed in 1964. I got involved in various other movements, such as the voters' registration movement and the cooperative movement, which sought to improve the quality of life for people in the community.

Then, of course, came Dr. Martin Luther King Jr.'s Poor People's Campaign of 1966–1967, through which he sought a "middle ground between riots on the one hand and timid supplications for justice on the other."[2] His initial plan was for two thousand poor people from all over the country to descend on Washington, DC, to meet with government officials and demand jobs, unemployment insurance, a fair minimum wage, and quality education for poor adults and children. I regret to say that even these many years after his death, outside of the integration of public schools, not much has changed. Even as I look back over my life, what came out of my being beaten in a Brandon jail was the opportunity for blacks to work in stores as clerks, cashiers, and so forth. Undoubtedly, cracks began to develop in the system by virtue of what King and others were doing, but so much more still needs to be done.

I didn't see much connection between the various movements I was involved in and the evangelical church. The white church in the South was still trying to use itself as a pacifying religion—sort of a peacemaker for blacks. For example, when some of us in the black church finally got involved in trying to win our freedom, many white evangelicals lumped us together with communists because we were protesting against the state. We heard the Romans 13 passage recited to us everywhere we went: "Let every soul be subject unto the higher powers. For there is no power but of God: the powers that be are ordained of God. Whosoever therefore resisteth the power, resisteth the ordinance of God: and they that resist shall receive to themselves damnation" (Rom. 13:1–2 KJV). These evangelicals believed their segregated power represented God's power, which made it hard for me to identify with them as brothers in Christ.

So from my experience, I welcome the growing movement of urban-suburban partnerships because it reflects the church as being God's ambassador of reconciliation. We at CCDA must look closer at the urban-suburban relationship and understand and affirm it. We have an opportunity to break down racial barriers, particularly among the poor and marginalized—those who are most neglected.

One of King's strategies in the Poor People's Campaign was to raise the economic issue in order to do something about the economic gap between the rich and the poor. As he reflected on his life and ministry shortly before his death in 1968, King was moving beyond civil rights to working toward *human rights*. He talked about a human rights revolution that would place economic justice at the center. In his book *To the Mountaintop*, Stewart Burns pinpoints that the aim of King's human rights movement was to achieve genuine integration, meaning shared power and genuine equality, a "radical redistribution of economic and political power." Burns goes on to interpret King's human rights aspirations: "There must be a revolution of values. Only by reallocating and redefining power would it be possible to wipe out the triple interlocking evils of racism, exploitation, and militarism."[3]

In order for urban and suburban churches to address the triple evils of racism, exploitation, and militarism addressed by King, they must take a hard look at their own materialism and their own support of militarism. For instance, nobody knows how much the war in Iraq is costing. I have heard the figure five hundred billion dollars thrown around, and some say it is actually going to end up well over a trillion dollars. So that's a trillion dollars taken out of our society that could have been used to improve healthcare, education, social welfare programs, and other desperately needed services among the poor in America.

How are we going to get churches—urban and suburban—to overcome materialism and militarism and to come together for purposes that align more with God's purposes? Perhaps the best picture of what God's church should look like is painted in Acts 4:32–36, where it tells of the followers of Jesus sharing everything in common. There were no needy among them. This is an absolutely remarkable statement because if we reflect on the Jewish society at that time, according to some scholars and depending on where you draw the line, at most only 5 percent of the people were classified as rich. Again, depending on where you draw the line, there were 10 to 15 percent considered middle class. On the other hand, 75 to 85 percent of the people were working poor or dirt poor. But the Spirit of the Lord moved so greatly on these people that the rich voluntarily sold their surplus land and houses. At least for a while, the power of the Spirit so moved God's people that poverty was abolished within the church.

I have come to the conviction that this is the number one evidence of the Holy Spirit at work. The church today must relearn this way, and urban-suburban partnerships can point the way. If the church today applies the economic sharing and mutual caring between rich and poor believers that was recorded in Acts 4, I believe we would be on our way to being the answer to Jesus's prayer that we be one in heart and purpose (John 17).

The massive response from the church in the aftermath of Hurricane Katrina shows that God's people can be galvanized for action in times of crisis. Ironically, however, as some volunteers went to New Orleans to give aid, they passed through the Mississippi Delta, which is the home of both the most fertile soil and the poorest people in the nation. It is a rich land full of poor people! In an article in the October 1989 issue of the *Wall Street Journal*, the Delta was described as "a region that epitomizes the extremes of American wealth and poverty. It is almost unbelievably fertile. . . . It has mansions and big cars and a wealthy gentry. . . . It has county poverty rates that range from 20% to 50%. . . . It has white as well as black poverty."[4] The point is that American Christians are better at responding to crises than they are at addressing the long-term poverty problem in our land. Partnerships that cross the urban-suburban divide can help us with blind spots such as this as we learn from one another the deep-seated needs of our poor communities. We need real partnerships—committed people working together who dare to tackle places like the Mississippi Delta.

If the church together could see that we are ambassadors of reconciliation and understand Paul when he says that the love of Christ compels us, we could really make a difference in society. We, who have come from many different kinds of backgrounds, have experienced the love of Christ, and as a result, we can reach out and embrace those who are different. The apostle Paul understood this better than anyone. As a once-ethnocentric Pharisee, he hated the followers of the Way with a passion. But in God's wonderful, almost humorous way, he saved Paul, called him, and sent him to live out the gospel among the Gentiles. Paul was a reconciler, and we need to be too if we want to change our society. And again, I believe urban-suburban partnerships point the way.

Thank you for allowing me to ramble. All I really wanted to say was that I have experienced adversity—brokenness, poverty, racial hostility, and so forth—and I have experienced the wonderful and profound love of God. God redeemed me and brought me into the kingdom through my white brothers and sisters in California. Then God called me back into the hostility of my birthplace—a place where racism was a way of life. Upon my return, the way I started to become a true reconciler was through a friendship with a local white pastor in Mendenhall. This pastor wanted to work with me, a black man—which was unheard of in that part of the country. The rejection he received from his own congregation for even considering this partnership with me was so severe that he committed suicide. After losing my friend, I began to see how deeply rooted racism was in both church and society. We had taken this wonderful gospel, this love that can burn through racial and cultural barriers and reconcile men and women to God, and had corrupted it by mixing it with American individualism, materialism, and racism.

I believe the church calls us to be that city coming down from God out of heaven, to be reconcilers in this world. I pray this book on urban-suburban partnership can help us along the way to fulfilling this call.

From Wayne Gordon, Pastor

What a privilege it has been for my wife, Anne, and me to have lived and worked for more than thirty years in the inner-city neighborhood of Lawndale, on Chicago's Westside. By living cross-racially and raising our three children—Angela, Andrew, and Austin—here, we have learned much about who God is and what he wants to do in the world. We have considered living as a family in an African-American community as a high calling and a wonderful opportunity. We learned fairly early that we had few answers to questions people were asking and few solutions to problems the community faced. Things began to change, however, when we became listeners to and partners with the people.

Now at the thirty-year mark of the Lawndale Community Church (LCC), of which I have served as senior pastor since its inception, we can see God's handiwork in amazing and remarkable ways. The seed of LCC was planted among a small group of high school students in 1975. Together we nurtured a dream of loving the community and making it a better place in Jesus's name. As we rediscovered God's great commands to love God and love people, we have been linking arms with our neighbors to rebuild a broken community. And God's blessings flowed and indiscriminately touched all of our lives.

I have had the privilege of being mentored by some of the great pioneers of urban ministry such as Ray Bakke, Jim Queen, Bill Leslie, Tom Skinner, and John Perkins. My wife, Anne, joined me in 1977, and it was through her gift of discernment and empathetic spirit that the dream of a church that serves the community holistically became a reality. Anne has been a partner in every respect in the work, and I am thankful to God for her. Our children have been partners as well. Having grown up in Lawndale, they have all developed a heart for the poor, an understanding of the value of working together for the greater good, and a genuine love for the city. We have learned much from them. For example, when our son Andrew was around ten, he posed to me an innocent but jarring question; he said, "Dad, why do you let all these white people come into our neighborhood?" I had to laugh inside because apparently my son didn't think he was white! When I asked what he meant, he said, "They come in and do a little work and think they've done a lot. They really feel good about themselves. But our people end up feeling bad about them when they leave." It was through this exchange that I began to consider that there are right ways and wrong ways for suburban churches to partner with urban churches. One thing is certain: true partnership cannot be paternalistic or demeaning to the people receiving help.

In 1989 John Perkins, Glen Kehrein, Mary Nelson, Spencer Perkins, Bob Lupton, and a few others of us got together and prayerfully decided to form a fellowship that learned together and supported each other in the often grueling work of urban ministry. Our efforts led to the birth of CCDA, a network of organizations, churches, and individuals who are committed to doing ministry in a biblical, holistic manner. We have developed eight key components that define a philosophy of ministry that is built around the conviction that the very people struggling with poverty have within them the solutions to their problems. For kingdom workers, this means developing the art of listening and building upon the peoples' dreams. I believe such a posture is the beginning of true partnership.

In Lawndale, partnership is one of the three Ps by which we practice holistic ministry. The first P stands for *people*—those who live in the neighborhood should be the ones to identify their own needs as well as determine what kind of help is necessary. The second P is *prayer*—we depend on God for guidance and wisdom to use our resources to meet community needs and bring about transformation. The last P is *partnership*—we must go about ministry together in order to solve our problems. In 1 Corinthians 12:26 it says that when one member suffers, we all suffer, which conveys the oneness there is in the body of Christ. When we come together side by side in mutual partnership, we are simply affirming our oneness in Christ for the sake of the community.

In Lawndale we have looked for partners who don't just want to give away food, money, and services but want to join us in helping the underprivileged help themselves. It is about empowerment. In Deuteronomy 24:17–24 and Leviticus 19:9–10 the Law provides for the alien, the orphan, and the widow through the gleaning system. From this system, four very important guiding principles of empowering the poor emerge:

1. The portion of the field left unharvested created an opportunity for the poor to meet their own needs. Much of community ministry is simply to create opportunity.
2. The unharvested portion required the poor to work in order to meet their needs. Food was not handed to them; they had to go into the fields themselves and pick up the fallen crops. Community ministry places responsibility and accountability upon the people and thus does not create an unhealthy dependency.
3. Gleaning was meaningful work—that is, it was purposeful and necessary. Community ministry creates meaningful service, developing life and vocational skills that will enable persons to contribute to the community.

4. Because the gleaning system required the poor to do the work of meeting their own needs, their dignity was affirmed. They felt good about themselves. If community ministry does not uphold the dignity of the poor, then it falls short of the gospel.

Space will not allow me to say more about these principles, but I encourage readers of this book to look at these biblical passages more closely, for in them lay the seeds of true partnership. The principles we have derived from the Old Testament practice of gleaning have certainly guided us in how we go about ministering with and for people here in Lawndale.

Over the years we have partnered with many suburban churches, nonprofit groups, businesses, foundations, corporations, and individuals. And some of the partnerships have been excellent experiences and some not so great. Again, we have learned that there is a right way and a wrong way to partner. True, effective partnerships that bring glory to God take time, work, and honesty, and both urban and suburban groups must mutually contribute and benefit.

Toward this end, we write this book. It is with a thankful heart to God, to the people of Lawndale, and to my family that I have contributed to this project along with my very good friend and ministry partner, John Perkins, and with my respected colleagues, Ron Sider and Al Tizon. It is our hope that this book will inspire partnerships around the country and beyond to eliminate poverty, racism, and unnecessary suffering in the world.

From Al Tizon, Missionary

The question, "How can my experience as a cross-cultural missionary contribute to the discussion?" caused me some hesitation when I was first asked to join this project. But the more I learned about the issues surrounding the urban-suburban divide in America, the more I realized the considerable overlap that exists between the urban-suburban encounter and the Western–non-Western encounter.

I spent the better part of the 1990s in the Philippines, working alongside Filipino sisters and brothers for the sake of the gospel among both the urban and rural poor. Although I am ethnically Filipino, I grew up in the United States. So other than looking Filipino on the outside, I arrived as the Western-raised, Western-trained, evangelical missionary that I was. As such, I am certain I brought along with me some of the cultural baggage of the *ugly American*, which included an aura of superiority, ethnocentrism, paternalism, and positional power due to large amounts of money, which when converted to Philippine pesos counted me among the rich in that country.

But I thank God for what I was able to learn due to the advances made in the vital field of missiology, a field that has done well to warn us of the ethnocentric baggage that we bring with us to the mission field. Therefore, instead of superiority, we need to affirm equality and practice humility. Instead of ethnocentrism, we ought to see the face of God in every ethnicity. Instead of paternalism, we should assume a learner's posture in submission to national counterparts. And instead of presupposing leadership in matters of theology and ministry, we need to share power and resources for the sake of the kingdom. Thanks to missiologists espousing such convictions, I believe I was able to curb at least a certain degree of colonial missionary practice. Furthermore, in retrospect, my national Filipino coworkers also taught me a thing or two about cross-cultural relationships that befit the kingdom.

As I reflect upon urban-suburban relationships, I believe these missiological convictions apply quite readily. In fact, in order for genuine partnership to happen between urban and suburban Christians, we *must* apply them. Because of the Third World conditions of many of our inner cities, well-meaning Christians from the suburbs desire to do something about it, and rightfully so. Unchecked suburban benevolence for the city, however, often leads to the exact same mistakes that many Western missionaries have made in non-Western settings. For example, suburban Christians often come to the city well resourced with a preset idea of what poverty alleviation and community transformation look like. As such, like many Western missionaries, they assume positions of leadership, dictating how ministry should be conducted, and taking their "rightful place" as teacher, trainer, and provider. And like many non-Western counterparts in the cross-cultural missionary relationship, the urban church acquiesces and plays the subservient role of recipient and follower.

I have painted a general but not inaccurate picture here. Just like in the Western–non-Western relationship, Christians involved or who desire to get involved in urban-suburban ministry partnership must strive toward equality, mutual respect, an affirmation of diversity, a biblical understanding of the rich and the poor in God's economy, and a shared sense of mission. I have compared the urban-suburban relationship with the Western–non-Western relationship simply to underscore the enormous task of partnering across the urban-suburban divide. It requires taking advanced missiological insights seriously, for this type of partnership is nothing less than a cross-cultural encounter. Our hope for this book is to help both sides of the divide to meet the great challenge of genuine partnership for the sake of the kingdom.

Part 1

Where We Do It

The Evolving Urban-Suburban Landscape

Today's world spins at a rate of unprecedented change. Information turns over so rapidly that innovations and trends are rendered obsolete even before they are fully understood. This astounding rate of change requires redefining old words on an ongoing basis, as well as creating new ones, just to know how to discuss the realities before us. Language itself cannot keep up!

Consider words like *urban* and *suburban*. In this book we issue a call not just for partnership but for partnership that crosses the urban-suburban divide. The changing patterns of migration, settlement, and resettlement in and out of cities in the past thirty years compel us to reconsider what we mean nowadays by these descriptors. New words like *exurb* and *technoburb* have cropped up in recent years in an attempt to define discernible changes in the nature of the urban-suburban relationship. What does it mean to be *urban* or *suburban* today? Are these strictly geographic terms, or do they go beyond location? Furthermore, what is the nature of this divide we are talking about, and how hard is it to cross?

Before anything else we do in this book, we first have the formidable task of understanding the ever-changing urban-suburban context. If we have gained anything from the missionary *faux pas* of the past, we have learned that knowing the context in which we serve matters, that *where* we do ministry determines in a major way *how* we do ministry. Chapter 1 will attempt to provide an aerial view of today's urban-suburban landscape, which is evolving apace with the rest of the world.

1

Location and Beyond

Directly on the other side of the southwestern border of Philadelphia sits the township of Upper Darby. Once a predominantly Irish- and Italian-American community, Upper Darby has experienced a remarkable influx of African-, Asian-, and Latino-Americans beginning in the mid-1980s. Immigrant populations from many different countries also began to move into the area in earnest. While the Anglo-American population decreased 8 percent by 1990, the black population increased 117 percent, Asians by 201 percent, and Hispanics by 30 percent.[1] Social researchers of multiculturalism would have a heyday in Upper Darby! Indeed what has happened in this area begs the question, "What is going on here?"

While several complex factors are at play, the many urban revitalization projects taking place in various parts of Philadelphia have undeniably contributed to this migration. Many ethnic minorities, particularly from West Philadelphia, have felt pushed out by these projects and consequently have moved into the emptying suburban community of Upper Darby. The exodus that has occurred in this suburb began markedly in the late 1980s and continues to this day, as the many *For Sale* signs that dot residential neighborhoods can attest. This is, of course, a generalization with which many can cite exceptions. But longtime Upper Darby resident and retired local historian Thomas DiFilippo confirms this trend:

Middle income minorities began to move into the area starting in the 1980s, where longtime, middle-income white residents had moved out. At the same time, many of the lower-income whites stayed, and many of the lower-income minorities from West Philadelphia eventually began to move into the area. Since the early 1990s, parts of Upper Darby have been turning into slums worse than you see in Philadelphia.[2]

Upper Darby is but one of many communities around the country that tell the same story of the changing, shifting, urban-suburban scene where, generally speaking, the rich are moving back into the city or creating plusher suburbs farther out, and the poor are moving into older, first-rung suburbs or remaining in inner-city pockets.

The Urban-Suburban Landscape Yesterday

How does this differ from yesterday's urban-suburban migration patterns? The word *urban* used to refer to economic opportunity and, with that, the promise of high culture. The city represented jobs, freedom, sophistication, and comfort, and in some ways, it still does. But at least two factors marred this idyllic picture from the perspective of many Euro-Americans who moved out of the city in the post–World War II era: the flood of nonwhites into the city and the poverty that came with many of them.

As the lights of the city beckoned, people of color began to pour into cities. Millions of African-Americans from the rural South, for example, began to migrate north and west to major city centers. According to journalist Nicholas Lemann, author of *The Promised Land: The Great Black Migration and How It Changed America*, five million blacks left the farmlands of the South and settled in cities between 1940 and 1970. He directly attributes this exodus to the invention of the mechanical cotton picker, which left countless African-Americans jobless and which greatly exacerbated the already stifling poverty experienced by so many Southern blacks. As economic drought pushed them out of the Southern countryside, economic opportunity in the cities pulled them north and west. In Chicago alone in the 1940s the "black population . . . increased by 77%. . . . In the 1950s, it grew another 65%. . . . By 1960, Chicago had more than half a million more black residents than it had had twenty years earlier." By 1970, Lemann says, "Black America was only half Southern, and less than a quarter rural; 'urban' had become a euphemism for 'black,' "[3] and more accurately, *black and poor*.

But *urban* meant more than *black and poor*; it meant more broadly *other ethnic minorities and poor*. It also meant *immigrants—white or nonwhite—and poor*. It essentially meant *different and poor* migrating into the city. Beginning in the early part of the twentieth century, migrants from Mexico and other Latin American countries steadily flowed to *El Norte* in search of refuge from revolutions going on in their countries as well as economic opportunity. They usually ended up in industrial centers, where more often than not they "found themselves trapped in a condition of cyclical unemployment as industries expanded and contracted."[4] Asians also flowed into the cities, with almost every major urban center having a significant Chinatown. Furthermore, refugees from Vietnam and Cambodia seeking safety from atrocities in their own countries came in earnest in the 1970s and 1980s. Europeans escaping persecution and coping with postwar displacement also began pouring steadily into the United States in general and cities in particular after World War II.[5]

This notion of impoverished different peoples defining the urban context certainly contributed to the urban exodus of the middle and upper classes, although there were many other factors involved in the suburbanization of America.[6] Indeed the post–World War II use of the word *suburban* referred in part to frustrated urbanites creating communities they considered safer, cleaner, and more spacious than the city had become, but yet close enough to commute into the city for work as well as to enjoy its bright lights, its creativity, and its nightlife. Made possible by federal subsidies after the war, the construction of detached homes on the outskirts of major cities increased dramatically from 114,000 in 1944 to 1,692,000 in 1950.[7] And those with means moved into these new homes, leaving those with little or no means within the declining city center. Urbanologists have employed the picture of the donut, where the outer rim constitutes its essence at the expense of the middle, to describe classical postwar suburbanization.[8]

The post–World War II road to suburbia not only had an economic class element fueling it, it had an undeniable racial driver to it as well. The postwar flight to create suburbs was predominantly a *white flight*, leaving the African-, Latino-, and Asian-American peoples in the deficient center, or the hole in the middle of the donut. In fact, *redlining*—the practice of making it extremely difficult if not impossible for minorities, especially African-Americans, to move into certain neighborhoods—guided (or rather, misguided) suburban development for at least the first two decades after World War II. Some claim the practice lasted much longer than that and in fact continues to exist today in more subtle forms.[9]

Gentrification and the Suburbanization of Poverty

This scene has changed dramatically, however, as the case of Philadelphia and suburban Upper Darby aptly demonstrates. "The twenty-first century signals a great reversal for U.S. cities," claims urbanologist Robert Lupton, "as wealth returns to the core and poverty is pushed to the periphery."[10] Tired of commuting to and from work, many suburban baby boomers and the generation that followed have increasingly moved back into the city, diverting both their resources and their power to transform notoriously hopeless urban areas into clean, modern business centers and avant-garde living spaces. Of course, not all moved back to the city; many suburban residents also stayed put or moved even farther away from the urban center.

The returnees to the city have begun to reshape the urban context, ironically, according to suburban values. Albert Y. Hsu, who recently conducted a popular, but well-researched, study of suburban Christianity as it relates to the city, states it succinctly: "Cities . . . are themselves changing to look more and more like suburbs."[11] Young suburban-raised business entrepreneurs, artists, actors, and musicians have begun suburbanizing the city, converting old industrial buildings and storefronts into state-of-the-art offices, studios, and lofts. Streets are being repaved and structures restored. Businesses are reemerging and growing. Art and music centers are regaining their glitz and attracting the avant-garde. Extraordinary urban revitalization programs have restored major sections of New York, Boston, Chicago, Atlanta, and Los Angeles to once again become thriving commercial, residential, and artistic centers. "House by house, brick by brick," as Harvard's senior research fellow Alexander von Hoffman puts it, the society's gentry are transforming American cities.[12]

In their optimistic book *Comeback Cities*, activists Paul Grogan and Tony Proscio have identified four trends in urban centers around the country that constitute "a surprising convergence of positives." They are (1) a growing network of grassroots efforts that are increasingly supported by politicians, academics, and clergy; (2) emerging markets; (3) dropping crime rates; and (4) deregulation of public housing, education, and welfare.[13] At the outset, who could argue with these improvements? Indeed, there is much to praise in the gentrification phenomenon, where the gentry, the cream of the crop, the elite, restore dilapidated neighborhoods.

Gentrification, however, has a major downside as sociological study after study has shown. These improvements, if implemented unchecked (as they often are), also increase the cost of living in these areas. As the value of real estate skyrockets, the poor once again find themselves *displaced* by circumstance and *replaced* by those who can afford to relocate into the renewed communities. To be sure, there is nothing new about the have-nots making way for the haves. The salient point here is that as lower-income families get pushed out of the city, many of them move into the emptying, decaying, older suburbs, creating what some sociologists aptly call the "suburbanization of poverty."[14] The flip side of gentrification, or the urbanization of wealth, is the suburbanization of poverty. Hsu prefers the "urbanization of suburbia" and the "suburbanization of the city."[15] Whichever wordplay one chooses, it conveys the same thing: a reversed flow of the rich and the poor that has changed the urban-suburban landscape. The donut metaphor no longer applies.

But lest we overstate the matter, cities, even as sections are being revitalized, continue to worsen in some pockets. Indeed, many of the poor have remained in the city, but not necessarily to reap any benefits of urban improvements. On the contrary, they go deeper into poverty, thus ensuring the ongoing existence of "islands of decay in seas of renewal" (i.e., the perpetuation of the inner city, the ghetto, the slums).[16] The "ghetto underclass," as sociologist William Julius Wilson describes those who live there, are "the truly disadvantaged."[17] Isolated from mainstream society, the ghetto underclass endure hardships that include political neglect, overcrowded and substandard housing, lack of easily accessible markets, lack of employment opportunities, poor education, drug trafficking, and an alarming number of single-parent households. The close proximity between these decaying neighborhoods and the sections undergoing gentrification in many cities embarrassingly reveals the injustice. Sociologist David Claerbaut observes, "Luxury hotels, an ESPN Zone, Planet Hollywood, multiplex theaters, Starbucks and shopping complexes dot downtown areas, while only a few blocks away, people live in the most blighted of neighborhoods. Often a single street separates a gated rehabbed community from one ridden with street crime, deteriorating housing and joblessness."[18]

Urban and Suburban in a Changing Context

In short, the last twenty-five years or so have made a mess of the urban-suburban landscape. Where do cities end and the suburbs begin? Wealthy suburbanites are turning cities into suburbs, and poor urbanites are turning suburbs into inner cities. As true as this is, many of the rich still live in and continue to move to suburbia, and many of the poor still live in and continue to move to the city. In this milieu, the rich and the poor of the multitudinous ethnic groups have migrated on the two-way bridge between city and suburb to the point where they now find themselves living closer together than ever before—at least geographically—on both urban and suburban turfs.

What does this scenario do to our understanding of *urban* and *suburban*? In light of the changing landscape, we quite simply have to go beyond geography to maintain any useful meaning for these terms. To suburbanites, *urban* can no longer mean some place *over there* where poverty abounds, danger lurks, and culture wars rage. Indeed, poverty, violence, crime, and multiethnic tensions have made their way into the suburbs. And to urbanites, *suburban* can no longer mean a glorious place *out there* where only the *rich whites* live and where spaciousness, cleanliness, safety, and wealth abound. Whether we find ourselves in the city or the suburbs, we can no longer view the *other place* as *over there*.

We propose, then, to downplay location as delineating *urban* and *suburban* and instead define them primarily in social terms—that is, by social realities that perpetuate the gap between the haves and the have-nots. By *urban*, we mean the world or worlds wherein the poor, the oppressed, and the excluded live, whether they do so in or out of the physical city. We understand *urban* as a social condition that results from enduring the daily grind of population density, poverty, substandard housing, substandard education, violence, crime, and drug trafficking. Fear, insecurity, and despair are palpable among the urbanized.

Furthermore, although there is no lack of a poor white population in America (especially in rural mountain regions), the urban condition correlates demographically with ethnic minorities, particularly African- and Latino-Americans. Claerbaut notes that African-Americans have been the most urbanized of all ethnic groups, and a sizable proportion (about one-third) are trapped in poverty.[19] As for the Latino community, it "is the fastest growing minority group in the nation," claims Temple University Professor John C. Raines. "It is also the poorest group."[20]

This urban condition no longer respects the traditional urban-suburban line; in fact, it knows no boundaries. As such, it is different from the physical city, which has geographic and political boundaries and which has positive, even glorious, aspects to it. Let us be clear: we are not saying that the city is all bad! We are saying that in the physical city and all around the outskirts we call suburbs, many people—especially African- and Latino-Americans—endure the miseries of the urban condition.

By *suburban*, we also mean a social condition and not primarily location—a condition that results from a growing gulf of wealth and privilege as well as the intentional social segregation from those of different ethnicities. Suburbia as ideology anesthetizes the human heart to the plight of the poor and the culture of the different. Christian sociologist Mark Bjelland criticizes regions driven by the suburban vision in light of the gospel: "Communities bound together by their desire to exclude lower status individuals and maintain property values certainly fall far short of the community God intends."[21]

Again, we differentiate between the suburban condition and the physical suburbs, for indeed some aspects that have shaped the suburbs are wholly understandable, such as the desire to provide quality education for our children and to enjoy the peace and beauty of nature. As Hsu argues compellingly, suburban living is legitimate.[22] However, as Hsu also argues, those who are consumed by the suburban vision, whether they live in the physical suburbs or not, fall prey to the suburban condition that can keep them blind to the plight of the poor and excluded, and thus inhibit the compassion of God from flowing through them.

The Urban-Suburban Divide

When we refer to the urban-suburban divide then, we mean nothing less than the ancient line that divides the poor and the rich, the underprivileged and the privileged, the powerless and the powerful.

Although the geographic line that divides the rich and the poor on the American scene eludes any easy understanding, the line we draw between social classes remains clear. For in spite of the fact that the rich and the poor and the black, white, and brown people live closer together than ever before, they continue to live worlds apart. Hsu's personal testimony illustrates this point, as he reflects upon his profound experience as a suburban high school student participating in a short-term urban mission: "What was most convicting for me was the fact that we were working in inner-city neighborhoods only about ten miles away from my suburban home. I lived in the very same county, but I had never ventured into the depths of the 'hood.' I had driven by on highway bypasses countless times, but I had never met these people, let alone considered them my neighbors."[23] Indeed, despite the blurring of the geographic line between urban and suburban worlds, the very real social divide between them remains far and wide, attesting to the extreme difficulty people face when trying to cross it.

Yet we believe this is exactly what God calls us to do: (1) to cross the divide, meaning that we allow God to redeem us from whichever condition we suffer with and to begin to see the whole world—urban and suburban (and for that matter, rural)—as God's domain; and (2) to partner together across this divide so that urban and suburban followers of Jesus of all classes from all tribes and nations can work together to bring the Good News to the poor and excluded.

Furthermore, this call to urban-suburban partnership is for the purpose of transforming our needy communities, not escaping from them. God does not call us to link arms and lives in order to help people leave the ghetto; he calls us together to transform the ghetto! Such a statement flies in the face of the popular notion that the answer to urban blight is to leave it. We resist this with all of our strength. With this book, we issue forth the call to partner together across the urban-suburban divide in order to participate in God's transforming work, which includes a kind of *gentrification without displacement*, a type of community reform for the sake of its residents by the power of the gospel.

But we are getting ahead of ourselves. As we have gained a better grasp of the changing urban-suburban context—the *where* question—let us now address the *why* question of urban-suburban partnership. And for this, we turn to the Scriptures to see what God's Word has to say about working together across racial and class lines in light of God's mission to transform the world.

Reflection Questions

1. What are your definitions of *urban* and *suburban*? How, if at all, has this chapter caused you to rethink those definitions?

2. Is gentrification all bad? What are some ways that it is good and other ways that it is not?

3. How does the *suburbanization of poverty*, where the poor are increasingly moving into what once were plush suburbs, impact our understanding of ministry to the poor?

4. Discuss *urban* and *suburban* as social conditions rather than as geographic locations.

Part 2

Why We Do It

The Biblical Demand for Partnership

Allow us to state the obvious: our Christian convictions must be biblical. While this should go without saying, we *need* to say it. As cultural interpreters in the postmodern age routinely point out cracks in once-trusted social, religious, historical, and even scientific foundations, we must reaffirm our belief in the trustworthiness of Holy Scripture. Let us remind ourselves that we are people shaped by the living Word as it is revealed in the written Word—people who meditate on the Bible's magnificent stories, who sing its songs, and who internalize its truths, believing that through the words of Scripture we hear God's guiding voice for today. Part 2 records what we have heard God saying to his people regarding the call to partner together across socioeconomic and racial lines in order to participate in God's transforming work.

The biblical demand regarding this special kind of partnership comes from two basic calls that flow out of the Bible's powerful theme of the reign or kingdom of God. The first is the call to radical community—the countercultural formation of God's people in the Bible from beginning to end. Chapter 2 explores this biblical call, which demands God's people take on a fundamentally different agenda than the rest of the world. "This is the original revolution," wrote the late theologian John Howard Yoder, "the creation of a distinct community with its own deviant set of values."[1] One of the core distinguishing values of God's community is economic justice, where the poor enjoy a profound level of dignity and participation. Directly related to this is the value of racial reconciliation that also distinguishes the community of God from the rest. This call to radical kingdom community, where God's justice and reconciliation reign, provides the biblical backbone for the notion of urban-suburban partnership.

The second call beckons the people of God to engage in holistic mission—word and deed ministries that serve all, but especially the poor, oppressed, and marginalized. God not only calls the redeemed to live in radical community in order to model justice and reconciliation; he also calls us to engage a needy and divided world *proactively* with the gospel, bringing the light of God's reign in places of darkness where people live in despair, poverty, oppression, inequality, and violence. Chapter 3 takes a look at the biblical mandate for God's people to engage in proactive kingdom mission—the call to proclaim by both word and deed the Good News of God's reign, which, by its very nature, especially touches the desperately underserved.

In stereo, these two biblical calls to radical community and to holistic mission produce an altogether distinct sound—namely, the call to transformational partnership that dares to cross the urban-suburban divide.

2

The Call to Radical Community

Hundreds of years of harsh slavery, and just like that it was over. The God of Abraham, Isaac, and Jacob heard the suffering cry of the Hebrew slaves in Egypt, and it was time to intervene. We know the story well: God used a progression of plagues to afflict Egypt until Pharaoh finally released them (Exod. 7–12). Led by Moses, who forsook a life of Egyptian privilege and chose to stand in solidarity with his people (Heb. 11:24–26), they miraculously crossed the Red Sea as the Lord parted the waters. When those same waters crashed down upon Pharaoh's army, which was hotly pursuing them, the former slaves found themselves on the other side of oppression. What could they do but celebrate God's acts of mercy and power (Exod. 15:1–21)?

While sojourning in the wilderness, with God's miraculous liberating acts fresh on their minds, the people received a nation-forming word from the Lord: "If you obey my voice and keep my covenant, you shall be my treasured possession out of all the peoples. . . . You shall be for me a priestly kingdom and a holy nation." To which the people replied, "Everything that the Lord has spoken we will do" (Exod. 19:5–6, 8). Insofar as the people succeeded in keeping the covenant and obeying all that the Lord had commanded, they held a unique and special place among the nations (Deut. 4:32–40; 10:14–15). This monumental exchange between God and the Hebrew people marked the birth of the community of God and the beginning of the fulfillment of God's promise to Abraham that through his seed a great nation would be born, a nation that was to bless all the families of the earth (Gen. 12:1–3). From conception to formation, the people whom God called into being had a mission—to bless the whole world or, as the prophet Isaiah described it later, to be "a light to the nations, that [God's] salvation may reach to the end of the earth" (Isa. 49:6). We will say more about this "to the end of the earth" mission in the next chapter. For now, suffice it to say that its starting point was the call to community—a radically different community in which God will reign as king.

The primary call upon this community was simply "to *be* the people of God,"[1] to reflect the kingdom of God, and to model a new kind of community for the benefit of communities around them that were ruled by humans. Indeed God's covenantal call to the newly formed people to model his reign reflected what God desired for the whole world. The formation of the people of God—where the redeemed enjoy justice, equality, peace, righteousness, and joy—was intended to model nothing less than the new humanity.

Among the central distinguishing marks of this community was God's justice. Poverty and oppression had no place where God ruled, for how could a community founded on Exodus liberation tolerate the sustained presence of the poor and oppressed in its midst (Exod. 22:21; 23:9)? In both law and liturgy, the people of God remembered their former state and celebrated God's mercy and justice (Deut. 10:17–22). From Genesis to Revelation, the Bible tells the story of this new community that, among other things, modeled a new kind of relationship between the rich and the poor.

Economic Justice in Israel

If the people of God obeyed the law of Moses to the letter, what would ancient Israel have looked like? The picture included every family having an allotment of land according to tribal size (Num. 26:52–56), which essentially meant that each would have had the means to meet its basic necessities as well as the opportunity to participate in the political and economic life of the community.[2] The picture included the implementation of the Sabbatical Year every seven years, when the ground was allowed to rest, slaves were freed, and debts were erased (Deut. 15). It also included the application of the Year of Jubilee every fifty years, when land was returned to the original owners, effectively wiping the socioeconomic slate clean for all (Lev. 25).

In addition, the picture included the nonpoor in Israel providing for the poor and marginalized, represented in the law by the orphan, the widow, and the resident alien (Deut. 24:17–18). In an ideal ancient Israel, the temple tithe every third year went to the needy as well as to the Levites (Deut. 14:28–29; 26:12). The edges of the harvest fields were left for the hungry to glean (Lev. 19:9–10; Deut. 24:19–21). The natural produce of the land during the Sabbatical Year was left for the disadvantaged to harvest (Exod. 23:10–11; Lev. 25:1–7). Freed slaves, also during the Sabbatical Year, were given enough by their former masters to support themselves on their own (Deut. 15:14), and no-interest loans were enjoyed by the poor (Exod. 22:25; Lev. 25:35–38).

These laws of land ownership, restoration, and poverty alleviation reflect one of the fundamental tenets of the theological ethics of the Old Testament—namely, God's economic justice. Sociologist Lowell Noble describes biblical justice as that which challenges oppression as well as creates the conditions for *shalom* (wholeness). It also provides access to the resources of God's creation for everyone.[3] Theologically, biblical justice reflects God's very character as the God of love and grace.[4] If God's people implemented divine justice according to the Mosaic law, then the world would have seen in Israel economic relationships between the rich and the poor that were wholly and radically different from anything it had ever seen before.[5]

But the ideal Israel never materialized. In fact, according to the historical and prophetic books in the Old Testament, Israel did not just fail, it failed miserably. Filled with injustice, corruption, oppression, political assassinations, exile, and foreign captivities, the Old Testament story does not hold back in recording the utter failure of God's chosen people to be the radically different community they were called to be. Israel failed to model God's kingdom; it failed to enlighten the nations and, in fact, participated in the same darkness as the rest of the world.

One of the chief sins of Israel was its failure to uphold God's economic justice in the community. For example, "the sabbatical year, unfortunately, was practiced only sporadically."[6] The God of the poor and oppressed voiced his displeasure over this through the prophets: "[My people] know no limits in deeds of wickedness," the Lord complained to the prophet Jeremiah. "They do not judge with justice the cause of the orphan . . . and they do not defend the rights of the needy. Shall I not punish them for these things?" (Jer. 5:28–29). Similarly, the Lord declared through Malachi, "I will draw near to you for judgment; . . . against those who oppress the hired workers in their wages, the widow and the orphan, against those who thrust aside the alien" (Mal. 3:5).

Among the prophets, Amos stood out as one who saw the hypocrisy of worshiping the God of justice while not living justly in the land. Consequently, the poor remained poor even as the people worshiped the God of the poor. "Take away from me the noise of your songs," Amos preached as the mouthpiece of God, "I will not listen to the melody of your harps. But let justice roll down like waters, and righteousness like an ever-flowing stream" (Amos 5:23–24). As Israel mistreated its poor and vulnerable, it fell under severe judgment.[7]

Invariably, however, hope followed the prophets' doomsday message as they assured the people that God would someday fulfill his promises (e.g., Jer. 33:14). One of the most vivid prophetic images of future fulfillment pictures everyone sitting under their own vine or fig tree, meaning that each person will enjoy the benefits of just land distribution (Ezek. 45:1–9; Micah 4:4; Zech. 3:10). The kingdom community that is to bless all of the families of the earth will become a reality; perhaps not through the state of Israel as the people knew it, but the kingdom of God in some very real and efficacious form will come.[8]

It should not surprise us that an integral part of the prophetic vision of the coming kingdom was a reaffirmation of God's justice, more particularly, the implementation of the Year of Jubilee. The Isaiah 61 passage, which Jesus himself used to inaugurate his ministry in Luke 4:14–21, clearly painted a picture of a community living by the spirit of the Jubilee.[9] In this picture the oppressed receive good news, the captives go free, the brokenhearted are made whole, and the afflicted are comforted (Isa. 61:1–3); "for I the Lord love justice," the prophet recorded (Isa. 61:6). Indeed God's community that the prophets envisioned—the community of Abraham's seed called to embody the kingdom of God—will be characterized in the future by what Noble calls "jubilee justice."[10]

Jesus, Justice, and the Community of the Twelve

When Jesus read Isaiah 61 from the synagogue pulpit at Nazareth, he announced the kingdom of Jubilee justice in accordance with the prophets (Luke 4:18–19).[11] To be sure, the kingdom that Jesus inaugurated meant more than justice. It meant nothing less than "a new creation, a new humanity, a redeemed community. [In Christ], the kingdom of justice, love, mercy, joy, peace, and reconciliation is now being realized."[12] Nevertheless, Jubilee justice was absolutely integral to the kingdom vision. As Donald Kraybill, author of the classic *The Upside Down Kingdom*, plainly states, "We . . . cannot conclude that the Christian's economic practice is a peripheral fringe of the Gospel. It stands at the very core of the kingdom way."[13]

After reading Isaiah 61, Jesus said, "Today this scripture has been fulfilled in your hearing" (Luke 4:21). These words marked the transition from the prophetic hope of Jubilee justice to present reality in Christ. "The time is fulfilled," Jesus proclaimed, "and the kingdom of God has come near; repent, and believe in the good news" (Mark 1:15). He preached this Good News everywhere, for he said, "I was sent for this purpose" (Luke 4:43). In Christ's person, the time had come to begin reestablishing the reign of God on earth, to bring the Good News to all, but especially to the poor and oppressed.

Jesus himself embodied the kingdom; as such, he lived out the justice and righteousness that the kingdom demands. He ate with sinners, tax collectors, prostitutes, and the outcasts of society (Matt. 9:10–13), meaning that he treated those whom society disdained with respect and dignity. He also ministered to their deepest needs. When John the Baptist sent his disciples to ask Jesus if he was the one to usher in the kingdom, he said to them, "Go tell John what you have seen and heard: the blind receive their sight, the lame walk, the lepers are cleansed, the deaf hear, the dead are raised, the poor have good news brought to them" (Luke 7:22; see vv. 18–22). Indeed, when Jesus ministered to the poor, the oppressed, the sick, the demonically possessed, and the socially dispossessed, he was living out the compassion and justice that God called the nation of Israel to live out.

But he did not model the kingdom alone. Even while Israel's religious leaders hardened to his teachings and practices, individuals began to respond to his invitation to "Come, follow me" (Matt. 9:9; Mark 1:17; 2:14; Luke 5:27; John 1:43). In Luke 6:13 Jesus "called his disciples and chose twelve of them, whom he also named apostles." And immediately after forming the community of the Twelve, Jesus gave his famous sermon, best known as the Sermon on the Mount (although in Luke it is more accurately the Sermon on the Plain),

outlining for his disciples the *upside-down values* by which they were
to abide (Luke 6:20–49).[14]

A radical view of economic justice, in which the poor hold a promi-
nent place, launches Jesus's sermon: "Blessed are you who are poor,
for yours is the kingdom of God" (Luke 6:20). Undoubtedly such a
value informed the new community of disciples in its view of possessions and wealth as well as the economic relationships among them.
For example, they shared a "common purse" (John 12:6), meaning,
among other things, that "the resources of the entire community of
obedient disciples would be available to anyone in need." In short,
Jesus and the community of the Twelve took up the responsibility
originally given to Israel to model kingdom justice. "Jesus and his
first followers vividly demonstrated that the old covenant's pattern
of economic relationships among God's people [was] not only to be
continued but also deepened."[15]

Economic *Koinonia* in the Early Church

The common purse of the Twelve only magnified after Pentecost,
resulting in sweeping economic sharing in the early church. As the
Holy Spirit empowered the disciples and increased their numbers, the
new order of the kingdom effectively dismantled the walls between
the privileged and the underprivileged, the powerful and the powerless, and the haves and the have-nots in the community. Luke reported
several times in the book of Acts how the Spirit-led followers of Jesus
"had everything in common. Selling their possessions and goods, they
gave to anyone as he had need" (Acts 2:44–45 NIV). And again, "All
the believers were one in heart and mind. No one claimed that any
of his possessions was his own, but they shared everything they had"
(Acts 4:32 NIV). Though hard to imagine today with our highly indi-
vidualistic mind-set, this economic arrangement among them seemed
only natural in the early church in light of the gospel. The experience
of fellowshipping with the risen Jesus (1 Cor. 15:5–8) and the coming of the Holy Spirit (Acts 2:1–47) registered such an impact upon
the first generation of believers that economic sharing—the spirit of
Jubilee justice—defined their relationships.

Indeed the first followers of Christ practiced "economic *koinonia*":[16]
the sharing of material resources so that none went without in the faith
community. Paul chastised churches under his charge that deviated

from this—those that reverted back to the economic ways of the world, which advantaged the rich over the poor. For example, when the Corinthian congregation neglected the poor in its practice of the Lord's Supper, Paul flatly denied that it was the Lord's Supper at all (1 Cor. 11:20; see vv. 17–34).[17] How could it be participation in the body and blood of Christ, Paul angrily reasoned, if "when the time comes to eat, each of you goes ahead with your own supper, and one goes hungry and another becomes drunk" (v. 21)? In Paul's kingdom thinking, the violation of economic *koinonia* between the rich and the poor ran contrary to the very nature of the redeemed community.

Second Corinthians 8–9, where Paul encouraged the Christians in Corinth to participate in the collection for the poor in the Jerusalem church, provides perhaps the most vivid picture of the economic *koinonia* experienced by the first generation of believers. Poverty abounded in Jerusalem, and the brothers and sisters there felt the impact of it, along with the rest of the city. Famine and drought, which the prophet Agabus foresaw in Acts 11:27–30 and which was documented by historians Josephus, Suetonius, and Tacitus, pervaded the region.[18] Moreover,

> The poverty of the Jerusalem church was . . . related to peculiar conditions in Jerusalem, especially the city's large number of poor pilgrims. The Jews considered Jerusalem the holy city. Hence large numbers of elderly poor flocked there to die. Also, the Holy City was the favorite location for the rabbis and their students who were dependent on charity. Since almsgiving in Yahweh's city was thought to be an especially meritorious act, the poor in general naturally drifted to Jerusalem.[19]

Add to this the members of the Jerusalem church being cut off from the standard Jewish sources of charity because of their association with the Way, and the picture of the impoverished church comes into sharp focus.[20]

The church at Antioch first sent an offering to Jerusalem via Paul and Barnabas (Acts 11:29–30). But far from a onetime gift, churches in the surrounding regions continued to give sacrificially through Paul, who obviously served as some kind of point person for the collection. Our typical approach to Paul makes it easy to picture the apostle planting churches throughout the Mediterranean region. But we seldom picture the equally accurate picture of missionary Paul coordinating a sustained relief effort among the believers. He, along with the other apostles (James 2:14–17; 1 John 3:16–17), simply could not stand the idea of the nonpoor in the body of Christ not doing what they could to meet the needs of the poor in the body. Paul urged the Corinthian church to display their maturity in the faith by out-doing the churches in Macedonia in their giving; he argued that the Macedonian churches, even out of their poverty, gave abundantly to help the impoverished brethren in Jerusalem (2 Cor. 8:1–6).[21] Indeed, economic *koinonia* defined the kingdom community of Christ, its members believing that when one part of the body suffered, the whole body suffered (1 Cor. 12:26).

Multi-Ethnic *Koinonia* in the Early Church

Furthermore, in addition to economic *koinonia*, a multi-ethnic *koinonia* eventually depicted the early church. Jews and Gentiles simply did not mix in ancient Roman society, but in the new society of Jesus, the power of the gospel effectively dismantled the wall between them. Of course the cultural diversity that eventually became the church did not come about without struggle. It took Peter's rooftop trance (Acts 10) for the church to begin to understand the multicultural nature of the gospel. "God shows no partiality," Peter concluded from the trance, "but in every nation anyone who fears him and does what is right is acceptable to him" (vv. 34–35).

As significant as Peter's experience was to bring salvation to the Gentiles, it was Paul's unwavering and passionate preaching of the free gospel—a salvation unencumbered by cultural requirements—that prevented the new faith from becoming just another sect of Judaism. As apostle to the Gentiles (Acts 9:15), Paul adamantly contended against anyone who compromised the boundlessness of the gospel. Even Peter was not exempt. When Peter refused to eat with Gentiles "for fear of the circumcision faction," he got a public tongue-lashing from Paul (Gal. 2:11–21). If Paul heard anything at all from God, it was this: both Jew and Gentile can come as they are and receive the Good News. Paul understood inclusion of the Gentiles as a divine mystery revealed at the appointed time to bring salvation to the world. He wrote in Ephesians 3:5–6, "This mystery . . . has now been revealed to his holy apostles and prophets by the Spirit: that is, the Gentiles have become fellow heirs, members of the same body, and sharers in the promise in Christ Jesus through the Gospel."

Of course the idea of God bringing people of different ethnicities together was not entirely new. In fact, the inclusion of Gentiles in the nascent church was in perfect lockstep with God's ancient proposal to form a people out of an ethnically mixed group of desert wanderers called the *Apiru* or the Hebrews. William Albright depicts the ancient Hebrews as "stateless persons of varied ethnic stock, scattered from Elam to Egypt."[22] Burton Goddard adds that they were "wandering peoples greatly restricted as regards financial means and without citizenship and social status."[23] Although the ethnic makeup of the land during Israel's formation continues to be a topic of scholarly debate, it is "safe to conclude that the Israelites of the Old Testament had numerous 'ethnic' affinities with their neighbors in and around Palestine and that the lines of ethnic demarcation were not hard and fast."[24]

The truth that the ancient Hebrews were made up of different ethnicities is often obscured by Israel's tenacious efforts throughout the Old Testament to maintain national purity—that is, its unique identity that set them apart from surrounding nations. But we must not forget the I Iebrews' multicultural origins. We may think diversity among God's people began when the Gentiles joined the Jews to make up the post-Pentecost church, but consider the Hebrews of old! God's multicultural, multiclass project of salvation in fact began when he sent out an ethnically mixed group of desert wanderers on a faithful search for the Promised Land. The newly formed Jew-Gentile church of Jesus Christ merely advanced the ancient plan.

Taking on the mantle to embody God's kingdom, the new people of God—the church—were defined no longer by Israelite ancestry but by a common faith in Jesus Christ. Insofar as the revealed mystery of the radically multicultural, multiclass church reflected the kingdom of God, it was God's "chosen race, a royal priesthood, a holy nation, God's own people, in order that [it] may proclaim the mighty acts of him who called [it] out of darkness and into his marvelous light" (1 Peter 2:9).

So what does this biblical call to radical community, where the rich and the poor enjoy Jubilee justice and where Jew and Gentile fellowship together, have to do with urban-suburban partnership? Everything! For it demonstrates the equality, respect, compassion, reconciliation, and humility between the rich and the poor and between Jew and Gentile (i.e., between all tribes and nations) that God desires among his people.

But partnership implies a working relationship, an arrangement by which two parties share a vision and engage together in activity to meet shared goals. Chapter 2 has shown that the rich and the poor and all tribes and nations enjoy a profound level of justice and reconciliation under the reign of God, and chapter 3 will emphasize the fact that this justice and reconciliation are integral to the biblical call to mission to take the Good News of the kingdom of God to the ends of the earth. We seek to understand this missionary call, which beckons the church to move from simply modeling the new order of God to proactively bearing witness to it in word and deed for the transformation of the world.

Reflection Questions

1. The biblical call for community is to *be* God's people. How does simply *being* the people of God inform our understanding of mission?

2. How does socioeconomic justice (economic *koinonia*) fit into the call to be God's radical community?

3. How does reconciliation (multi-ethnic *koinonia*) fit into the call to be God's radical community?

4. How does this call inform our understanding of urban-suburban partnership?

3

The Call to Spirit-Empowered, Holistic Mission

In the beginning God created *shalom*. He paused to look at his handiwork at various intervals in the process and "saw that it was good" (Gen. 1:10, 12, 18, 21, 25, 31). *Shalom*—wholeness in every area of life, where God, creature, and creation enjoy harmonious relationships—defined existence.[1] *Shalom* was, because God ruled the universe. And God charged humankind, made in his image, to steward *shalom*, to rule over it with care (Gen. 1:26–31) as man and woman enjoyed God, each other, and all of creation (Gen. 2:7–25).

But tragedy of tragedies: the serpent, the most cunning of creatures, sweet-talked Adam and Eve into eating of the tree from which God forbade them to eat (Gen. 3:1–7). They disobeyed God, and *shalom*-destroying sin entered into the world. With *shalom* contaminated, "widespread deception, distortion, and domination in all forms of human relationships—with God, within one's self (and family), within the community . . . and with the environment" cursed the world.[2] Brokenness, fear, selfishness, and greed—which resulted in all manner of rebellion, violence, oppression, injustice, poverty, and unrighteousness—tore at the very fabric of existence; indeed the earth was full of corruption (Gen. 6:11–12).

But even as Satan gained a foothold in creation, God had a plan to mend it. Instead of looking to the brightest and the best of humanity to counter this evil, however, God set his eyes on the nomadic Hebrews, out of which he formed a nation. God called one of them, Abram of Haran, and instructed him, "Go from your country . . . to the land that I will show you. I will make of you a great nation, and I will bless you, and make your name great. . . . In you all the families of the earth shall be blessed" (Gen. 12:1–3). To lift up a homeless, ethnically mixed group of people, make a great nation out of them, and bless all the families of the earth through them constituted God's plan to redeem creation and everyone in it.

We retell the Genesis story to remember the backdrop of God's plan of salvation—a fallen world, a paradise lost, a world that had forgotten how to love God and each other, a world far away from *shalom*. And God formed Israel to heal and redeem it. God formed a people he could call his own in order to redeem *all* peoples. We retell the story of creation, fall, and redemption to remember that the biblical notion of mission begins here.

Whereas we emphasized the *great nation* part of the plan in the last chapter, we now necessarily emphasize the part that through them *all the families of the earth will be blessed*. These two parts form an inseparable whole: in one breath, God sought to form a nation (community) for the sake of *all* the nations (mission). This organic relationship between radical community and world mission is key in understanding justice and reconciliation as an integral part of the church's missionary activity in the world. As we saw in the last chapter, economic and multi-ethnic *koinonia*—where the rich and the poor enjoyed a relationship of justice, respect, and dignity, and where all tribes and nations fellowshipped together—held a central place in the biblical community. So as God's people in the New Testament began to take the gospel of Christ to the ends of the earth with proactive missionary fervor, it was simply extending the values of the kingdom to the rest of the world as they themselves lived them out in the redeemed community.

The Cross, Resurrection, and Great Commission

Jesus paid the ultimate price for ushering in the new order of God, for it threatened both the religious and sociopolitical establishments.[3] As those in power captured, tortured, and killed the itinerant preacher from Nazareth, his disciples scattered (Matt. 26:47–56), their hopes dashed and their lives wracked with confusion, fear, and despair (Matt. 26:69–75; Luke 24:13–27). But three days later, the single most significant event in human history took place: The large stone covering the entrance to the tomb was rolled away (Matt. 28:2). The linen wrappings inside just lay there, and "the cloth that had been on Jesus' head . . . [was] rolled up in a place by itself" (John 20:7). The crucified Messiah defied the powers of death and was alive again. Jesus had risen! A group of grieving women first discovered the empty tomb. And after they encountered heavenly messengers, who reminded them of Jesus's words about being raised on the third day, the women told the disciples (Luke 23:55–24:9). At first they did not, could not, believe the women, until Jesus himself appeared and showed them his nail-scarred hands and side, which had been pierced with a spear (John 20:19–29).

The resurrection of Christ gave the disciples reason to hope again. As long as Jesus lived, the community of disciples could see once again the possibility of the reign of God in their midst. Furthermore, his resurrection gave ultimate meaning to his crucifixion. What humanity meant for evil—crucifying the trouble-making prophet—God transformed into good, raising him from the dead so that all may choose life (Acts 2:22–47; 3:12–26; John 20:31). Through their worship of the crucified and risen Lord (Luke 24:52–53), the disciples in essence became the community of the cross and resurrection. Insofar as this community worshiped the living Christ and served one another, it testified to the power and love of God. The believing community rejoiced, and appropriately so, for the disciples saw once again the attainability of the glories of the kingdom, including Jubilee justice and reconciliation for all who came to faith in Christ.

Lest the believers keep the glories of the kingdom to themselves, however, the risen Jesus charged them to move beyond the confines of the believing community and "Go . . . and make disciples of all nations, baptizing them in the name of the Father and of the Son and of the Holy Spirit, and teaching them to obey everything that I have commanded you" (Matt. 28:19–20). The other three Gospels record similar charges, but the Great Commission in the book of Matthew has inspired more missionary movements around the world than any other biblical passage.

We cannot miss the profound shift that occurs here. From God's call to Israel to *be* his people, the mandate went forth, out of Jesus's mouth no less: "Go into all the world and proclaim the good news to the whole creation" (Mark 16:15), and, "As the Father has sent me, so I send you" (John 20:21). The Great Commission (along with the *lesser commissions* in Mark, Luke, and John) calls for more than simply modeling the kingdom; it calls for bold initiative: Go. Tell. Baptize. Make disciples. These proactive verbs catapulted the new community of Christ out of itself and into the world.

But certainly it did not render obsolete the call to *be* the people of God; on the contrary, *to be* and *to go* were two parts of the one call of God upon his people to bear witness to the kingdom. Social activist Melba Maggay's description of the church's witness today as "proclamation and presence" depicts well the New Testament practice of mission.[4] To be sure, missionary zeal did not replace the commitment to one another in community; rather, it flowed *out from* their community experience of joy, worship, and mutual care. From the worshiping community of the cross and resurrection (presence), Holy Spirit–empowered mission flowed out, thus beginning an extraordinary transformational, global movement that continues to this day (proclamation).

The Great Commission in the Power of the Spirit

The commission of the crucified and risen Christ gave the community of disciples its confident sense of mission, but it was the coming of the Holy Spirit that gave them the boldness and power to implement it. As missiologist Bryant Myers puts it, "The Holy Spirit is the source of power that transformed a fairly ordinary group of disciples, who had abandoned their Lord, into a fearless group of witnesses who would not surrender their mission even under threat of death (Acts 4:19)."[5] Jesus knew the significance of the Spirit and instructed his disciples to wait for the Spirit's coming before they attempted to do anything in his name (Luke 24:49). Only after you receive power from on high, Jesus said, will you "be my witnesses in Jerusalem, in all Judea and Samaria, and to the ends of the earth" (Acts 1:8). And sure enough, as recorded in Acts 2, when the Spirit came, Peter preached a sermon that resulted in three thousand conversions (Acts 2:1–41), which was only the beginning!

What role did the Holy Spirit play in empowering the disciples to engage in mission? The Bible suggests at least four activities of the Spirit that inspired them to go: First, the Spirit verified the truth of Jesus in the hearts of the disciples (John 14:17, 26) by allowing them to experience God in a deeply personal and motivational way. The baptism in the Holy Spirit, "a profound experience of the reality of God's presence," so moved the disciples that they were compelled to share the faith with others. Indeed, the connection between Spirit baptism and witness is undisputed.[6] Specifically referring to Pentecostals today, missiologist Douglas Petersen, himself a Pentecostal, asserts that they "have always emphasized experiential Christianity as the way to validate the authenticity of [their] doctrinal confession."[7] This authenticating experience in the Spirit motivated the first believers to take the gospel anywhere and everywhere.

Second, the Spirit creates the unity of the Body (Eph. 4:3–16), demonstrating the reconciliation that can happen in Christ between men and women, black, brown and white, and rich and poor (Gal. 3:3, 23-29; Col. 3:11). Such Spirit-empowered unity in Christ in and of itself attested to the power of the gospel, and it gave the New Testament church the right—the integrity—to preach the gospel of peace and reconciliation to the world.

Third, the Spirit convicts the world regarding sin, righteousness, and judgment (John 16:8–11). In other words, the Spirit goes ahead of the church in mission, paving the way for a visible witness. We can infer from this that the Spirit did just that in the case of the apostles, for when they preached the gospel, thousands were obviously ready to hear. The experience of Peter and Cornelius in Acts 10 exemplifies particularly well the Spirit's preliminary work. Peter was still speaking, it says; he wasn't quite through spelling out the way of salvation when "the Holy Spirit fell upon all who heard the word" (v. 44). Cornelius's household began worshiping God and speaking in tongues (v. 46), to which Peter rhetorically asked, "Can anyone withhold the water for baptizing these people who have received the Holy Spirit just as we have?" (v. 47).

And fourth, the Spirit provides the power that transcends the natural world (Acts 2:17–21), a power that overcomes the pain and suffering of the masses—broken bodies, hunger, powerlessness, oppression, and so on. This power enabled the first disciples to go out with the ability to discern, heal, cast out demons, and perform many miracles, which left the people awestruck (Acts 2:43). This power enabled them

to minister to both the bodies and souls of those whom they encountered. Empowered by the Holy Spirit, a missionary fervor began to
sweep the land as the disciples proclaimed the Good News of Jesus
by way of "word, deed, and sign."[8]

The Church's Proclamation: The Gospel of the Kingdom

What exactly did the early church take to the ends of the earth in the
power of the Spirit? In light of the inseparable connection between
the radical community and its proactive mission in the world, we can
affirm that the disciples proclaimed nothing less than the gospel of
the kingdom of God, which included the justice and reconciliation
that they themselves were experiencing within the faith community.
Grasping this truth enables us to see the integral place that a ministry
to the poor has in the Spirit-empowered mission of the church.

But did the disciples in fact preach the gospel of the kingdom?
This question warrants some attention since not a few scholars have
pointed out the fact that whereas Jesus proclaimed the gospel of
the kingdom, the early church primarily proclaimed the gospel of
Christ.[9] Some point this out to suggest that the disciples lost the
social vision of Jesus's teaching and replaced it with the gospel of
individual salvation. This shift in the proclamation of the kingdom
to the proclamation of Christ most certainly occurred; the late missionary theologian Leslie Newbigin argues that it had to because the
kingdom "had now a name and a face—the name and the face of the
man from Nazareth."[10]

It is crucial to see, however, that the substance and scope of the
message did not change for the early disciples. But now, to explain the
kingdom, they drew the peoples' attention to the one who embodied
it. The kingdom—God's reign of peace, justice, righteousness, and
reconciliation (*shalom*)—was still the Good News to be proclaimed
to the ends of the earth. And by proclaiming the crucified and risen
Jesus, the disciples did exactly that. When Philip proclaimed "the
good news about the kingdom of God and the name of Jesus Christ"
(Acts 8:12), he exemplified the seamlessness by which the disciples
understood the kingdom of God and the person of Jesus.

Mortimer Arias's groundbreaking work *Announcing the Reign
of God* claims that the contemporary narrow view of evangelism,
which focuses on personal salvation and individual conversion, stems

from an eclipse of the kingdom of God not just in language but in substance.[11] The early church may have shifted its language from the kingdom of God to the person of Christ, but it did not lose sight of the broad scope of salvation that the kingdom demanded—personal *and* social transformation. Because justice and reconciliation held a central place in the kingdom, they found concrete expression in the holistic mission of the early church.

The Holistic Mission of the Early Church

Indeed today we can describe the early church's proactive mission in the New Testament as *holistic* or as some prefer, *wholistic*[12]—that is, ministry that proclaimed the Good News of the kingdom of God in Christ and its full scope of salvation, touching the whole of human existence from social structures to individual hearts. As such, it ministered especially to the poor, oppressed, and marginalized.

First of all, the fact that the first believers announced the message of the kingdom to both Jew and Gentile—the full range of human races and cultures—speaks volumes regarding the geocultural scope of their mission. Paul's well-documented journeys, which brought him and his missionary band to many lands, testify to the cultural wideness of God's salvation. In the book of Romans, Paul wrote a sophisticated theological treatise regarding God's great mercy and grace, which crossed the Jew-Gentile barrier. He concluded his complex argument in chapter 11 by explaining how Israel's disobedience led to the salvation of the Gentiles and how the salvation of the Gentiles will lead to the salvation of Israel. "Through [Israel's] stumbling," he wrote, "salvation has come to the Gentiles" (v. 11), and then, "I want you to understand this mystery: a hardening has come upon part of Israel, until the full number of the Gentiles has come in. And so all Israel will be saved" (vv. 25–26). So mission in the New Testament was holistic, first of all, in the sense that it encompassed the whole world.

Second, it was holistic because the practice of mission entailed at least two activities: (1) calling individuals to faith in Jesus Christ (Acts 2:38; Rom. 10:9–13) and, thus, into the reconciled, multicultural community called the church (Rev. 7:9–10); and (2) demonstrating the power of the kingdom to transform broken human situations, from sick bodies to evil social structures. The mission of the early church

was holistic in that it proclaimed the kingdom by both word (evangelism) and deed (social concern) in the power of the Spirit.

While verbal proclamation or evangelism in the New Testament
seems like a given in the mission of the church, the social action aspect
may not be as clear. The social dimension of the church's proactive
mission expressed itself mainly in miraculous signs and wonders
that brought God's Good News to the poorest and most desperately
oppressed in Roman society. As part of their missionary fervor in
proclaiming the Good News of Christ, the believers performed many
healings in the name of Jesus. For example, " 'I have no silver or gold,' "
Peter declared to a lame man, " 'but what I have I give you; in the name
of Jesus Christ of Nazareth, stand up and walk.' And [Peter] took
him by the right hand and raised him up; and immediately his feet
and ankles were made strong" (Acts 3:6–7). Many healing incidents
of this kind occurred throughout the ministry of the early church.

The apostles also continued Christ's war against evil spirits by
casting out those that held people captive (Acts 19:11–20). They even
occasionally raised the dead to testify to the power of the God of
life (Acts 9:36–42). Biblical scholar Thomas Hanks makes a compelling case that we should view the disabled, the leper, the ill, and the
demon-possessed in the New Testament as part of the oppressed
class. As a viable interpretation of Acts 10:38, where Peter described
Jesus's healing ministry among "all who were oppressed by the devil,"
Hanks writes, "We ought to understand all the healings that Jesus
and his disciples performed in Luke-Acts as *liberation of oppressed
persons.*"[13] If Hanks's analysis has any merit, then these healings,
exorcisms, and resurrections testified to God's profound mercy and
awesome power, which challenged the many varied forms of oppression in society.

The point is, these supernatural acts of the apostles—which went
hand in hand with their proclamation of the Good News—upset
the prevailing social order, as thousands of people came to faith
and joined the new community. And by upsetting the social order,
the church essentially challenged society's religious, political, and
economic practices in light of the kingdom of God. In Philippi for
example, after Paul exorcised a spirit of divination from a slave girl
whose gift of fortune-telling yielded big business, her owners incited a
mob against Paul and Silas and dragged them to the local authorities
saying, "These men are disturbing our city" (Acts 16:19–21). In other
words, their mission to manifest the kingdom of God was bad for

business; it was an affront to the prevailing economic order. It was also an affront to the powers that be. In that same story, the city officials tried to release Paul and Silas without explanation after beating them publicly and chaining them in prison. Propelled by kingdom justice, Paul demanded not just to be released but to be exonerated as well. He forced the magistrates in Philippi to do right by them and to practice justice, which they reluctantly did in the form of an apology (Acts 16:22–24, 35–39). Paul and the early church undoubtedly threatened the status quo on the essential social levels of economics and politics as they proclaimed and demonstrated the dangerously transforming gospel of the kingdom and of Jesus Christ to the ends of the earth. This is holistic mission at its best.

It's Biblical

This brief biblical review of the early church's holistic mission should remind us of the reason we are writing a book about partnership in the first place namely, to resume the mission of bearing witness to the kingdom of God by both proclamation and presence "in Jerusalem, in all Judea and Samaria, and to the ends of the earth" (Acts 1:8). This mission, insofar as it reflects the kingdom, most certainly includes ministries of compassion, justice, and reconciliation among the poor, the oppressed, and the marginalized.

As we listen to this call to engage the world in holistic mission along with the call to be the radical community of God—where the rich, the poor, and all tribes and nations fellowship together as a sign of God's justice and reconciliation—a distinct call begins to form, the call to affirm the multicultural, multiclass people that we are and to begin working together to extend the amazing goodness of the kingdom of God to our neighbors. More specifically, it is the call to link arms and lives across the urban-suburban divide to transform our communities. Picture it: the rich and the poor among the black, white, and brown in the redeemed community together extending their experience of justice and reconciliation to all, especially the poor.

This picture of urban-suburban partnership ultimately comes from the *Magna Carta* of our faith: the Holy Bible, God's Word. So we urge the people of God to obey the biblical call to partner together across the seemingly sturdy divides between the rich and the poor and between the culturally different. We must walk in obedience over the ruins of these walls, which the hammer of the gospel has effectively destroyed, link arms with one another, and work together to bring about lasting change in our world in Jesus's name and by the power of the Spirit. "For the love of God is this," wrote the apostle John, "that we obey his commandments. And his commandments are not burdensome, for whatever is born of God conquers the world" (1 John 5:3–4).

Reflection Questions

1. Discuss the transition from the call to be God's people to the call to engage in proactive mission. Put another way, what is the relationship between *being* God's people and *doing* God's mission in the world?

2. What is the role of the Holy Spirit in the mission of the church?

3. How are works of compassion, justice, and reconciliation related to the mission of the church to take the gospel to the ends of the earth?

4. What does Spirit-empowered holistic mission have to do with urban-suburban partnership?

Part 3

How We Do (and Don't Do) It

Principles and Practice of Partnership

We have heard the biblical demand to partner together for the sake of the kingdom, but how does one even begin to cross the seemingly ever-widening divide between urban and suburban realities? As we have already established in chapter 1, despite the blurring of the geographic line that separates urban and suburban territories, "there [remains] a great barrier of distrust between the rich and the poor today."[1] The lines that divide the races also remain solidly drawn. Regarding the black-white divide, which still predominantly defines the race problem in America, some social scientists have not hesitated to describe the United States as essentially two separate nations—one white and the other black.[2]

Unfortunately, the church is not exempt from these dividing lines. Wealthy, middle-class churches—intentional or not—behave in ways that repel the poor. And poor churches, try as they might to attract the nonpoor, do not succeed. Furthermore, and not unrelated to the economic homogeneity of our churches, white, black, and brown churches remain remarkably white, black, and brown. Sociologists

Michael Emerson and Christian Smith cite the 1998 National Congregations Study as saying that "about 90 percent of American congregations are made up of at least 90 percent of people of the same race."[3] In short, poor and rich and black, white, and brown churches (i.e., urban and suburban churches) simply do not mix.

Gripped by the biblical vision of economic and multi-ethnic *koinonia*, we ultimately cannot condone these divides in our churches. Think about it: The haves flock together in prosperity while the have-nots remain empty-handed in the body of Christ, and black, white, and brown people redeemed in Christ segregate for worship and ministry. We suspect that Moses, the prophets, Jesus, Peter, Paul, and the whole cloud of biblical witnesses would have something to say about this! The church today needs to strive in the Spirit to be that multiclass, multiracial kingdom community that by its very existence challenges the many divisions that exist in the world.

Part 3 seeks to translate the biblical call to urban-suburban partnership into visible, relevant, practical form. What does this type of partnership look like in today's world? What needs to happen in order to pull off such a thing? In other words, how can urban-suburban partnership work? Chapter 4 lays out the absolute essentials that make it possible—essentials that define redeemed human relationships in Christ. Chapters 5, 6, and 7 follow this with practical Dos and Don'ts, of which much of the substance comes from practitioners of cross-cultural ministry partnerships. Part 3 ends on a positive note as chapter 8 discusses the fruit of urban-suburban encounters from the perspective of practitioners who have engaged in ministry partnerships.

4

Partnership Essentials

In the early 1980s an international group of theologians met for an important consultation on "Sharing Jesus in the Two-Thirds World."[1] It was important not just because of the insights resulting from the consultation but also because it led to the formation of the International Fellowship of Evangelical Mission Theologians (INFEMIT). The twenty-five participants, the majority of whom came from Africa, Asia, and Latin America, intentionally gathered to exercise their right to theologize on their own terms. Space will not allow us to tell the whole story behind the formation of INFEMIT, but it was at the core a strong statement against Western missionary dominance, which has defined global Christianity for the last two millennia.[2]

In retrospect, things could have become divisive; an intercontinental theological war could have broken out between Western and non-Western missiologists. But participant Chris Sugden put into words the true spirit of the visionaries who propelled the INFEMIT movement: "They did not reject partnership with Western Christians. . . . They wanted to build that partnership on a proper basis of equality and mutuality. . . . They wanted a partnership with Western Christians and churches that expressed a relationship of reconciliation and mutual sharing in place of dominance and subservience."[3] INFEMIT did not want to create division, and it certainly did not want to start a war. On the contrary, it sought genuine partnership—the kind built upon shared power and shared vision. As part of the fruit of its efforts, INFEMIT developed functioning branches in Europe and the U.S., even as it maintained its non-Western focus and identity.

This example from the global scene highlights the challenge to cross cultures as well as to move away from dominant-subservient relationships to genuine partnership. We contend that the urban-suburban divide poses strikingly similar challenges, for indeed the city and the suburb are in essence two different cultures representing different levels of power in society. Whether across the exotic seas—which divide ethnic cultures—or across the street—which divide urban and suburban cultures—there are essentials that must be in place in order for true partnership to form and flourish. In light of the partnerships like INFEMIT being forged between Western and non-Western missionaries, we have narrowed these essentials to three absolute, irreducible minimums: deep reconciliation, authentic relationship, and collaborative action.

Deep Reconciliation

Reconciliation, a rich theological and sociopolitical concept, which the limits of this book cannot fully take up, necessarily begins the road toward genuine partnership, for the process of reconciliation compels us to view one another with dignity, equality, and mutual respect—the basic ingredients of true partnership. Practically speaking, reconciliation means the hard work of overcoming distrust, misunderstanding, bitterness, and even hatred between peoples of different ethnicities and economic class. These sentiments run deep because they have developed and simmered over time. From the injustice endured by Native Americans to black slavery and Jim Crow laws to Japanese relocation, our history has led to what Emerson and Smith call a "racialized society." According to them, the racialized society of post–civil rights America is

> one in which intermarriage rates are low, residential separation and socioeconomic inequality are the norm, our definitions of personal identity and our choices of intimate associations reveal racial distinctiveness, and where "we are never unaware of the race of a person with whom we interact." In short . . . a racialized society is a society

wherein race matters profoundly for differences in life experiences, life opportunities, and social relationships.[4]

Generally speaking, the urbanized in our racialized society represent those who have received the short end of the stick as oppression, marginalization, and poverty define their existence. On the other hand, the suburbanized represent those who have enjoyed—sometimes at the expense of the oppressed and marginalized poor—the place of privilege, wealth, security, and comfort. It is precisely this scenario that those who wish to establish a partnership between urban and suburban Christians must begin to overcome through a process of reconciliation.

The experience of injustice and oppression has left open sores not only on the community at large but also on the body of Christ, and the Band-Aid remedies of Christian niceties will not do. Trite phrases like "Let bygones be bygones," or "It's all under the blood now," or "Why can't we all just get along?" mock genuine reconciliation in Christ, especially when they come from well-intentioned but nevertheless patronizing idealists from the privileged class. Theologian Robert Schreiter contends that the process of reconciliation needs to come from the lineage of the victims, not of the oppressors.[5]

But haven't we resolved the race problem in America? Haven't we overcome our prejudices via the civil rights movement, the women's movement, and other liberation movements in the 1960s and 1970s? Why the need to call for reconciliation again and again? The fact is that the residual effects of the history of blatant racism still inform our society today. The Los Angeles riots, inflamed by the Rodney King case in the early 1990s, are a case in point. Those riots should have reminded us of the black-white tensions that seem ever ready to shoot up from the ground like a geyser. Moreover, the riots demonstrated the fact that racial tensions go beyond the black-white divide as "more Latinos than blacks were arrested [during the riots], and Korean-American stores suffered some of the worst devastation."[6]

But we certainly do not have to go back as far as the Los Angeles riots to prove how racialized our society is. For example, profiling—the practice on the part of law enforcement of singling out individuals on the basis of their color or appearance for questioning and arbitrary checks—has been outlawed in many states, but it continues to be a problem.[7] The rise of hate crimes against people of Middle Eastern descent or of the Islamic faith since 9/11 provides another tragic story.

For example, the Muslim Student Association (MSA) officially condemned an attack made January 20, 2007, against three Palestinian students by five football players at Guilford College in Greensboro, North Carolina. The MSA reported that the victims were "beaten with fists, feet and brass knuckles early Saturday by attackers who called them 'terrorists' and used racial slurs." The report quoted MSA President Mohamed Sheibani, "We are very concerned by the recent trend of increased hate crimes directed at Arab and Muslim students on campuses across North America."[8]

As plausible as this may be in light of 9/11, it should nevertheless serve as a tragic reminder of the ease with which we can slip back into pre–civil rights behaviors. The 2005 Academy Awards Best Picture, *Crash*, perhaps illustrates most vividly the racialized society of which Emerson and Smith speak; it shows on the silver screen the underlying distrust and dislike between people of different racial, social, and economic backgrounds. As long as these types of tensions exist between human beings made in the image of God, the call to reconciliation must be heralded.

And it should be heralded the loudest by God's people—people who have supposedly experienced deep reconciliation with God and with each other in Christ. Yet the famous words of the late Dr. Martin Luther King Jr. that eleven o'clock on Sunday morning is the most segregated hour in America still rings true.[9] Christians must enter into the process of deep reconciliation with each other, which is at the heart of the call to urban-suburban partnership. We must face up to our own racial and socioeconomic prejudices. "Our love for Christ should break down every racial, ethnic or economic barrier. As Christians come together to solve the problems of their community, the great challenge will be to partner and witness together across these barriers."[10]

Partnership between urban and suburban Christians necessitates a reconciliation of a deep and humble kind—that is, reconciliation based upon confession of and forgiveness for the sins of racism past and present. Stories of Christians engaged in this kind of reconciliation process are few and far between, but examples do exist that testify to its possibility in the power of Christ.

One night during worship at the 1996 Urban Poor Network Consultation in Hong Kong, a participant from Japan walked up to a woman from Korea and publicly apologized to her. The man said he needed to do so, on behalf of his country, because of the atrocities his forefathers committed in the 1940s and 1950s against Korean women, who were forced to "comfort" Japanese servicemen. After getting over the awkwardness of the moment, the Korean woman teared up and suddenly embraced the Japanese man in a visible act of forgiveness. Their exchange of confession and forgiveness set off a domino effect among the rest of the participants. For the next thirty minutes or so, while the music leaders appropriately played the song "Break Dividing Walls," based on Ephesians 2:14, Americans approached Filipinos and confessed their sin against them, the English did the same to the Indians, the Dutch to the black South Africans, and so on—all in the name of Jesus Christ through whom God promised the reconciliation of all things (Col. 1:20). Jackie Pullinger, founder and director of the St. Stephen's Society in Hong Kong, was scheduled to speak that night, but she decided to forego her message, for all concurred that the Spirit of God had already spoken a word—the word of reconciliation—to which the people of God could only respond.

The intentional interracial community that Anglo-American Chris Rice and the late Spencer Perkins (John Perkins's son) formed in Jackson, Mississippi, also serves as an example of deep reconciliation as six families—three black and three white—lived and ministered together in an extremely racialized community in the 1980s and 1990s. They document their story in their award-winning book *More Than Equals.*[11] Another book, *Breaking Down Walls*, also lays out a model of deep reconciliation in inner-city Chicago.[12] Authors Raleigh Washington, an African-American, and Glen Kehrein, a Euro-American, tell their story of how God brought them together to highlight racial reconciliation as integral to community transformation.

Both sets of men—Perkins and Rice; Washington and Kehrein—claim that whatever principles of reconciliation their stories modeled have resulted from their profound personal struggles to develop the kind of unique relationships they enjoyed. The honesty in their stories of both the pain and the reward of overcoming racial and cultural barriers demonstrates how deep into ourselves and with one another we must go in the work of reconciliation.

Authentic Relationship

Partnership that dares to cross the urban-suburban divide must begin with reconciliation, but it must proceed to the next indispensable principle: authentic relationship. It must strive for authenticity in relationship as an inseparable part of deep reconciliation. Authenticity and reconciliation undoubtedly go together, but not sequentially. For this reason we could have discussed these two aspects together, but authenticity has properties that are distinct enough to discuss separately.

By *authenticity* we mean a relationship that goes beyond toleration of one another. Speaking as a presenter at the American Society of Missiology in 2004, Maggay summed up well the formidable task of striving for authentic relationships across cultures. She said:

> Cross cultural contact does not necessarily lead to cross cultural understanding. . . . It is one thing to see other cultures on TV, with their exotic habits and colorful costumes; it is another thing to see them invading our living spaces and smell their cooking. Once contact becomes real rather than virtual; once it engages that part of us which has to do with perceptions, values, beliefs and world-views, coming together becomes awkward, tense, messy and often painful. This is the kind of discomfort we all go through once we truly cross cultures.[13]

Maggay had crossing the ethnic divides in mind, but does this not also describe the crossing of the urban-suburban divide?

Perkins and Rice essentially answer "Yes" to that question when they distinguish between integration and reconciliation in American society. They write, "Integration and reconciliation are not the same. . . . America may be more integrated, but it is far from being reconciled."[14] In other words, the laudable progress of America to desegregate society and cultivate the attitude that has accepted increasingly more minorities in places of civil leadership (integration) has not necessarily resulted in better interracial understanding and, even less so, full acceptance of one another (reconciliation).

As we apply this distinction to the urban-suburban encounter, we see clearly that truly partnering together requires a commitment that goes beyond integration and reaches for a kind of reconciliation that is marked with relational authenticity. It must go beyond working together for the greater good of ministry. It must go beyond: "I'll work with you because the gospel demands it, but I don't have to like you!" Perkins and Rice profoundly point out that "the mark of reconciliation is not a truce but an embrace."[15] God calls those who stand on the two sides of the urban-suburban divide to cross over and fully embrace one another—that is, fully accept, affirm, and trust one another toward the development of something called friendship.

Friendship marks the transition from mere integration to reconciliation. Rice's relationship with Spencer Perkins obviously taught him the indispensability of friendship in ministry, for he has since formed other friendships that cross the urban-suburban divide; for example, his friendship with Emmanuel Katongole, an African Catholic priest-theologian, who co-directs the Center for Reconciliation at Duke Divinity School with Rice. Despite the many divides that would work against them—black-white, Africa–North America, and Catholic-Protestant—a friendship-based ministry partnership has developed. "We work together," Rice says, "but our work is grounded in our friendship. Emmanuel is a family friend as we've hosted him many times in our home, and he has hosted me a number of times with his family in Malube, Uganda."[16] Rice traces the beginning of a real friendship when they roomed together in Pattaya, Thailand, as they participated in the 2004 forum organized by the Lausanne Committee on World Evangelization. It solidified from there as they took each other to significant landmarks in their personal faith journeys; Rice took Katongole to Jackson, Mississippi, where his discipleship was deepened by his firsthand experience of genuine Christian community across the black-white divide in the Deep South, and Katongole took Rice to Malube, Uganda, where his Christian commitment was profoundly shaped by village life under the regime of Idi Amin as well as the genocide occurring in neighboring Rwanda. To share with one another personal places of pain and hope, along with other intentional relationship-building efforts, has resulted in an authenticity of relationship, a friendship.

Urban-suburban partnership requires striving for this kind of authenticity in relationship, but there is nothing easy about it. Indeed, all who have entered into that process testify to its hard challenges that go along with the rewards. Referring back to the friendship between Perkins and Rice, they report that they almost threw in the towel on a number of occasions. In fact, at around the ten-year mark of their partnership, they came close to going their separate ways due to what they considered to be irreconcilable differences. With the resolve of genuine commitment to each other, however—not unlike a marriage!—they chose instead to call upon spiritual mentors to help them do the hard, painful, risky, and vulnerable (i.e., authentic) work of deep reconciliation. Of his late friend, Rice writes, "For the sake of the Gospel Spencer loved me 'till death did us part.' For the sake of the Gospel, I loved him like a brother. Because of God neither of us was ever the same."[17]

A telltale sign that a ministry relationship has attained a level of this kind of authenticity is that it goes beyond the *business of ministry* as it begins to work itself out during the *off hours*. The relationships formed between the early leaders of LIGHT Ministries in the Philippines provide an interesting case study of this kind of authenticity, not between people of different ethnicities—because they were all Filipino—but between people of different socioeconomic backgrounds. Both the poor and the nonpoor made up the leadership, and they described their relationships like this: "We not only worked together, we also played together; we not only designed community development strategies together, we also shared family problems together; we not only organized projects in impoverished areas together, we also went on retreats in the mountains together. [We] . . . went beyond the workplace."[18] Indeed, authentic relationships between the rich and the poor and between the black, white, and brown in the community of Christ pave the way for genuine partnership—the kind of partnership that transcends professionalism in ministry; the kind of partnership that flows out of friendship.

Collaborative Action

This friendship, however, must ultimately graduate to collaborative action—the final essential principle of partnership. Without it, the relationship never truly matures into a partnership, for the very word *partnership* implies working together on the basis of shared vision and toward the fulfillment of shared goals. At the end of the day, a relationship that seeks to be a partnership must move on to shared action. Whereas reconciliation and authenticity seek to accomplish understanding, trust, and mutual respect between persons, collaborative action moves the relationship from mere friendship to genuine partnership in ministry.

"Faith without works is dead," wrote the apostle James (James 2:14 KJV). As works activate faith, so too does partnership activate friendship. In other words, if our efforts at reconciliation and authenticity stop when we become friends and we do not mature to collaborative action, then we have not yet attained partnership. We must become more than buddies if we want to live out the vision of partnership. God ultimately calls us to action—or to do good works, in the language of James—in the service of humanity and to the glory of God; *collaborative* action conveys the idea that we fulfill this call in partnership with each other. If urban-suburban partnerships are to reflect the gospel of Christ, then they must ultimately mature to collaborative action.

In light of the challenges of reconciliation and authenticity posed by the urban-suburban divide, to rush into attempts at collaborative action seems ill-advised. Indeed, trying to work together for the kingdom without acknowledging and dealing with latent prejudices and relational conflicts only invites trouble.[19] On the other hand, if we wait for the fruit of reconciliation and authenticity to ripen before we take action, then we might never take the first step! Reconciliation can always go deeper, and relationships can always be more authentic; in short, these are lifelong processes. As we strive toward these things, however, we must also work in collaborative action if we want to develop something resembling a partnership. We believe that partnership in Christ develops when all three of these processes are moving forward together.

Perkins and Rice drive this point home when they distinguish between friends and yokefellows. We know what a friend is, but what is a yokefellow? Interacting with the way Paul described his brothers and sisters in Philippi, Perkins and Rice write: "A commitment to advancing the Gospel—a cause much too big for a lone individual, no matter how heroic—was what 'yoked' Paul to his fellow workers. It is also the cause of the Gospel . . . that supplies [us] with the fuel to cultivate and maintain our unlikely relationship."[20] *Yokefellows* then describes friendships bound together by a common purpose—friends with a mission: a mission too big for individuals *as* individuals to try to accomplish; a mission that requires partnership. Needless to say, the mission to bring the full implications of the gospel to bear upon society, especially the poor and oppressed, is too big for individuals to handle. It requires cooperation, collaboration, and teamwork. "Friendships are built for the benefit of the friends," Perkins and Rice explain. "Yokefellows come together for the benefit of the kingdom."[21]

For example, the yokefellow relationship between Perkins and Rice provided the impetus for an interracial community and church in Jackson, Mississippi, in the 1980s and 1990s. Before Perkins's untimely and tragic death in 1998, he and Rice took their gospel message of racial reconciliation and justice around the country as they conducted workshops in colleges, universities, churches, and civic organizations. The impact of their partnership was immeasurable, influencing countless people in the pursuit of racial and socioeconomic justice in the name of Jesus. One school, Belhaven College in Jackson (the alma mater for both Perkins and Rice), recognized their achievements by granting them the Outstanding Service to Mankind Award, an honor given only one other time in the history of the institution.[22] The special memorial issue of *Reconcilers* (the changed name of *Urban Family* magazine from 1996 to 1998), released in the spring of 1998, was filled with testimonies of the impact of Perkins's and Rice's message upon their lives as well as their ministries surrounding race and poverty.

Although very different from the yokefellow relationship between Perkins and Rice, Katongole and Rice can also be considered yokefellows, as their friendship has resulted in fruitful ministry together. As founding co-directors of the Center for Reconciliation at Duke, they not only serve the divinity students at Duke by offering courses and formation programs in reconciliation (Katongole and Rice co-teach a course called "Journeys in Reconciliation"), they also have started a book series called Resources for Reconciliation as well as travel extensively around the U.S. and the globe. One major area of focus for their travels is the African Great Lakes region, partnering with organizations like World Vision, the Mennonite Central Committee, and ALARM (African Leadership and Reconciliation Ministries) in order to nourish and develop Christian leaders who understand and are committed to the ministry of reconciliation.

The yokefellows Washington and Kehrein began a faith-and-works partnership in 1983 that continues to this day to be salt and light in West Chicago and beyond. Rock of Our Salvation Evangelical Free Church, pastored at the time of this writing by Washington's brother Abraham Lincoln Washington, and Circle Urban Ministries, for which Kehrein continues to provide key leadership, have been an enduring partnership of indigenous leadership development, discipleship, evangelism, community restoration, health care, shelter, and many other ministries that have addressed the great challenges of the city.

These men—Perkins, Rice, Katongole, Washington, and Kehrein— and their ministries have modeled deep reconciliation, authentic relationships, and collaborative action across the urban-suburban divide. Their examples demonstrate the possibilities and the hope.

Reflection Questions

1. "Despite the advances made in racial integration, we remain a racialized society." Do you agree or disagree with this statement? How important is racial reconciliation in the success of Christian mission?

2. How can we form authentic relationships across the urban-suburban divide? In what ways have you seen the diverse in Christ truly embrace each other as sisters and brothers?

3. What is the difference between friendship and a yokefellow relationship? Discuss the importance of collaborative action to accomplish God's mission.

4. How do the three irreducible minimums of deep reconciliation, authentic relationship, and collaborative action make for an effective urban-suburban partnership?

5

Dos and Don'ts for Both Urban and Suburban Groups

Laying out the essential principles in the last chapter has provided the groundwork for partnership; this chapter will read like the follow-up handbook. This is only natural, for as the Christ-centered processes of deep reconciliation, relational authenticity, and collaborative action take hold among us, we poise ourselves for implementation, for the *how-to*s of coming together in partnership for transformational ministry.

Partnership ultimately requires that we identify certain practices that can either make or break our attempts at crossing the urban-suburban divide. Based on the many experiences of ministry practitioners, we have highlighted certain essential Dos and Don'ts—first for both sides of the divide, since any healthy partnership necessitates some level of reciprocity (chapter 5), and then for each side of the divide given the different strengths and struggles that each side brings to the table (chapters 6 and 7). Taken together, we hope these lists of Dos and Don'ts provide the nuts and bolts of effective urban-suburban partnership.

In light of the processes of reconciliation, authenticity, and collaborative action, there are at least seven pairs of Dos and Don'ts that equally apply to both urban and suburban worlds.

1. Do Begin with Existing Relationships/Don't Attempt to Partner with Brand New Contacts

Unless our heads have been buried in the proverbial sand and we have had absolutely no contact with fellow Christians on *the other side*, chances are good that we have had some association across the divide. This could be a personal friendship that goes way back, a referral from a friend or coworker, or a denominational connection. It could be as personal as one's own parents—like the supportive parents of the first relocaters in Lawndale Community Church in Chicago[1]—or it might be as impersonal as having gotten on some ministry's mailing list and receiving its regular newsletter. The point is, start here. As we prayerfully consider partnering with a church or organization for transformational ministry, it is optimal to begin with an existing relationship. Such a head start will enable the two entities to consider partnership almost immediately.

If partnership does not have such a starting point, the two sides of a very green relationship will have to undergo a process of getting to know each other first. This is not necessarily bad, of course, but developing something resembling a working ministry will not happen anytime soon. It could take months or even years before they can consider ministry together. We do not recommend even talking about partnership unless some level of trust and communication has been established.

We liken premature partnership to rushing into a marriage before getting to know your future spouse. Partnering right away with a new contact is a bad enough idea that it has ended up on our Don'ts list. It is certainly possible that a partnership can eventually bloom out of a relationship that began out of the blue, but not without much preliminary relational work.

Do begin with an existing relationship, and don't go to the Yellow Pages and pick a church or organization with the expectation of developing an immediate partnership.

2. Do Let Human Need Motivate Us/Don't Forget to Love God!

Both parties agree to the idea of ministry partnership because of the reality of human need. Considering partnership does not come about because two groups just want to get to know each other; on the contrary, the needs of a poor community have beckoned the faithful on both sides of the urban-suburban fence. The late Mother Teresa, who dedicated her life to the poorest of the poor in Calcutta, India, often said, "Calcuttas are everywhere if only we have eyes to see. Find your Calcutta."[2] A burden for the poor and oppressed comes from God, and to acknowledge this together establishes compassion and justice as the drivers of the partnership.

In allowing human need to motivate us, however, we cannot forget to love God. We must keep our interior life intact by staying connected to the one who alone can ultimately meet human needs. We have heard too many stories of people whose eyes have been open to the plight of the poor and have become social activists, but tragically at the expense of their own spiritual health. Being motivated by the many needs of the community is one thing; being consumed by them is quite another.

At least two consequences occur when the needs of the community consume us: First, the needs overwhelm us. The sheer amount as well as the gravity of human need in an impoverished community can feel like quicksand—the more we move to help others, the more we feel like we have sunk in over our heads. Instead of standing on the solid rock of Christ, we sink down into the quicksand-depths of debilitating despair. Second, the tone of the ministry becomes primarily pragmatic, devoid of deep spiritual meaning for both the server and the served. Put these two consequences together, and you have the formula for disillusionment and burnout.

Author-activists Brenda Salter McNeil and Rick Richardson lament, "Far too often, those who seek to be reconcilers and peacemakers have anemic worship—both individually and corporately. This is a mistake. Racial and ethnic problems are too immense to be addressed with spiritual anemia and cynicism." More positively, they write that the "process of renewal and transformation takes place in worship and prepares us to be prophets who criticize the world's status quo, and it energizes the imagination for what is possible through God."[3]

A partnership between urban and suburban people must eventually grow to worship God together and celebrate the spiritual ground upon which their partnership is built—namely, upon Jesus Christ, the rock of their common salvation. Loving God together reminds both parties that for all of the economic, cultural, and racial differences between them, they stand united in the grace, mercy, and power of God. "God is delighted," write McNeil and Richardson, "when his people come together in worship and prayer to live out the power of the cross to break down dividing walls of hostility."[4]

Furthermore, solidarity in prayer and worship reminds both parties of the very reason for the partnership—namely, the transformation of persons and communities in Christ's name—and it maintains the spirituality of holistic ministry. As Mark Labberton, senior pastor of First Presbyterian Church in Berkeley, California, writes, "Worship sets us free from ourselves to be free for God and God's purposes in the world. The dangerous act of worshiping God in Jesus Christ necessarily draws us into the heart of God and sends us out to embody it, especially toward the poor, the forgotten and the oppressed."[5] Insofar as this kind of worship defines the ministry, urban-suburban partnership flows out of a vital faith that both sides share.

Do let the partnership be driven by compassion and a desire for justice to address the needs of the poor, but don't forget to love God together—to pray and worship together, reminding yourselves of the power and provision of God.

3. Do Strive for Equality and Joint Ownership of the Ministry/Don't Allow Inequality to Define the Partnership

As we stand together upon Christ the Rock, we must necessarily develop a partnership that reflects God's justice—a relationship that reflects equality and joint ownership of the ministry. We will say more about what each side of the urban-suburban partnership must do to ensure this in chapters 6 and 7. For now it is enough to acknowledge that if the partnership is to have a chance, both must mutually submit to Christ's lordship and commit to God's justice. On her own Dos and Don'ts list for partnership, research analyst Heidi Unruh puts it this way: "Do begin from a position of mutual strength," and "Do build joint ownership by ensuring that each partner is bringing something valued to the table. A true partnership is an equal exchange."[6]

By contrast, if we let the standards of our racialized and class-based society define the relationship, then color, money, and positional power determine a one-way flow, where one side contributes (usually the suburban partner) and the other receives (usually the urban partner). Such an arrangement describes something other than a partnership, and it does nothing but perpetuate—perhaps even widen—the very divide we long to cross. Having said that, Carey Davis, founder and coordinator of an urban-suburban community organization in Philadelphia called CityLights, makes an important point when she writes that partners "must acknowledge the inequalities of our world that often filter down into our partnership relationships."[7] These inequalities of wealth and privilege are real, and both urban and suburban partners cannot deny them. Again, we will say more later about what each side must contribute to make the partnership truly equal.

Suffice it to say here that both sides must strive for equality, mutual respect, and mutual power—the stuff of true partnership—and they must resist the very real inequality that exists in the world.

4. Do Foster Interdependence and Mutual Service/Don't Be a Burden and a Liability to the Other

Christ-centered partnership takes the third point one step further: not only should the partnership be equal, each side needs to acknowledge its need for the other, which fosters interdependence and mutual service. This can be accomplished by taking seriously the words of the apostle Paul that we should try to "outdo one another in showing honor" (Rom. 12:10). What can happen if each side of the partnership strives to serve the best interest of the other? We can play with the words of JFK and say, "Ask not what your partner can do for you, but what you can do for your partner." To the extent that both sides take on this posture, an interdependent relationship develops wherein each side recognizes its need for the other as well as its contribution to the other.

Anything less than this kind of interdependence jeopardizes a healthy partnership and in fact fosters relational dependence and codependence. At that point, each side becomes a burden and a liability to the other, which breeds frustration, resentment, hurt feelings, and inevitable conflict. Unruh says it this way: "Don't allow an unequal partnership to reinforce patterns of dependency." In fact, she advises, "Enter a partnership [only] if each [side] can honestly say, 'I need you because . . . ,' "[8] meaning that independence/dominance and accompanying dependence/subservience should not be tolerated by either side.

Do foster interdependence, and avoid unhealthy patterns of one-sidedness and overdependence.

5. Do Cultivate a Relationship that Transcends the Ministry Project/Don't Forget to Play

As we established in the previous chapter, relational authenticity constitutes the foundation of partnership, and a mark of that authenticity is when the relationship goes beyond professionalism and develops into friendship. As authentic friendships form between urban and suburban Christians (yokefellows), they begin to invite one another to each other's homes for meals, go to each other's kids' soccer games, play together, retreat together, confide in each other, and so on. "The best urban-suburban church partnerships . . . include the development of meaningful personal relationships based on mutual trust and respect. Both suburban and city churches must make an intentional effort to go beyond the superficial."[9] Of his relationship with Spencer Perkins, Chris Rice writes, "Our lives are so intertwined that often people, even close friends, will call me 'Spencer' on the phone and refer to him as 'Chris.' We work together. Our children almost think they're brothers and sisters."[10]

Because of the differences between urban and suburban realities, this kind of relationship will require intentionality as well as perseverance to endure periods of awkwardness and tension. Regarding his early years at the interracial Voice of Calvary Church, Rice confesses, "I realized that I had not won any deeper relationships with black people in the process. I came to the uncomfortable realization that for two years I had lived in a black neighborhood, worked in a black-led ministry and worshiped in a majority-black church, but had not gained a single close black friend."[11] It was not until he, along with the others who made up the interracial community, went at it with intentionality that genuine, true friendships began to form between them.

The *Don't* of this Do and Don't couplet is a negative way of saying the same thing: Don't forget to play. "Don't get so busy doing or planning projects," says Unruh, "that [you] fail to get together on a regular basis to pray, talk and hang out."[12] For example, one year when the Berkeley Covenant Church in the suburban north side of Berkeley, California, and New Hope Covenant Church in neighboring inner-city Oakland decided to do their annual church retreat together, the joint gathering had a decidedly recreational purpose to it. Bound together by denominational ties, these two churches had linked arms on various levels of partnership through the years, including starting a preschool together to serve low-income families in East Oakland.

But this was the first time they had ever come together primarily to play. From ultimate Frisbee to basketball to Ping-Pong, the two churches played together heartily. Many also went on nature walks together, swam together, and gathered around a campfire together to sing folk songs. Every night of the retreat, the two churches were refreshed with song and teaching by musical artist and pastor Glenn Kaiser from Chicago. Through play, the two churches solidified their partnership.

Do grow beyond ministry projects, and don't forget to play!

6. Do Commit Long-Term/Don't Give Up Too Easily

Partnership does not happen overnight. It requires patience, creativity, flexibility, listening, and learning, and no microwave approach will do. On the contrary, effective urban-suburban partnership needs more of the Crock-Pot, slow cooker approach to make it happen. Partnership is a long-term commitment; it is for people who are in it for the long haul. Having said that, Davis points out the importance of a time frame within which partners can evaluate at certain points—the one-year mark, three-year mark, and so on—whether they should continue. Furthermore, she states that there are legitimate levels of commitment to the partnership. While some partners come and go to do specific projects that have a beginning and an end, others become "lifers" in the work of the ministry.[13]

The point here is that both sides must have a tenacity to stick with the partnership when problems arise. This applies to both short-term and long-term levels of partnership. We should *expect* problems— small and large, ranging from cultural *faux pas* to annoying personality quirks to differences in goals and strategies—partnerships of the enduring kind are made as iron sharpens iron. If partnership is going to work, both parties need to commit to the relationship and demonstrate a willingness to do what it takes to work out problems that arise between them. Partners cannot give up too easily.

While we should not completely equate ministry partnership with a marriage, we can certainly make valid comparisons. As in a marriage, partnership takes strong resolve to stay in it when the going gets tough. It requires the confidence to know that sticking it out will result, by the grace of God, in a better, stronger, more effective relationship.

The partnership that has formed between two of the four authors of this book—Wayne Gordon and John Perkins—exemplifies such stick-to-it-tive-ness. Although they live in two different parts of the country, they make it a point to have face-to-face meetings, staying at each other's respective homes on a monthly basis, and they talk over the phone almost everyday regarding both personal and ministries issues. They are yokefellows who do not mince words in keeping each other accountable and who are not afraid to disagree with each other on how things should be run in their respective ministries as well as in ministries that they share, such as CCDA. They rely on each other to tow the line of ministry integrity, and as a result, their partnership has endured the test of time and adversity. Their daily, lovingly candid phone conversations are reminiscent of the "summits" that Washington and Kehrein used to have in the 1980s at the original Pancake House, where both men came together once a month to air out differences, resolve conflict, seek understanding, and pray for each other.[14]

As in a marriage, urban-suburban partnership is doomed to fail if either side is poised to pull out once problems arise, because problems *will* arise. Washington and Kehrein say, "Only when 'divorce' is not an easy option will the relationship have a chance."[15]

Do commit to the partnership, and don't give up too easily.

7. Do Aim for Quality Partnerships/Don't Partner Indiscriminately

Finally, precisely because an effective partnership takes deep investments of time, effort, and heart, we should aim for quality and not just team up with any organization or individual who happens to be there. It is not as important that we form many partnerships as it is to cultivate deep ones that truly make an impact. Investing deeply with a few not only makes sense from a time management perspective but also in terms of ministry effectiveness. To be sure, there are working relationships based on time-limited projects that do have their place. There are also strictly financial partners or prayer partners from a distance, and these also have their place. But then there are *deep* partnerships, which long-term practitioners have deemed as the ones that make the enduring, significant impact upon the community. In this light, longtime community activist Scott Oostdyk advises, "Pick a quality partner carefully."[16]

For example, Strategies to Elevate People (STEP) in Richmond, Virginia, is "a nonprofit that facilitates partnership between suburban

and urban neighborhoods for the transformation of all involved."
It was started in 1983 by a handful of inspired urban and suburban
Christians who independently attended a conference in Washington,
DC.[17] In 1998 Oostdyk described STEP this way: "Two groups of
people, coming together at a conference, and for 15 years those same
people have been walking together, building this ministry that now
touches thousands of people."[18]

This kind of effectiveness, achieved through long-term partnerships,
can also be found in the partnerships between Circle Urban Ministries and Rock of Our Salvation Church in Chicago, the interracial
members of the Voice of Calvary Church in Jackson, Mississippi, and
many others. In light of these testimonies of effectiveness as a result
of the long-term commitment that the partners have demonstrated
to each other and the ministry, do aim for quality partnerships and
don't just partner with anyone.

Reflection Questions

1. Do these Dos and Don'ts, which apply to both urban and suburban partners, make sense to you?

2. Which of them particularly stands out for you?

3. Are there any that you would add?

6

Dos and Don'ts for Urban Partners

In addition to the seven Dos and Don'ts that apply to both, at least seven more Dos and Don'ts apply primarily to urban partners. Before we single out the urban partners in this chapter and the suburban partners in the next, we need to emphasize that the following urban-only and suburban-only lists cannot stand alone; they need the foundational support of the seven Dos and Don'ts for both. We must therefore see lists in the next two chapters in the context of the *meta-list*. Furthermore, we point out the overlap of these lists. Just because we deem one set of Dos and Don'ts as urban-specific does not mean that suburban partners can skip that section, and vice versa. Indeed, many if not all of the Dos and Don'ts apply to some degree to both sides.

With these important caveats in mind, let us look at what urban partners primarily need to know about what to do and not do in order to develop a healthy and effective partnership with their suburban sisters and brothers.

1. Do Be Motivated by the Larger Gospel Truths of Reconciliation and Mission/Don't Let Financial Needs Define the Partnership

In the face of the urgent and desperate needs of their context, urban workers tend to have more difficulty than their suburban counterparts in maintaining theological truth as that which drives ministry, but they simply must. The tyranny of the urgent—desperate needs require desperate measures—often poses the danger of unreflective theology. A disdain for theology can even develop, claiming it is impractical theorizing and useless navel-gazing. While we sincerely resonate with the urgency to meet the needs of the moment, we cannot stress enough the need to maintain the theological motivation for the practice of ministry. In fact, urban ministries should not even consider entering into a partnership with a suburban entity until they have undergone a process of biblical and theological orientation. Studying part 2 of this book, for example, will orient them to the larger theological framework, thus securing the gospel as the basis of the partnership. Of course the same call to theological orientation goes to suburban partners as well, but since they do not face daily, urgent, practical needs like their urban counterparts, they do not have as difficult a time keeping theology in focus.

To put it bluntly, if their understanding of God, church, and mission does not inform the partnership, then urban partners will find that their relationship to suburban brothers and sisters can easily become one of financial convenience disguised in spiritual clothing. In the urban mind-set, unless the gospel serves as plumb line, the suburban partner easily can be reduced to one primary use—to finance urban projects. At that point, the suburban partner simply serves as a kind of cash cow, even though urban counterparts will not ever express it in this way. In time the suburban partner will catch on and feel manipulated and used. They will find themselves fighting off thoughts like, "It's not us they want; it's our money," or worse, "Partnership looks good on paper, but it's a bad idea."

The matter of finances, however, cannot and should not be avoided. In fact, it must be discussed and worked out by the partners. But this should be done in the context of the big vision of the ministry, with the urban partner being careful not to allow suburban resources to be the primary reason for the partnership. This can be tricky, but it is not impossible if urban partners keep their eyes on the ministry vision.

Do be guided primarily by a kingdom theology of compassion and justice, and don't let the financial needs of the ministry define the partnership.

2. Do Be Honest about Your Struggle/Don't Sabotage the Partnership with Unforgiveness

If historical and political realities have taught the urbanized anything, it is to assume a posture of reticence and even suspicion toward those who hold positional and financial power. In fact, as Claerbaut sees it, it would be stranger if the poor were *not* hesitant, even a little paranoid.[1] From the history of slavery to redlining to racial profiling to the displacement of the poor by gentrification, the urbanized have borne the brunt of American-style oppression. These historical and current realities affect the psyche of the urbanized, and we cannot overemphasize the importance of acknowledging any harbored resentment or anger that comes from woundedness.

Referring to the role of African-Americans in the black-white divide, community organizer and pastor Eugene Rivers states bluntly, "Black people's responsibility is to tell the truth. Most of us don't tell the truth, because we know that many white folks would walk out that door."[2] Of course, as Christ commands, the truth must be expressed in love (Eph. 4:15), but it needs to be expressed nonetheless. The reconciliation meetings at Voice of Calvary (VOC) in Jackson, Mississippi, modeled this. Initiated by several black members, these gatherings convened "to challenge what they said was racism within [their] own church and ministry."[3] These meetings enabled black members to express their deep-seated struggle with how white members seemed oblivious to the residual effects of historical and institutionalized racism. Both Perkins and Rice admit how hard these meetings were; the fellowship even lost members as a result. But the long-term fruit of such pruning made those gatherings worthwhile: a deepening of the interracial experience within VOC as well as a strengthening of the church's witness in the community.[4]

On the other hand, bitterness and unforgiveness will deep-six any effort to partner with a suburban entity. Expressing our reticence and suspicion allows us to overcome them with honesty, transparency, and effective communication rather than lashing out against the privileged. Moreover, chances are good that those suburban partners who are attempting to minister together with urban ministries do so because they have responded to the call of the gospel to challenge the racism and classism that define our society. Sustained bitterness and unforgiveness will only discourage them.

Three days before his untimely death, Spencer Perkins preached a powerful sermon on grace in which he urged all involved in reconciliation ministries to "play the grace card." Without it, the pain and humiliation experienced at the hands of oppressors prevent anything resembling friendship—and forget about partnership! He preached to everyone the need to extend radical grace, but he especially addressed his fellow black Christians, stating that they needed to forgive the white community for their own sake and for the sake of the gospel. He said, "Being able to extend grace and to forgive people sets us free. We no longer need to spend precious emotional energy thinking about the day that [our oppressors] will get what they deserve. What tremendous freedom! . . . Being able to give grace while preaching justice will make our witness even more effective."[5]

Do be honest about deep-seated feelings and fears, and don't sustain a partnership-killing grudge.

3. Do Have Confidence in What You Bring to the Partnership/Don't Play the Victim

Few deny that sustained impoverishment and marginalization among the urbanized have resulted in a damaged self-image, which manifests itself in many ways—fatalism, mischief, despair, hopelessness, feelings of inferiority, and various combinations thereof. In light of what urban counterparts need to do for a healthy partnership, we view these socio-psychological consequences as resulting in a lack of self-confidence, "a learned powerlessness,"[6] which needs to be overcome. Insofar as urban partners can rise above this and thus increase their confidence in who they are in Christ and what they bring to the partnership, a healthy, effective ministry relationship with suburban workers can flourish.

"Easier said than done," some may say. And we should *all* say it, for to overcome generations of oppression, poverty, and hardship requires superhuman resoluteness; it takes nothing less than submitting to the Lord of liberation and justice. We do not place this particular *Do* on the list lightly. We include it trusting that urban brothers and sisters have submitted themselves to the transforming power of God, for what is impossible for mortals is possible with God (Luke 18:27). As the level of confidence increases in urban partners, the insights borne out of struggle, the vision to transform their communities (which they know as insiders), and their various gifts and skills can appropriately inform the partnership.

Without this type of confidence, the urban-suburban partnership will most likely form (or malform) according to the default patterns of our racialized and class-driven society, relegating urban counterparts to passivity and timidity. Such an arrangement plays right into the world's categories of power, where the rich and privileged call the shots. As such, urban partners inadvertently play the part that the world dictates: victims who are incapable of contributing because of their circumstances. Granted that a very real level of victimization among the urbanized exists, but to play the role instead of attempting to overcome it in Christ surely undermines genuine partnership.

A ministry such as Young Urban Black Males (YUBM), which seeks to develop male black leadership at the intersection of Christ, urban realities, and hip hop, exists precisely to challenge victim consciousness. Under "Why YUBM" on its website, its leaders ask, "What are we to do when we face a life that is statistically harder, shorter, meaner and poorer; a member of an under-reached, under-served and under-developed people group?" They provide the following answer: "We minimize the 'victim' mentality and maximize the 'victor' mindset through Him that loved (and even now loves) us and gave Himself for us."[7] It is this kind of nonvictim confidence that urban workers must bring to the urban-suburban partnership.

Do be confident through Christ who strengthens us, and don't settle for victim status.

4. Do Provide Key Leadership in the Partnership/Don't Acquiesce to the Default Posture of Subservience

This fourth Do and Don't couplet is the mature, older kin of the third: urban partners need to occupy key positions of leadership in the partnership. In fact, given their insiders' knowledge of the city, where the partnership will most probably be implemented, the urban counterparts need to play a key role, if not *the* key role, in setting both the agenda and the strategy for ministry. This takes intentionality in an urban-suburban partnership because leadership often defaults along racial and class lines.

Regarding black-white relations, Perkins and Rice observe, "When blacks and whites come together for a common cause, the whites tend to feel more secure taking on the leadership roles. . . . So we decided to make an intentional effort to affirm black culture and encourage black leadership."[8] Without this type of intentionality, urban partners will likely assume the default posture of subservience, and suburban partners will likely oblige.

The National Hispanic Christian Leadership Conference (NHCLC) provides an excellent example of strong urban leadership, which sets the agenda and then seeks partners to accomplish it. In NHCLC's self-description with regard to its partners, its website reads, "The NHCLC seeks to establish life-long partnerships and covenants with organizations and institutions that share the same core values and seek to transform society via the enhancement of the Judeo/Christian ethos in addressing the issues of poverty, social injustice, inequality, moral relativism, cultural decay, class warfare, educational and political disenfranchisement."[9] The strength in this statement lies in the confidence of the NHCLC to set the agenda as it seeks partners "that share the same core values."

For example, Samuel Rodriguez, cofounder of NHCLC, has worked hard to form ministry alliances with fellow evangelicals, but these may be in jeopardy due to NHCLC's commitment to immigration reform. In an interview with *Christianity Today*, he states, "Immigration puts us at odds with our white evangelical brothers."[10] This saddens and frustrates Rodriguez, remembering how the civil rights movement created a rift between black and white Christians in the 1960s and 1970s. Even in light of such a risk, however, the NHCLC will continue to work on an agenda it believes in—immigration reform that better reflects the biblical image of hospitality and that benefits the Latino community in America.[11]

Urban partners need to aspire toward this kind of leadership, which brings insiders' knowledge to bear strongly and confidently upon ministry vision and strategy. Do take the lead in the partnership, affirming the supportive role of the suburban partner, and don't conform to the social default pattern of subordination.

5. Do Listen to the Insights of Suburban Partners/Don't Let the Oppressed in You Become the Oppressor

Suburban partners do have something valuable to bring to the table besides financial resources, and it is important that urban partners listen to their insights. An outside perspective can often point out what otherwise are blind spots to an insider, so urban partners do well to take suburban insights seriously. Regarding insider-outsider roles, anthropologist Charles Kraft writes,

> [Insiders] have . . . an understanding that outsiders rarely attain, though insiders can often be quite naïve in their understandings and evaluations [of their own context]. Outsiders, however, if they learn to understand

and appreciate the insider's point of view, can often be very helpful in the process of cultural evaluation, for informed outsiders can often see certain things more clearly than the insiders themselves.[12]

Besides just the practical fruit of listening to their suburban partners—valuable outside perspective, assessment and evaluation, strategy proposals, and so forth—this kind of respect is fundamental to human relationship. It harkens back to our discussion in chapter 4 on partnership essentials, especially the part regarding deep reconciliation. We say it again here in the form of a practical *Do* because equality and mutual respect finally need to transcend the realm of principle and take concrete expression.

One may interpret this demand to work toward equality and respect as something we should be saying to suburbanites, who default to a *teacher-leader complex* (more on this later), but there is something here for urban partners as well because they cannot let the past experiences of oppression turn them into oppressors. They cannot turn a deaf ear to the valuable insights of their suburban sisters and brothers and insist on *their way or the highway*. Developing urban leadership cannot ultimately mean urban domination.

In his classic *Pedagogy of the Oppressed*, the late Brazilian educator Paulo Freire developed the idea that the oppressed must overcome equating success in life with the life of the oppressor; in other words, liberation does not mean attaining the same kind of lifestyle, values, and behavior as the oppressor. Taking on an antidialogical posture toward outsiders indeed takes on the oppressor mentality.[13] Not only does such a mentality undermine the personal relationship between the partners, it also undermines the very transformational work for which they came together in the first place.

Do genuinely and respectfully listen to the insights of suburban partners, and don't take on the ungodly characteristics of oppressors.

6. Do Be Open to New Ways to Understand Time/Don't Dismiss the Virtues of Timeliness

No one would argue that the concept of time differs between Western and non-Western cultures. Many cross-cultural workers on both sides can cite instances of miscommunication and frustration, as one culture views time loosely and the other lives by the clock. The same can be observed in urban-suburban relationships. Enough conflict and misunderstanding over the time issue has occurred between urban and suburban workers that we felt compelled to include it on the Dos and Don'ts list.

In a lecture given for an urban mission class at Palmer Theological Seminary in Philadelphia, African-American pastor and seminary president Wallace C. Smith explained why Sunday services in many black churches do not begin on time: "Church is not an abstract concept to us; church is people gathered together. So how can church begin at 11:00 AM if the church hasn't arrived yet? Church begins when the church gets there!"[14]

People from the suburbs have a hard time with this one. If they say the church service begins at 11:00 AM, for example, then at 11:00 AM sharp the service begins, even if only a handful of people are sitting in the sanctuary. If they err, they err on the side of "Timeliness is next to godliness." In order to prevent frustration and misunderstanding, we highly recommend that urban workers give a little here and open themselves up to understand time in a different way, affirming the virtue of timeliness. Of course suburban counterparts need to try hard as well not to make time a make-or-break issue (we will get to them soon enough). But just as suburban partners need to learn softer ways to understand time, urban partners need to see the virtue of timeliness. Otherwise, urban partners can stick to their guns, affirming uncompromisingly the more relational and less mechanistic approach to time. But such a stance has yielded nothing but the unpleasant fruit of misunderstanding, hard feelings, and conflict.

Instead of hanging on too tightly to the relational concept of time, do be open to learning new ways to understand the suburban way of viewing time.

7. Do See Enriching Suburban Culture as Part of the Task/Don't Ignore Suburban Culture

Finally, urban partners should see the enrichment of, and the challenge to, suburbia as part of their task in the partnership, for suburban culture has much to learn from urban culture. Shane Claiborne, cofounder of The Simple Way in Philadelphia, shared how he went to the city to incarnate the gospel among the poor, but he learned so much from the poor about the gospel that now he sees himself as a missionary to the suburbs. In an urban mission lecture at Palmer

Theological Seminary, he stated plainly, "It's the suburbs that need to hear the radical implications of the gospel."[15]

After all, as Albert Hsu has pointed out, urban and suburban realities relate best when they see each other interdependently. "Our destinies are intertwined," he says. "Suburbanites and urbanites together must affirm that to care about one requires that we care about the other."[16] Carey Davis of CityLights claims something similar when she describes how each side of the partnership has benefited the other. Through City-Lights, suburban Wayne Presbyterian Church has effectively connected organizations in Southwest Philadelphia to each other as well as connecting suburban people to the work. Likewise through CityLights, urban partners from Southwest Philadelphia have contributed to the life of Wayne Presbyterian Church in a variety of ways, including enriching and diversifying peoples' spiritual experiences as well as challenging them to live free from the material trappings of this world.[17]

In light of what urban partners can contribute to suburban culture, for them not to take advantage would be a missed opportunity to share the gospel. In order to be open to this, urban workers must resist the tendency to disdain suburbia and thus ignore it as if it is not worth redeeming. Hsu challenges this notion among urban Christians and writes, "Indeed the problems and challenges of suburban living are significant. . . . But for Christians, nothing is beyond redemption."[18] In other words, God loves the suburbs too! And urban workers who partner with suburban entities have a great opportunity to participate in what God is doing in the suburbs.

Do seize the opportunity to minister in the suburbs for the benefit of suburbanites, and don't ignore them.

| Reflection Questions

1. For urban Christians, do these Dos and Don'ts capture the issues that need to be addressed in a partnership with a suburban agency?

2. For suburban Christians, do these Dos and Don'ts make sense to you? Are there any that you did not understand?

3. From your experience, what Dos and Don'ts could be added to this list?

7

Dos and Don'ts for Suburban Partners

We come now to the suburban partners' list, which consists of nine Dos and Don'ts. Again, urban counterparts should not skip this chapter, just like suburban counterparts should not have skipped the previous chapter. These lists overlap enough that they cannot be seen in isolation from one another. Nevertheless, we have suburban partners primarily in mind with the following list.

1. Do Remember That Jesus Is Lord of the City/Don't Be Overly Critical of the City

Humanity has had a long history of antiurbanism—a view of the city as the domain of evil—despite the trajectory of the world moving undeniably toward one global metropolis. Missiologists Harvie Conn and Manuel Ortiz note, "One particular image continues to capture and summarize many others into one popular ideology—the city as an urban wasteland. Christian joins with non-Christian in a stereotype of concentrated chaos and disorder, the city as a maze of disruption and dislocation, bewildering sprawl and confused worldviews."[1] Such an antiurban notion is ubiquitous, especially among those living outside the city limits. Viewed from the outside, intense urban problems can and often do create blind spots to the positive aspects of the city. But Jesus is Lord of the universe, which includes the city.

The first *Do* for suburbanites, therefore, has to do with remembering the positive, beautiful, and redeeming aspects of the city as seen through the eyes of God. "We can look at any place in London or Chicago as sacred," claims urbanologist Ray Bakke, "because God is present and at work there." Indeed, God loves the city, and God's people—rich and poor, black, white, and brown, urban, suburban, and rural—need to love it also. Bakke admonishes, "We cannot work in our city unless we love it—its architecture, sewer system, politics, history, traditions and neighborhoods."[2]

The importance of cultivating a positive theology of the city lies first in the truth that there are in fact many aspects to celebrate—for example, cultural diversity, economic opportunity, global influence, and inspiration for innovation in the arts. Second, a positive urban theology lays the foundation for a ministry of humility. It prevents suburban missionaries to the city from viewing themselves as God's holy representatives to the rescue! Albeit a stereotype, the belief that suburban people are cleaner, safer, wealthier, more educated, and more sophisticated informs the American psyche. If city-bound suburban workers do not resist this belief, they come as rescuers.

As such, their efforts cannot but come across as old-fashioned paternalism: "We have the high ground, so listen to us, do it like us, become like us." Indeed, an overly critical view of the city implies the moral superiority of those outside it. In order to minimize this faulty but prevalent thinking, suburban workers need to view the city as God sees it in all of its richness, creativity, and potential.

Do remember Christ's lordship over all realms of life, including the city, so you don't make the mistake of demonizing it.

2. Do Make It Personal/Don't Objectify the Urban Poor

In addition to seeing the positive side of the city, suburban workers must also view its inhabitants as fellow human beings. We cannot stress enough the importance of viewing the urban context personally—that is, expecting to find complex human beings with names, faces, and fascinating stories with which one must interact with both head and heart. Some suburbanites might feel insulted that this is even on the list. We include it because outsiders often enter into urban ministry sincerely but with an underlying abstractness in their view of poverty. Suburbanites likely get involved in urban ministry because they were inspired by a Scripture, a sermon, or a book, and so they tend to develop a romantic notion of working with the poor. But "the poor" often refers more to a concept, a category, a faceless mass than to real people. Suburban workers would do well to heed the words of social worker Ruby Barcelona, who reminds us that "the poor are not primarily a class; the poor are people."[3] Becoming increasingly aware of this fundamental notion paves the way for genuine relationship building with urban dwellers, which makes urban ministry personal.

The opposite of this is to objectify the poor, to view them as projects or broken things that need to be fixed. Needless to say, this makes it high on our Don'ts list. Relocaters—suburban Christians who intentionally move into the city for ministry purposes—understand acutely the trap of objectification. Bob and Peggy Lupton and Gloria Yancy introduce the practice of *neighboring* over against *fixing*. They write,

> No one likes to be someone's project. But we all like to be considered someone's friend. Treating our neighbors as objects of ministry can define those relationships in unhealthy ways. . . . Healthy relationships are reciprocal. Each has something of worth to contribute to the other. Good neighbors keep watch on each other's house. Neighbors borrow from and lend to each other. Neighbors watch each other's kids. . . . When we move in as fixers rather than neighbors, we set ourselves up to be used. And that isn't healthy for anyone.[4]

Do practice *neighboring*, and don't come primarily to fix the urban situation for the benefit of a faceless mass of people called *the poor*.

3. Do Understand the Initial Distrust and Resentment That May Come from Urban Counterparts/Don't Be Too Defensive

As we have encouraged urban partners to be honest about their suspicion toward outside partners but also not to sabotage the partnership with bitterness and unforgiveness (see number 2 on the urban Dos and Don'ts list), we now encourage suburban partners to do their best to understand the initial distrust and resentment that may come their way from their urban counterparts and not be too defensive. This might sound like we are speaking from both sides of our mouth, but we are convinced that in order to move beyond this impasse, forged out of a cruel history of racism, classism, and oppression, both sides will have to do their respective parts. The suburban part entails taking seriously the hurts of the past that may have been inflicted on city dwellers—from abandoning them, as many fled to create racially defined suburbs, to displacing them via unjust gentrification practices. Time alone does not heal these things, and distrust and resentment among many urban dwellers exist precisely because they have not yet been heard. Suburban workers do well to listen, to understand—even if it feels like the painful words are being directed at them—and to be part of the necessary process of reconciliation.

The black-white reconciliation meetings at Voice of Calvary once again provide a great example of the fruit of understanding and endurance. Rice admits, "I hated going to those meetings. I felt like a pig that was voluntarily walking into a slaughterhouse." But despite feeling accused of racism week in and week out, Rice continued to go, slowly realizing the depth of anger and resentment that many blacks had for whites. "I began looking beneath the anger," he writes, "to the hurt behind it. I realized that their anger came from personal wounds—experiences in which they had suffered wrong—and just plain weariness with being black in a white world."[5] Obviously, Rice's deepening understanding of the black experience enabled him to stick it out and be part of a genuine modern-day model of reconciliation and justice.

Crossing the urban-suburban divide more than likely will take wading through the dangerous currents of racism, and suburban partners must learn to discern the hurt behind the anger and to develop a humble, understanding posture. One thing is certain: dismissing too easily the anger of urban sisters and brothers will subvert any attempt at genuine partnership. Easy dismissal demonstrates a lack of identification with the hurting, a lack of understanding toward the lingering effects of the experience of oppression, and, finally, a defensive posture to ward off what may feel like accusation and attack.

In a 2000 Urban Mission Consultation held in Quezon City, Philippines, an American community development worker proposed a plan to work together with Filipinos to do the church's part in Manila's transformation. It sounded like a good enough plan, but during the Q&A a brave Filipino raised the issue of reconciliation that Americans and Filipinos have yet to undergo. Furthermore, he pressed, without this kind of reconciliation, genuine partnership between the two peoples cannot happen. The American worker annoyingly replied that we had to leave the past behind, that we could not waste precious time on licking each other's wounds, and that we needed to move forward together for the sake of Manila's urban poor. Although he felt justified in his reasoning, the American worker lost his Filipino audience.

Do maintain an understanding posture toward any form of distrust, anger, or resentment that may come from urban counterparts, and don't maintain a defensive or dismissive posture.

4. Do Establish Presence in the Community/Don't Be Aloof

Relocation—the call to demonstrate God's love and our love for the poor by moving into their neighborhood—is one of the three Rs of Christian community development.[6] Those who have uprooted and taken up residence among the poor continue to inspire the church at large as they share testimonies of the power of God, of community love, and of practical solidarity with the poor. It is hard to argue against the effectiveness of such Christ-centered sacrifice, even though some contend that physical relocation might not be for everyone.[7]

Regardless, however, of the degree to which one understands the incarnational model for ministry, "there is a growing consensus among committed urban practitioners that being a vested member of the community one is called to serve is an important key to effectiveness."[8] Being a vested community member, as Lupton, Lupton, and Yancy put it, or establishing one's personal presence in the community, drives the concept of relocation, not the belief that the only faithful act of Christian development is to move into the slums. As Lupton, Lupton, and Yancy have argued, one can actually live in the community and be virtually invisible, referring to "people who live on our street but contribute nothing to the well-being of our street."[9] Relocation, then, in and of itself does not necessarily translate into incarnational presence. It is not physical relocation that is demanded of all who care for the city; it is, rather, real and faithful presence.

Assuming that the primary context for an urban-suburban partnership is the city, this Do applies primarily to suburban partners. They must see establishing their presence alongside their urban partners as essential to effective partnership in ministry. What can this look like? Again we cannot overstate the value of physically relocating to the neighborhood and establishing presence that way. Suburban Christians—especially singles and young marrieds—have chosen this approach. For example, six graduates of Eastern University in St. Davids, Pennsylvania, began a ministry in 1997 called The Simple Way in one of the poorest sections of Philadelphia. Cofounder Shane Claiborne describes their relocation:

> In January 1997, six of us moved into a little row house in Kensington, one of Pennsylvania's poorest neighborhoods. . . . It felt like we were reinventing the early church for the first time in two thousand years (we were quite ignorant). We had no idea what we were getting into. We had no big vision for programs or community development. We wanted only to be passionate lovers of God and people and to take the gospel way of life seriously.[10]

Physically relocating into the community is one way, perhaps even the best way, to establish presence; but working regularly and faithfully with existing urban churches and organizations while maintaining residence in suburbia is another way. The many suburban volunteers through CityLights in Philadelphia, for example, have established their presence in the city by going to the notoriously dangerous southwest section of the city to work with organizations like Cornerstone Christian Academy, the Southwest Community Development Corporation, and the Philadelphia Training Program. Although these faithful volunteers continue to live in surrounding suburbs, they have established their presence, supporting and strengthening existing churches and organizations through CityLights. Whether it is forming a new monastic order in the slums (The Simple Way) or investing in the effectiveness of existing urban churches and organizations (CityLights), suburban partners must establish their presence in the community.

The other side of this *Do* is "Don't be aloof." Suburban partners cannot maintain aloofness—that is, cautious, measured involvement in the community at best or, at worst, no direct involvement at all—and expect to fulfill their part of the partnership. *Old-school missions* unfortunately provides a prime example of aloofness in the form of the missionary compound, which serves as the place where missionaries can live as if they never left their *natural habitat*. Within it, missionaries eat their own food, wear their own clothes, talk their own language, educate their children with their own curriculum, and so on, away from the people of the host culture. The high walls and locked gates of the compound serve as apt symbols of aloofness, distance, and separateness.

Can the same danger of the compound mentality also lurk insidiously among suburban Christians regarding the city? Like most of those who end up on the mission field, suburbanites may be touched somehow to serve the less fortunate in the city, enough that they actively seek out urban partners. But if they spend little or no time in the urban context, maintaining safe distance not just physically but also emotionally and spiritually, then the suburbs may be serving as just another form of the missionary compound. In light of the ineffectiveness of such an approach, aloofness rates high on our Don'ts list.

Do establish real and positive presence in the community, and don't be aloof.

5. Do Live by the Principles of Servant Leadership/Don't Always Feel You Have to Lead and Teach

Few issues of partnership carry more weight than the question of leadership. What does leadership look like as urban and suburban worlds come together? Who should lead? The biblical call to servant leadership applies to all, but because of the propensity of suburbanites to take the lead in ministry situations, this *Do* is primarily directed at them—namely, to take the servant part of servant leadership seriously. Suburban partners should be willing to take part in leadership if appropriate, but it should be the kind of leading that manifests equality clearly, taking the insights of their urban partners seriously and humbly offering any insights they may have.

In light of the fact that their urban partners know more about the urban context because of their insiders' experience, servant leadership logically takes on a more supportive role. Regarding missionary-national leader relations, missiologist Bernard Adeney makes the point that missionaries are guests, and "as guests we must always remember that our hosts are superordinate. We are on their turf."[11] The same can be said of suburban workers entering into an urban community; their guest status compels them to assume a submissive posture toward their urban partners, who need to take the lead in both the vision and strategy of the ministry.

Such a posture does not come easily for idealists from the suburbs who sincerely want to change the world but who also think
they know how to do it! Armed with altruism and an agenda,
suburbanites can fall prey to what Maggay calls "an awful teacher
complex"[12]—a disease of well-meaning know-it-alls who conde-
scend to help the less fortunate in the city. Suburban workers may
interpret their financial, educational, technological, and political
resources as the unquestionable right to teach and train, to assume
leadership, to take charge. They must resist this voice and not feel
compelled to teach and lead.

Having said that, it is also not desirable to set up an artificial
leadership structure, which can manifest in a variety of ways: an ill-
prepared urban worker is thrust into leadership just because of his
or her social status; outsiders continue to lead but through puppet
indigenous leaders; or the suburban worker says nothing and does
nothing for fear of violating the ideal of indigenous leadership.[13]
These artificial leadership structures will only result in frustration,
resentment, and ineffectiveness.

For example, if a suburban expert on AIDS attends a meeting
about community health but then says nothing in order to give room
for an urban counterpart to take the lead, then a travesty has been
committed. Offering a viable solution to this kind of situation, Davis
says that if urban leaders are the ones who have identified the problem
of AIDS, who call the meeting, and then who facilitate the meeting,
introducing at some point the AIDS expert from the suburbs to speak,
then the suburban counterpart can contribute greatly while urban
leadership is upheld.[14]

There is no getting around the fact that leadership is tricky in an
urban-suburban partnership. For that reason, we strongly encourage
suburban partners to maintain a counterintuitive posture—a posture
that resists the predisposition to call the shots and emphasizes instead
the *servant* part of servant leadership.

6. Do Show Generosity as the Ministry Calls for It/Don't Mistake Wanton Handouts for Generosity

The only other matter that comes close to rivaling leadership as a
make-or-break issue is money, which this and the following Do and
Don't couplets attempt to tackle. The first *Do* in this area encourages

the suburban partner to be generous. In an urban-suburban partnership, the suburban entity is most likely the one who has access to financial resources, which ultimately calls for generosity. Suburban partners should only heed this call, however, when the ministry warrants it. In other words, they cannot enter into the partnership flashing green and handing out goodies indiscriminately in the name of generosity. This is the first *Don't* with regard to money, but let us first talk about the *Do*.

A process of discernment with their urban partner regarding timing is absolutely essential for wise financial disbursement and management. Visioning, dreaming, and planning together need to precede financial giving so that the giving has a meaningful, intentional purpose. But once plans have been discerned, don't hold back; or to say it positively, practice generosity, the kind that the Scriptures praise—a generosity wrapped in humility, sacrifice, and joy.

Giving indiscriminately may feel generous, but suburban workers must not mistake wanton handouts for generosity. Despite good intentions, to give prematurely to the ministry or to be overzealous and give even before their urban partners are ready to use the resources can undermine the partnership. First, it can immediately set up a giver-recipient relationship between urban and suburban entities rather than a true partnership that discerns together how funds are to be used. Second, indiscriminate giving, especially to community residents, establishes the outsider as the one in control.

LIGHT Ministries in the Philippines models a way to prevent unwise generosity. Its policy to channel all outside funds through the organization for its Church-to-Church Partnership in Community Transformation Program exists precisely to avoid these pitfalls. It states that no funds may be transferred directly from a U.S. church to a Filipino church. Communication between the churches should also go through the LIGHT leadership structure. All funds (and communication) then must go through LIGHT to ensure accountability monitored by the national organization.[15] An urban-suburban partnership should have similar policy guidelines. The bottom line is that suburban partners need to disburse and manage financial resources with the full knowledge and authorization of urban partners.

Do practice generosity, but avoid indiscriminate giving at all costs.

7. Do Share the Responsibility of Managing Financial Resources/Don't Allow Finances to Manipulate and Control the Ministry

The other money-related Do and Don't has to do with control, which the first Do and Don't couplet touches on as well. Although the primary funds may flow out of the suburban sector, suburban workers need to share the responsibility of managing financial resources with their urban partners. First, it makes sense because the inside perspective of urban partners allows them to know the situation better and therefore they should be part of determining where and how funds should be used. Second, it also sends a statement that in kingdom relationships, finances do not dictate leadership.

To seize control because one pulls the purse strings aligns more with the world's rules, and needless to say, such a posture undermines any attempt at partnership. Money-based overcontrol can manifest in a variety of ways, including deciding which projects are worth funding and which are not—if they do not agree with a certain project then they simply withhold the funds. For example, an outside mission group initiated a community organizing effort in a large squatter community in Quezon City, Philippines. But when the residents said that what they needed most was a basketball court, members of the mission group began to debate among themselves whether a basketball court was worthy of the group's limited funds. Community leaders explained that a basketball court could serve as an important unifying place for deliberations, youth recreation, and community festivals. The mission group came close to doing the wrong thing—namely, withholding funds because they did not agree with the people on the significance of the project. But fortunately, kingdom heads prevailed as the group listened to the community leaders' aspirations and helped to construct the basketball court.[16]

Another manifestation of overcontrol includes micromanaging, insisting on certain people to lead, deciding if too much money is allotted for this part and not enough for that part, unrealistic and strict reporting standards (e.g., requiring urban partners or community beneficiaries to fill out long, involved report forms), and so forth. Although financial stewardship and accountability require a certain level of reporting in order to ensure integrity and transparency in financial dealings, dense, complicated report forms that are completely alien to urbanites can create an inadvertent top-down structure that has the feel of the wealthy, smart people on top making demands of the needy on the bottom. Whenever possible, the content and mode of financial reporting should be formulated with the urban partners. Suburban entities need to avoid the trappings of money-based overcontrol and learn to share the power to manage financial resources.

8. Do Learn the Art of Being Flexible with Regard to Time/Don't Be Impatient and Too Quick to Judge Tardiness

This couplet is the counterpart of number 6 on the list of Dos and Don'ts for urban partners. As mentioned earlier, the differing concepts of time across cultures have created all sorts of problems. As we have encouraged urban workers to take timeliness more seriously for the sake of the relationship, so we now encourage suburban workers to exercise the art of being flexible with regard to time. No, timeliness is *not* next to godliness. It merely represents a cultural way to express efficiency (let's not procrastinate and just get it done) and respect (mustn't make people wait for us). But there are culturally different ways to express efficiency and respect, and suburban partners must be open to these ways. They must learn to flex with the rhythm of their urban counterparts for the sake of the partnership. For example, some suburban workers have begun to retrain themselves with regard to time—for instance learning how to be satisfied to accomplish just one or two tasks a day instead of a longer To Do list with ten to twelve items to check off. Another small habit may seem trite, but one missionary to the city reports that his wristwatch was only serving as a reminder of how behind he always felt, so he has simply chosen not to wear it when he enters into the urban neighborhood in which he serves.

But perhaps the most important part in this *Do* for suburban partners is to remember that people matter over programs and relationships over tasks. Suburban workers must proceed with margin—that is, space set aside in the day that is uncluttered by an overcrowded, impossible agenda—for the sake of the people to whom God called them. In his popular book *Margins*, Dr. Richard Swenson urges people to reclaim margins in their lives not only for their own emotional health but also for the cultivation of interpersonal relationships. He states that "margin exists for relationship."[17] Those who live by the clock are the most susceptible to a marginless lifestyle and often have poor, broken relationships to show for it. The call to be more flexible with time is but another way to call for the creation of margin, where urban and suburban workers have the space to get to know each other and thus cultivate a genuine partnership of people-centered ministry.

By way of contrast, suburban workers could hold their urban counterparts to a rigid understanding of time and thus perpetuate the old conflict. With time inflexibility comes impatience as well as the propensity to judge the tardy as disrespectful, irresponsible, and unreliable. Needless to say, such a stance undermines the partnership on a fundamental relational level. So unless suburban partners are willing to jeopardize the relationship over time, we strongly suggest that they learn the rhythm of the lives of their urban partners.

Do be flexible with time and structure the day with margin, and don't let impatience and a judgmental attitude get the better of you.

9. Do Provide Ways for Suburban Volunteers to Participate in the Work / Don't Make a Showcase of the Poor

Finally, suburbanites ministering in the city through an urban partnership should intentionally pave the way for fellow suburbanites to get to know the city, to get to know fellow Christians working in the city, and eventually to get involved with the work in the city. Many suburbanites do not ever venture to "the other side of the tracks," and suburban partners should not pass up this opportunity to broaden the horizons of fellow suburbanites who need to know about urban life. "It isn't enough to live in a suburban bubble," writes Hsu, "isolated from a larger context, both immediate and global." He remembers his first exposure to urban life in Minneapolis-St. Paul as having the most impact on him "precisely because it was geographically so close to home." He continues,

> No longer could I consider myself just a resident of Bloomington, the individual suburb. I needed to reckon myself a resident of the Minneapolis-St. Paul metropolitan area. I came to understand that my county was home to both million-dollar mansions and crack houses. I could no longer say that the problems of inner city Minneapolis were none of my business. It has become part of my world. I needed to broaden my sense of citizenship and ownership and consider myself part of a larger reality.[18]

Suburban workers have a chance to offer this important opportunity to expand the world of others in suburbia.

There is a fine line, however, between teaching fellow suburbanites about urban culture and showcasing the poor, and suburban partners need to avoid the latter. While it is necessary and even good to share with others what God is doing in the city, the cry of the urban poor is, "Don't show us off. Don't exploit us." For example, an urban mission student at Palmer Seminary shared his concern in a journal entry regarding a class tour of a poor neighborhood in Northeast Philadelphia. He writes, "As we walked around, I couldn't help but notice the curious looks people were giving us. Being from the hood myself, I'm sure they felt like they were being observed like animals in a zoo."[19]

How does one walk this fine line? Carey Davis of CityLights recalls a time when she arranged a tour of murals in Southwest Philadelphia for fellow members of suburban Wayne Presbyterian Church. The invitation to an art show appealed to a number of people, and the tour gave them a chance to appreciate expressions of urban beauty while at the same time inevitably noticing evidences of hard living all around them.[20] They were exposed to both the joys and the struggles of urban life, while maintaining the dignity of those who lived there. One of the results of the tour was that some participants overcame their fear of the inner city and became part of the pool of volunteers who helped with the urban-suburban networking ministry of CityLights.

Do seize the opportunity to enrich the outlook of fellow suburbanites, but don't make a showcase of the poor.

These three chapters of *Dos* and *Don'ts* come from the varied experiences of reflective ministry practitioners from many different corners of the world. We hope they serve as helpful guidelines for both present and future kingdom partners working together for the sake of the gospel.

Reflection Questions

1. For suburban Christians, do these Dos and Don'ts capture the issues that need to be addressed in a partnership with an urban agency?

2. For urban Christians, do these Dos and Don'ts make sense to you? Are there any that you did not understand?

3. From your experience, are there any Dos and Don'ts you could add to this list?

8

Partnership Fruit

Urban-suburban partnership yields a sweet harvest. If we have not yet emphasized this awesome truth, then allow this chapter to shout it from the rooftops. This is not to deny the other truth that this type of partnership requires hard work, sustained vision, strong commitment, and relentless perseverance in the midst of huge relational and ministry challenges. Indeed, those who have crossed the urban-suburban divide for transformational partnership not only acknowledge the great challenge, they also readily testify to the gratifying fruit it produces.

At least four types of fruit hang from the vine of urban-suburban partnership: (1) theological, (2) sociological, (3) cultural, and (4) practical. Of course there is also personal fruit—transformation that occurs within the individual partners themselves. This should not go unacknowledged; in fact, we could have easily identified it as a fifth type of fruit. But ultimately, we see personal spiritual growth as integral to each of the other four. In other words, part of the very core of what grows from an urban-suburban partnership includes the personal development of the partners themselves. With this personal dimension constantly in view, let us now look closely at and appreciate the kingdom fruit that healthy urban-suburban partnerships can produce.

Theological: The Joy of Obedience and Expectation

God has called the redeemed to model the kingdom so that relationships between races and socioeconomic classes reflect God's power to reconcile peoples and to establish justice between them (see chapter 2). God has also called us to take this Good News of salvation, reconciliation, and justice to the ends of the earth (see chapter 3). A genuine ministry partnership that crosses the urban-suburban divide effectively fulfills the call both to model and to proclaim the kingdom of God. The joy of knowing that we are doing the kingdom will of God in the world constitutes the theological fruit of urban-suburban partnership, which brings the joy of obedience.

Generally speaking, joy comes with obedience, or as pastor and author John Piper insists, "Joy is not just the spin-off of obedience to God, but *part* of obedience."[1] According to Piper, a person who obeys God in righteousness and mission but does not rejoice in it is not in complete obedience. Regardless of whether we find Piper's well-known teaching on *Christian hedonism* persuasive, he does elevate the place of joy or delight in the Christian life.[2] How tragic that so many evangelists, pastors, and social activists carry on their important work without ever pausing to taste the fruit of joy.

Crossing the urban-suburban divide for holistic ministry is finally a matter of obedience as it breaks down the walls that separate people according to race and socioeconomic class. The motivation to cross the color lines does not come from political correctness, asserts Pastor Ken Fong of Evergreen Baptist Church in Los Angeles, but rather, it comes profoundly from the Bible.[3] Pastor Adam Edgerly of New Song Church, also in Los Angeles, adds, "We look at [crossing these lines] as a mandate . . . not an option."[4] The point here is that those doing the hard work of urban-suburban partnership can and should rejoice in their obedience.

Moreover, this joy of obedience deepens when we view the racial reconciliation and socioeconomic justice that urban-suburban partnerships model as *eschatological*—that is, as a preview of the things to come. Fong describes his own transformation toward this truth:

Most Christians would not argue with the picture they read in Revelation 5 where a diverse multitude gathers to worship around the throne of God. The critical question is what is going to happen between now and the day that scene actually occurs. A "static hermeneutic" would say that we basically stay the way we are now—ethnically and culturally separate. [But] as I have been reading Scripture what I see is a "redemptive hermeneutic" where we are moving toward this reality as a preview of what it will be like in heaven. We should be actively pursuing that reality now.[5]

This kind of thinking has changed his understanding of his role as a pastor as well: "I used to think my job was to make you all as comfortable in this life as possible so you wouldn't be uncomfortable in eternity, but I think I got it backwards. I now think my job is to make us all uncomfortable so we can be comfortable together forever. We need to start rehearsing the future."[6] Serving together in an urban-suburban partnership, which fosters multicultural and multiclass fellowship and ministry, better prepares us for the day when all tribes and nations gather together in unison to worship the living God (Rev. 7:9–10). For those involved deeply in urban-suburban partnership, the joy of obedience as well as the joy of expectation are theirs for the taking.

Sociological: Social Capital and Biblical *Koinonia*

Contributing significantly to community building via deep relationships constitutes the second discernible fruit of an urban-suburban partnership as it creates, solidifies, and mobilizes relational networks. In her excellent dissertation on the successful urban-suburban partnership of CityLights, Carey Davis documents the degree to which the partnership between community organizations in urban Southwest Philadelphia and suburban Wayne Presbyterian Church has done its part to build up what social scientists have identified as *social capital*, which basically refers to the power of relational interconnectedness that allows community members to work together to strengthen and maintain a quality of life for all.[7] There are two kinds of social capital: (1) bonding, which enables community members to work together for the good of the community; and (2) bridging, which enables community members to look outside of the community and take advantage of the larger interconnectedness that exists when interacting with those from a different background or experience.

Urban-suburban partnerships have the potential to combine these two types. For example, as a ministry focused in the specific region of

Southwest Philadelphia, CityLights has first of all contributed to the
bonding type of social capital by facilitating sustained relationship
building between neighborhood entities, which include Cornerstone
Christian Academy, Kingsessing Recreation Center, Mitchell Elementary School, New Spirit Community Presbyterian Church, and the
Health Annex. It has done this by holding monthly meetings, initially
just to get to know each other and eventually to discover what each
can do to assist one another for the good of the whole community.

Davis recalls a seemingly minor incident in the first network meeting that demonstrated to all present the potential power of simply
knowing each other. Pastor Rosa Drummond of Redeemed Learning
Center mentioned that her church needed a computer, at which point
Leroy Barber of Cornerstone Christian Academy said, "We have a
spare one that we can give to you. I can put it in my car and bring it
over." And the transaction was made. This small incident, where a
small congregation mentioned a need and another organization met
the need, seemed to open the eyes of the participants to the tangible
benefits of networking.[8]

Being a ministry consisting of both urban and suburban entities,
however, CityLights has also enhanced the bridging type of social
capital, where members of very different communities—inner-city
Southwest Philadelphia and suburban Wayne—have found their interdependence mutually benefiting:

> Through this partnership . . . leaders have worked to improve the qual-
> ity of life for residents of [Southwest Philadelphia] while simultane-
> ously encouraging growth and understanding within and between both
> communities. Helpful projects, programs, and advocacy efforts have
> been generated that have led to lasting change—social, economic, and
> spiritual—for participants from city and suburbs alike.[9]

The CityLights experience demonstrates the fruit of both the bonding
and bridging types of social capital, which have contributed to community building in Southwest Philadelphia as well as intercommunity
building between an urban neighborhood and a nearby suburb. These
interconnections between people and organizations serve as reinforc-
ing threads that strengthen the very fabric of the community.

In addition to social capital, community building that has enduring
value from a Christian perspective necessitates the cultivation of the
spiritual life in the community. Going beyond the powerful but limited

idea of social capital, Davis's dissertation also makes the case that urban-suburban partnerships between Christians also facilitate the experience of the biblical reality of *koinonia*. She defines *koinonia* as a "transcendent inter-relatedness [wherein] partners participate in something far greater than just interpersonal connectedness; namely they participate in the very coming of the kingdom of God."[10] *Koinonia* refers to the deep experience of community that is based upon God and God's *shalom*, and urban-suburban partnerships enable believers to work toward it as a kind of invitational model for the larger community to experience as well. While believers potentially experience the fullness of biblical *koinonia* through their bond in Christ and his mission, community members who do not yet profess faith in Christ can also taste of its fruit. Davis, for example, mentions her growing relationship with an atheist in the community who has acknowledged on a number of occasions how she has experienced genuine love and concern as a member of CityLights. "Of course, my hope is," says Davis, "that the *koinonia* experienced between Christians in the group will lead my atheist friend [and others] to experience Christ more deeply."[11] And as all benefit from the experience of biblical *koinonia*, all also have the capacity to participate in the coming kingdom of God. Unruh hints at this idea when she writes, "Government, businesses, banks, schools, non-profit organizations, and hospitals all play an important role in promoting the biblical vision of *shalom*. . . . Ideally . . . the church is to come alongside local institutions and strengthen them to do their part with [kingdom] justice, integrity and effectiveness."[12] Between social capital and biblical *koinonia*, an urban-suburban partnership creates more than a working relationship; it creates strong social and spiritual bonds that result in the overall good of the community. The fruit of genuine relationships that transform lives and address social problems hang sweetly from the vine of urban-suburban partnerships.

In addition to the experience of CityLights, many other urban-suburban partnerships affirm the value and the power of personal relationships for community building. For example, even though a significant work has been accomplished by the long-term partnership between Lawndale Community Church in inner-city Chicago and two nearby suburban churches—Glen Ellyn Presbyterian Church and Christ Church of Oak Brook—it is the personal relationships that have been most valued. Regularly shared luncheons among the women of the churches, exchange of Christmas and birthday cards, and regular nonministry contact all reflect how personal the partnerships are that have developed.[13] As a result of these personal relationships formed through the years between the people of these urban and suburban–crossing churches, Lawndale Community Church has developed into a major contributor of community transformation in both the urban district of Lawndale and the two church communities in the suburbs.

We can cite more, such as the experience of city and small town churches that came together in the early 1990s in Zambales Province in the Philippines. Faced with the formidable task of rebuilding their communities that were destroyed by the massive volcanic blast of Mt. Pinatubo in 1991, churches in Olongapo City joined hearts and hands with many churches of surrounding small towns (somewhat equivalent to U.S. suburbs in their relationship to a central city) to form LIGHT Ministries. As a network of city and small town churches, LIGHT did its part in rebuilding their communities in post–Mt. Pinatubo Zambales Province. But equally and inseparably significant to its accomplishments have been the enduring relationships formed between the churches, thus demonstrating a "relational community development" model that has accomplished much through personal bonds.[14] Formed and maintained properly, urban-suburban partnerships can significantly contribute to community building as they help build and harness social capital and facilitate biblical *koinonia*.

Cultural: Intercultural Perspective in a Globalized World

When urban and suburban worlds come together, nothing less than a cross-cultural encounter occurs, an encounter that lends itself to equipping the border-crossers themselves to live more adeptly in a diversifying world. Charles Kraft, for example, commits an entire chapter in his *Anthropology for Christian Witness to* pointing out the weaknesses of a monocultural perspective—such as naïve ethnocentrism and a tendency to disrespect difference—in favor of a cross-cultural one.[15] Futurist Tom Sine says plainly, "We must get to know people who experience life very differently from the way we do." He speaks to parents in particular and advises them: "You could give your children no better gift or preparation to live in an increasingly cross-cultural future than to live in a different cultural environment for a couple of years."[16] The potential mutual good of this kind of culture-crossing—namely, an intercultural worldview that enables one to get along in a globalized world with more understanding and flexibility—constitutes the third fruit of urban-suburban partnership.

By *globalized* we simply mean that due to intensified migration across cultures and the proliferation of Internet technology, peoples from all parts of the world intermingle more than ever before through interacting in cyberspace to moving next to each other on the same street. Increasingly, cultures of the world come together, and in order to live more competently and serve more effectively in it, our worldview must be informed by an intercultural perspective.

Closely related to *cross-cultural*, the term *intercultural* refers to what can *result* from crossing the boundaries of our cultural comfort levels—namely, the integration of a number of cultural perspectives that make up our worldview. The idea of this kind of integration subtly suggests that people can simply cross cultures but remain essentially unchanged in their worldview —their experience is only cross-cultural. On the other hand, to be intercultural—or some prefer *third cultural*—means they have crossed cultures and have allowed the other culture to meld with their own and thus modify their overall understanding of life. Adam Edgerly defines "third culture people" as those "who have been shaped by two or more cultures and have developed the ability to adjust."[17]

Understanding urban and suburban communities as culturally worlds apart, a partnership that crosses this divide can indeed contribute to the development of this intercultural perspective. New Song Covenant Church based in Southern California provides an excellent model-in-progress of mutual intercultural learning.[18] A multisite network of local congregations, New Song has developed churches in Irvine, Los Angeles, Dallas, Bangkok, and London. It seeks, however, to maintain the ideal of one church, one budget, one mission, and one leadership team for all of the sites. In order to accomplish this, New Song leaders have formed a group they call the Third Culture Alliance through which the local site churches agree to a common vision and common values and engage together in leadership development, joint mission projects, and the launching of new sites. The Third Culture Alliance attempts to bring the cultures of the world together by the power of the gospel for the sake of the gospel.

Take, for example, the relationship between two of the congregations—the original site, which is located in suburban Irvine,

California, made up predominantly of second- and third-generation Asian-Americans, and the one located in Crenshaw, a district of Los Angeles that is predominantly African- and Latino-American. Inspired by the multicultural vision of lead pastor Dave Gibbons at New Song Irvine, fifteen people from the church, led by Edgerly, were commissioned in 2003 to plant another church in Crenshaw in order to be the Good News of cultural and socioeconomic reconciliation there. But as members of the Third Culture Alliance, New Song in suburban Irvine and New Song in urban Los Angeles intentionally *cross-pollinate*—exchanging leaders, helping each other in their respective services, consulting each other, praying for each other, and so on—and thus they culturally enrich one another in fellowship, leadership, and ministry.

Crossing the urban-suburban cultural divide for ministry partnership enables us to develop an increasingly indispensable quality—an intercultural perspective that better equips us to live in a globalized world. According to urban missiologist Roger Greenway, such intercultural coalitions can contribute significantly to the life of both urban and suburban fellowships. "City and suburban churches could experience major renewals if they would get together and learn from one another." He even adds—perhaps as a bit of an overstatement, perhaps not—that "the welfare of the nation may depend on [these types of coalitions]."[19] What urban and suburban entities can learn from each other can only further develop this intercultural worldview, which opens up the possibilities of both church renewal and community transformation.

Practical: Personal and Social Transformation

It is transformation on both personal and social levels that inspires us to cross the urban-suburban divide in the first place—which finally begs the questions: Does urban-suburban partnership work? Does it produce any kind of practical fruit? Is it effectively leading people and communities to genuine transformation? We believe unequivocally that it does. Practical fruit may ripen slowly, but the power that urban-suburban partnerships demonstrate leaves an impression that beckons people and communities toward genuine change. Indeed, a healthy urban-suburban partnership has an inherent evangelistic element to it. Unruh asserts that "when Christians of different denominations, races, and socioeconomic backgrounds come together around the banner of holistic ministry, people take notice."[20] Edgerly tells of a time when an unbelieving man of another faith felt drawn to the multiculturalism of New Song: "A Muslim came into our midst to ask if he could help pass out flyers inviting people to the church because he saw the diversity and thought it was beautiful. Churches need to consider the evangelistic aspect of being a diverse church. . . . Racial justice . . . can attract people to the Gospel. It's evangelistic."[21] This should strike us with astonishment: a Muslim man promoting New Song and encouraging people to come and experience what he himself has experienced in this Christ-centered church. Go figure! What a demonstration of the attractive power of racial and socioeconomic justice, which is the essence of urban-suburban partnerships.

As for transformation on a social scale, Mary Nelson, president emeritus of Bethel New Life, a community development corporation in West Chicago, shares a number of ways that Bethel's suburban partners have contributed and continue to contribute significantly to its multifaceted ministries.[22] For example, Our Savior Lutheran Church in nearby Naperville has taken on the ongoing responsibility of keeping Alberta's Pantry—the convenience store for Bethel's elderly and disabled residents—replenished with basic necessities. For several years Lutheran Church of the Cross and Our Savior Lutheran, both in Arlington Heights, subsidized children in the Bethel neighborhood to go to camp, while at the same time enrolling their own children in the same camp so that urban and suburban youth could have an opportunity to get to know each other and learn from each other. Willow Creek Community Church, a suburban megachurch, partnered with Bethel in 2001 to do a massive workday of construction, cleanup, and maintenance—a day that was capped off by a joint praise service. All of these suburban efforts were initiated and managed by the urban staff of Bethel New Life, thus maintaining a true partnership characterized by equality and shared responsibility.

The most powerful story of social transformation that Nelson tells, however, is when urban and suburban forces came together in 1985 to advocate on behalf of the poor who needed affordable housing. Bethel New Life and other urban NGOs proposed the Cook County Multi-Family Tax Reactivation Program to local officials, a program that would enable Bethel to convert tax-encumbered properties into affordable housing. Besides these properties being general eyesores, they saw these neglected land plots as potential places to build much-needed apartments for low-income residents.

But County Commissioner Carl Hanson did not pay much attention to the proposal—that is, until Bethel New Life called upon its suburban partners in Hanson's district to support the cause. When Hanson heard his own constituents tell him of the genuine heart for the poor that Bethel New Life has as well as their own desire to see the program approved, Hanson was won over and became an advocate of the program as well as a friend of Bethel New Life. As a result, the Cook County Multi-Family Tax Reactivation Program passed, and more affordable housing was eventually built for many poor families. Urban and suburban voices came together in partnership to advocate on behalf of underserved families, and the result was urban beautification and affordable housing for the poor. Not only is urban-suburban partnership evangelistic by its very nature, it is also a powerful force to transform society.

Urban-suburban partnership may have its challenges, but the kingdom fruit that it can potentially bear—theological, sociological, cultural, and practical—make the endeavor worthy of our affirmation and our uncompromising commitment. As we said in the beginning of this chapter, these partnership fruits translate into the personal transformation of the partners themselves. For how can we remain unchanged when God is at work in, through, and sometimes in spite of us? How can we not become better people as we grow in our love for God and neighbor? Indeed, as God's diverse people apply themselves in partnership together for the sake of the kingdom, deep personal transformation occurs within each of them.

Reflection Questions

1. What is the connection between obedience and joy? (If indeed working together for the kingdom is a biblical mandate, we should expect to experience joy.)

2. What is social capital, and how can urban-suburban partnership strengthen it? Furthermore, what is the relationship between social capital and biblical *koinonia*?

3. What does it mean to be intercultural? Why would this be a great advantage in today's world?

4. The authors claim that urban-suburban partnership bears practical fruit; in other words, it really does change lives and communities. Have you seen or experienced practical fruit that results from people daring to cross the socioeconomic class and cultural divides?

5. In what ways do you see the partners themselves personally changing as a result of an urban-suburban partnership?

Part 4

How Others Have Done It

Practical Models of Partnership

Few things annoy ministry practitioners more than an idea that sounds wonderful but ultimately has no practical value. *Does it work? Is it realistic? Is it doable? Has it been tried? Does it yield real fruit in the lives of real people?* Some may be asking these kinds of questions regarding the idea of urban-suburban partnership. We have tried to draw upon reflective practitioners of holistic ministry from beginning to end in this book, but we also think it is important to present real working models of what we are talking about. Part 4 seeks to do just that.

We have focused on partnerships that cross the urban-suburban divide. Of course there are other kinds of partnerships, for example between Christian groups and government, or between parachurch organizations and educational institutions, or between two congregations of different denominations, or between mission organizations from different countries. But these and other kinds of partnership may or may not develop across the urban-suburban chasm. We have concentrated on the ministry issues that arise from that particular divide—issues that stem from racial, cultural, and socioeconomic differences and that alienate even the most well-meaning Christians. The models presented here, therefore, represent relationships between urban and suburban Christian workers and institutions that have found a kingdom way of respecting and harnessing difference in order to model and work toward reconciliation and justice.

With this in mind, we identify four types of urban-suburban partnership. The urban church or agency provides the constant because we assume the urban milieu to be the primary context for ministry. So by *types* we mean four different kinds of suburban entities that partner with an urban church or agency. These entities are: (1) a suburban church, (2) a suburban parachurch, (3) a business or company, and (4) a suburban individual. The next four chapters that make up part 4 correspond to these four types of urban-suburban partnerships, and we offer real models for each. Indeed, the call for urban-suburban partnership does not issue forth from an ivory tower but from the real-life experiences of real people who are engaged together in holistic, transformational ministry across the urban-suburban divide.

9

Leap of Faith

Urban-Suburban Churches in Partnership

If you want to catch a glimpse of the whole gospel at work in a community, plan a visit to Lawndale Community Church (LCC), a growing, nondenominational, multicultural, urban congregation located on the west side of Chicago in an area known as North Lawndale. Wayne Gordon, one of the authors of this book, started LCC in 1978. He hesitated at first to have this book focus on LCC lest he be accused of tooting his own horn. But the other authors decided that the story of LCC simply must be told, for as we considered churches that have combined word and deed ministries in their respective communities, LCC stands out as an extraordinary model of a local congregation that is holistically engaged. Its outreach ministries include a transitional discipleship home for ex-offenders, a state-of-the-art health center (with over 340 staff), business and vocational development ventures, an affordable housing development ministry, and of course, contextual worship services—one that serves the hip-hop generation in the community. We believe the church at large can learn some important missional insights from what God has done and is doing in and through LCC.

The story of LCC has been told elsewhere, so there is no need to retell it here in detail.[1] But the richness of its story reveals crucial substories that are worth developing more fully. For our purposes, the partnerships formed between urban LCC and surrounding suburban churches—particularly the one with Christ Church of Oak Brook (CCOB)—deserve a deeper retelling, because the CCOB partnership in particular testifies to the exciting possibilities of personal and social transformation when two churches resolve to cross the urban-suburban divide.[2]

Partnership of Lawndale Community Church and Christ Church of Oak Brook

On Thanksgiving morning 1983 the *Chicago Tribune* ran an article featuring LCC.[3] It described the hopes and dreams of this urban church, which despite its youth (barely four years old at the time) and its size (about forty people in attendance) dared to believe in the power of the gospel to transform the inner-city community of North Lawndale.

The feature story of the young, ambitious church in the notoriously drug-infested, high-crime area moved many, including certain members of a local congregation called Christ Church located in suburban Oak Brook, about fifteen miles west of Lawndale. After reading the article, these members approached the senior pastor, who at that time was the Reverend Dr. Art DeKruyter, and expressed their desire to see if CCOB could be of any service to LCC. Christ Church, a large, affluent, established nondenominational congregation, already had mission commitments both globally and locally, and it did not necessarily need another project. Nevertheless, DeKruyter authorized contact with LCC, eventually sending Ed Rose, chairman of the missions committee at the time, to visit the young urban church. What he saw impressed him, as he sensed the burning, relentless vision of this small fellowship to be a transformational agent in Lawndale. After a reciprocal visit by LCC leaders to CCOB several months later, the seed of a partnership between two churches that cross the urban-suburban divide was planted—a seed that has since sprouted magnificently and continues to bear fruit today.

At first the financial support from CCOB defined the partnership, but it did not take long before it went beyond merely *sending a check* as church members began giving of their talents and expertise toward the fulfillment of LCC's vision. For example, CPA Gene

Eleveld helped set up the computer system for the health center as well as the accounting system for the church. He also volunteered to keep the church's financial books for a decade. Businessman Victor Warren, who owns Farrington Transport, began hiring young men from Lawndale to work for him. He also bought LCC a van so the people he hired had a way to get to and from work. Another successful business executive, Dave Beré, who had been president of Quaker Oats Company and was now president and COO of a Fortune 500 company, took the time to help Sheranda "Shaun" Brooks, a businessperson in Lawndale. The younger, inexperienced Brooks had a great food product to sell—breaded flour with a unique blend of seasoning that she sold to local groceries—but she did not have the business and marketing savvy to make the business turn a profit. Beré met with her at least twice a month, three hours at a time, for several years, helping Brooks transform her fledgling operation into a profit-making business.

Beyond the business world, Barbara Beré, Dave's mother, set up a scholarship fund for the church so that eligible Lawndale youth can go to college. Karen Beré, Dave's wife, and Anne Gordon, Wayne's wife, began coordinating an annual beautification project in which every spring a group from CCOB joins a group from LCC to plant flowers. The Beré family of CCOB reflects the spirit of the whole church. Construction workers of all kinds (contractors, carpenters, bricklayers, electricians, plumbers, etc.) have also volunteered through the years to renovate old buildings and construct new ones.

Medical professionals from the church (doctors, nurses, aides, etc.) have also volunteered through the years to care for patients at the health center. One doctor in particular, radiologist Dr. Simon Chiu, has been volunteering regularly at the center for the past twenty years, not only reading X-rays and ultrasounds but also recruiting fellow doctors to lend their expertise in the service of the patients.[4] These examples represent the strong volunteer corps of CCOB members who have given of their time, skills, and love toward the effectiveness of LCC's ongoing outreach ministries.

These examples of the partnership that are beyond the monetary, however, are not intended to downplay the significance of CCOB's direct financial support. The church's generous, faithful giving in the early days enabled LCC to pay its bills as well as forge ahead in establishing the church's community ministries. CCOB gave (and continues to give) corporately, but so did many individual church members.

For example, when Bob Roque sold his successful trucking business, he gave some of the proceeds to finance LCC's housing ministry. Individual members who were in positions of influence in the financial world also used their clout to release funding for LCC projects. For example, as a member of the board of the Chicago Community Trust, the late philanthropist Jim Beré (yes, another Beré—Dave's father) undoubtedly influenced the decision to approve a major grant proposal submitted by LCC to the trust in 1983 to make the dream of a full-service health clinic a reality. With the grant approved, the Lawndale Christian Health Center opened its doors in 1984 and began ministering holistically to the sick. Between corporate and individual giving, CCOB has easily been LCC's largest financial supporter.

Moreover, every penny given by CCOB had no strings attached even when LCC had not yet quite proven itself (the church consisted of two storefronts for a small sanctuary and a church office when CCOB began to support it). The confidence that motivated CCOB to give in this way has resulted in incalculable dividends toward LCC's ministry effectiveness.

But true partnership is two-way. How has Christ Church of Oak Brook benefited from the partnership with LCC? In *Real Hope in Chicago*, Gordon writes, "Dr. DeKruyter told me recently that I talk too much about how greatly we appreciate the people of Christ Church of Oak Brook. 'You're the ones who have changed our lives,' he said. 'It is your people who have enriched the people of Christ Church of Oak Brook.' "[5] DeKruyter was referring to a nonmonetary and nonmaterial but nonetheless invaluable benefit—namely, the opportunity to participate in kingdom activities, which has resulted in the deepening discipleship of many members of CCOB. The Reverend Dan Meyer, DeKruyter's successor in 1997, concurs and adds,

> LCC is way ahead of our church in understanding and enfleshing [a truly holistic] approach to mission. . . . As we seek to be an influence on the neighborhoods around our church building, we look to LCC as a model and teacher from which we can learn. They are showing us what it means to "exegete your neighborhood" and pursue a distinctly "Christian" approach to relationship-building and community development which gains a hearing for the gospel and expands the kingdom of God on a spiritual, social, and physical level.[6]

In addition to the opportunity to grow in holistic mission, CCOB can claim the kingdom fruit of that mission. In light of their vested involvement in LCC's many outreach ministries, CCOB co-owns LCC's successes! The future jewels from the many wonderful community ministries in Lawndale will be placed in the heavenly crowns of both LCC and CCOB members.

When Rev. Meyer succeeded DeKruyter at CCOB, it would not have been unusual for such a leadership transition to result in partnership like the one with LCC to lose momentum and eventually run out of gas. But this did not happen. As a testimony to how deep the sense of ownership has permeated Christ Church, when DeKruyter retired, many church members made it clear to the new pastor how they felt about LCC. As people "spoke about LCC with misty eyes or charged excitement in a way that clearly said, 'God is in this and it is really good,' "[7] Meyer felt compelled to take the partnership seriously. He eventually arranged a visit to LCC to see for himself what the people of CCOB were talking about with such excitement. He reminisces about that 1997 visit in a recent correspondence: "I went to Lawndale myself and saw the profound renewal taking place, sensed the passion of the leadership, and imagined what might yet be done."[8]

The trust built between the people of the two churches constitutes the backbone for the partnership; the personal relationships that formed from the partnership have enabled it to stand the test of time and adversity. To begin with, the friendships that developed between Gordon and the two pastors of CCOB over the past twenty-five years—fifteen with DeKruyter and ten with Meyer—have undoubtedly contributed to the lasting power of the partnership. But the personal connections only begin there. The deep friendship formed between the Barnhart family in Oak Brook and the Ratliff family in Lawndale is a case in point. In the last sixteen years, the love between them has manifested in regular family get-togethers, going to each other's children's graduations, praying for each other, walking together through trials and tribulations, and countless other ways that define true friendship. "We have walked together through good and bad," write Bill and Nan Barnhart. They depict their relationship with the Ratliffs—Stan, Antonette, and their two boys—as a part of their own family.[9]

The personal trust factor has also enabled the two churches to be honest with each other. For example, as a Christmas project, CCOB members bought, wrapped, and gave gifts to needy children. But when this project yielded detrimental results in Lawndale—many children began to display greed as a result of the handouts, and parents felt

disempowered to be able to provide for and bless their own kids—
LCC leaders told CCOB that the program had to change drastically
or be discontinued. Rather than feeling resentment over what could
have been taken as rejecting the church's benevolence, CCOB leaders listened and helped LCC to implement something different—the
creation of a Christmas store that sells toys at 10 percent of the cost
so parents can choose gifts they can afford, buy them, wrap them,
and personalize them for their children. Such an arrangement models
generosity that leads to empowerment. The store has been an overwhelming success, and as LCC leaders use proceeds from the sales to
replenish the store, it is able to continue serving families in this way
for the next Christmas season.

The personal relationships have contributed significantly to the success
of the partnership, but their common faith and vision in Christ has
undergirded it all. The two churches have shared together in their
common, but diversely expressed, worship experiences in a number of
ways, including the pastors swapping pulpits—Gordon has preached
at CCOB a number of times as has Meyer at LCC. The LCC choir has
also ministered in music at CCOB, and different groups of people from
CCOB have often taken part in Sunday morning worship at LCC. The
two churches also participated in a joint short-term missions trip to
Timisoara, Romania, in 2007. Headed up by CCOB members Bill and
Nan Barnhart and LCC member Bo Delaney, a basketball team from
Lawndale and several adult chaperones from both churches went to
Romania to participate in an evangelistic tournament. Meyer captures
the personal depth of the ministry partnership: "When we meet the
people of LCC, we are not meeting a group of people we 'support.'
We are connecting with another part of that larger 'self' that is the
Body of Christ, moving on God's mission."[10]

The partnership between LCC and CCOB models what can happen
when an urban church and a suburban church decide to come together
for the sake of the kingdom—the transformation of all involved.
President George W. Bush said as much in a 2003 speech regarding
faith-based initiatives when he asserted, "When a suburban church
and an urban church become full partners, great things can happen."
He went on to honor exemplary models of this kind of partnership,
citing LCC and CCOB among them: "The Chicago Christ Church of
Oak Brook, and Lawndale Community Church are working together
to serve the sick in Lawndale's health care clinic for the poor."[11] Although he honed in on what the two churches have done for the sick

through the health center, the same praise could have been showered upon all the outreach ministries the LCC-CCOB partnership has accomplished in the last twenty-five years (and we assume for many years to come).

Other Urban-Suburban Church Partnerships

Indeed the LCC-CCOB partnership stands out, but there are other noteworthy models of urban-suburban church partnerships throughout the country. For example, the relationship between Mt. View Presbyterian Church (MVPC) in White Center, Washington—an at-risk, ethnically diverse, unincorporated neighborhood just south of Seattle—and University Presbyterian Church (UPC) reflects a partnership that has formed across the urban-suburban divide. One of its unique features is how this partnership reflects the changing social landscape, which we attempted to describe in chapter 1. MVPC represents the urban counterpart to this partnership even though it is located on the outskirts of the city where suburbs usually flourish, while UPC represents the suburban counterpart even though it is located in the urban heart of Seattle's University District.

Despite the *reversed roles*, these two churches typify the key differences between urban and suburban congregations. About sixty people attend MVPC, while over seven thousand attend UPC in five Sunday services. MVPC is ethnically diverse, reflecting White Center's population of Euro-, Asian-, African-, Latino-, and Native Americans, while UPC is predominantly Anglo-American. MVPC generally serves people of low socioeconomic status, while UPC generally serves the educated and well-to-do. The partnership began in 2001 when UPC sought to place some of its college interns in an impoverished community through the Urban Intentional Community Program, which was run by its denomination—Presbyterian Church (USA). MVPC made its parsonage available for the UPC interns assigned to White Center, and the partnership developed from there. The relationships that formed through this arrangement grew and strengthened as a number of the students stayed long after their internships ended to join in the life of both MVPC and the community on a long-term basis.

Mutually beneficial relationships indeed reflect the strength of this partnership. Mike McCormick Huentelman, urban ministries coordinator for UPC, emphasizes the intangible rewards of deepening discipleship at UPC: "Our relationship with the faith community of Mt. View helps our members to connect to the larger body of Christ, which is the Church. And it helps us to deepen in our discipleship journey—learning from one another across cultural, racial and economic lines, and to mature in the heart and mind of Christ."[12]

As for the benefits to MVPC, Lina Thompson, a commissioned lay pastor, concurs with these intangible rewards because the partnership has encouraged and strengthened the people of MVPC as well. But in addition to these intangibles, MVPC has also enjoyed some tangibles through the partnership—most significantly, the complete renovation of the church's much-used facility. UPC not only approved a large sum of money toward the project, which the two churches called "Build Up the House," it also supplied more than eight hundred volunteers over a span of two weeks to get the job done efficiently and in a timely manner. "It was a renovation project that impacted every inch of our facility," writes Thompson.[13] With the indispensable help of UPC, MVPC basically got an *extreme makeover*, or as local Seattle television station King 5 News headlined in its June 9, 2007, broadcast, "White Center church gets 'a divine makeover.'"[14]

But the partnership does not just benefit the two churches, as if they have come together simply to enhance the lives of their respective congregations. On the contrary, they have partnered for the sake of the community of White Center. The "Build Up the House" project, for example, was driven by a desire on the part of the two churches to make the facility safer for the seventy-five children and youth of the community whom MVPC serves via its after-school tutoring and recreation programs. The two churches have also come together for the last several years to put on a harvest party for the elementary school across the street from MVPC. At the time of this writing, the two churches are also seriously considering moving UPC's Language Institute, a ministry of love and language learning among refugees and immigrants, to MVPC. Such a move would certainly deepen the partnership between these two churches, but more importantly, it would provide an important service for the growing immigrant population in White Center.

The two churches work together with other Christian organizations in the community, such as the Union Gospel Mission and the YES Foundation, and thus broaden the partnership base. As Huentelman says, "Our partnership is not exclusive; we engage and welcome others in, and the community impact continues to grow."[15] The MVPC-

UPC partnership is only six years old, but its willingness to extend the partnership to other groups and ministries, the strong personal relationships between the two churches, and the common passion to live out the gospel in Seattle hold great promise for an enduring partnership that will yield kingdom fruit for years to come.

Strategies to Elevate People (STEP) in Richmond, Virginia, provides yet another type of model for urban-suburban church partnership in that it takes it to the organizational level. As we mentioned in the introduction, STEP came into being as a result of urban and suburban church leaders desiring to come together for the sake of the poor in Richmond, more specifically in Gilpin Court—an at-risk, impoverished, African-American housing project in inner-city Richmond. The original vision of STEP to bring together the church, in all of its diversity, to be the transforming presence of Christ in Gilpin Court continues to drive its many ministries, which include a literacy program that serves about forty elementary-age children, a summer enrichment program that provides weary youth sorely needed respite from the pressures of urban life, and wholesome family-oriented activities such as an annual back-to-school carnival and a fall family festival. In addition, STEP organizes family share teams that are designed to come alongside struggling families, offering prayer, friendship, support, and guidance.

STEP as an organization does the necessary planning and preparation for these ministries, but individual men and women come from both urban and suburban churches in the area to actually make it happen. Executive Director Timothy Cole explains further that STEP takes the lead in urban ministries and then provides relationships and structure for urban and suburban churches to become engaged together.[16] In close partnership with two urban churches in Richmond—Victory Life Fellowship and Eternity Church—STEP reaches out to suburban churches to participate in its exciting urban ministries. In this way, "STEP is a bridge ministry linking together the resources (people, finance, and material) of the suburban Church with the poor in urban Richmond."[17]

For example, STEP recently organized a Vacation Bible School that intentionally brought urban and suburban children together. The volunteer teachers, administrators, musicians, cooks, and chaperones came primarily from four churches, two from nearby suburbs—Third Presbyterian and Hope Church—and two from the city—Victory Life and Eternity Church. By virtue of this VBS, the children came together from both the city and the suburbs and received spiritual and social nourishment in a racially and socioeconomically diverse context. The over one hundred children who attended came from both predominantly black Gilpin Court and predominantly white suburban churches. Such an event, where churches cross the urban-suburban divide in order to foster gospel-inspired friendships between black and white children, serve as an affront to deep-seated racial tensions that are all too pervasive in that part of the country.

Other organizations, like Word & Deed Network (WDN) of the Evangelicals for Social Action, seek to facilitate similar urban-suburban church partnerships.[18] For example, WDN currently serves as a coordinator for a budding partnership between City Line Church, a young predominantly Asian-American congregation whose membership includes many people in the medical profession, and Sweet Union Baptist Church, a predominantly African-American congregation in West Philadelphia that seeks to be a place of holistic healing for the community. At the time of this writing, WDN is helping the two churches plan a medical outreach in West Philadelphia, bringing together the gifts, resources, and vision of both churches.

Strong cross-cultural friendships, deep discipleship and spiritual growth, richer experiences in God and each other, encouragement, empowerment, pooled financial and human resources to serve the poor, and bearing witness to the power of the gospel to dismantle the walls between black, white, and brown and between the rich and the poor—these are the fruit that urban-suburban partnerships yield; and churches that dare to partner across this great divide get to feast on them! These very real, on-the-ground models of urban-suburban church partnerships that we have featured here (and others that space simply did not allow us to share) should tell us that this kind of intentional border-crossing in the gospel is doable and effective.

What would happen if churches across the country and around the world resolved to come together like these churches? Transformation. Reconciliation. Revival!

| Reflection Questions

1. What characteristics do both Lawndale Community Church and Christ Church of Oak Brook have that has made their partnership work?

2. In light of these stories of partnership, what challenges do churches face by crossing the urban-suburban divide?

3. In the same light, what benefits do churches enjoy by crossing the divide?

4. How open do you think your church is to engaging in a partnership of this kind?

10

Expanding to the City

Urban-Suburban Parachurch Organizations in Partnership

Many parachurch organizations have contributed to the development of the global, holistic ministry movement around the world, but a strong case can be made that InterVarsity Christian Fellowship (IVCF) is at the top of the list. In terms of inspiring a cadre of holistically minded leaders, which includes John Stott, Melba Maggay, David Gitari, Miriam Adeney, William Pannell, and Samuel Escobar (to name a few), IVCF has no rival as these global leaders have done their part in galvanizing the worldwide evangelical Christian community toward integrated works of evangelism, social justice, racial reconciliation, and theological reflection.[1]

It seems odd then that a full-blown urban ministry within IVCF—at least in the United States—has only recently developed. After all, the historical root of campus ministries—which many trace as far back as 1827 when Anglican minister Charles Simeon preached a sermon on the church's responsibility to the poor—was precisely focused on works of compassion and justice in the inner city. Simeon's sermon inspired a group of Cambridge University undergraduates to begin an outreach in the Barnwell slum, a poor district of Jesus Lane in London. An urban vision, therefore, constitutes the very DNA of the world Christian student movement.[2]

Despite this history and despite its remarkable track record of holistic ministry, racial equality, indigenous leadership, and multiethnic ministries,[3] IVCF/USA had only sporadic involvement in American cities until the 1990s. But there were certainly important precursors to what is today a significant urban thrust within the organization:

> Former IVCF/USA staff worker Barbara Benjamin's ministry in the late 1960s among inner-city youth in Brooklyn, New York—in which she involved students, alumni, and faculty of Brooklyn College—provided a picture of what a university-based urban ministry could look like.[4]
>
> Pete Hammond's work to bring black and white students together in Mississippi in the 1960s, along with decades of cultivating a culture of racial justice within IVCF, certainly did its part in paving the way.[5]
>
> Tom Skinner's memorable address, "The U.S. Racial Crisis and World Evangelism," challenged the 12,000 attendees at the 1970 Urbana Conference to take racism seriously in their evangelistic efforts. According to many, Skinner "laid out the agenda for the thousands of future evangelical leaders who listened to his passionate charge that day."[6]
>
> Among those whom Skinner's words affected deeply was Paul Gibson, the first African-American to join the IVCF/USA staff in the post–civil rights era. Inspired by Skinner and encouraged and mentored by Hammond, Gibson began an urban work in New York City in 1976 and then another one in Los Angeles in 1978.

These ministries undoubtedly laid important groundwork for urban mission in the city. But even then, according to Brenda Salter McNeil (speaking as a former IVCF staff worker), urban ministry—a ministry of college students going *into the city* to minister to the poor in the areas of justice, reconciliation, and evangelism—struggled to find an integral place within mainstream IVCF/USA, which continued primarily to attract and serve white (and increasingly Asian-American), middle-class university students from the suburbs.[7]

It was not until the early 1990s that urban ministry made significant strides toward full acceptance in IVCF/USA, due in large part to the growing desire among students for more experiential and service-oriented types of learning.[8] As the aspirations of socially conscious students went in this direction, IVCF/USA's urban vision strengthened, allowing the experiences of Benjamin, Hammond, Gibson, and others to reshape the organization. This reshaping took on the form of what is now called "Urban Projects"—student placements in urban contexts for a designated period of time for learning and ministry. Since Gibson's Urban Projects in New York and Los Angeles, city ministries of this kind have multiplied to over thirty major cities across the United States, increasingly occupying an integral place in the overall vision and strategy of IVCF/USA.[9] The appointment of Randy White in 1995 as national coordinator of Urban Projects indicates the way in which this urban thrust has gained prominence (or rather, regained prominence, if we take into account its origins and ethos) within the organization.

Urban Projects Are All about Partnerships

The implementation of Urban Projects is especially appropriate for this book because it happens in partnership with existing urban ministries or churches. In fact, they do not just happen *through* partnerships, they *are* partnerships—between predominantly suburban college students under the auspices of IVCF/USA and urban ministries. The vision statement of the Fresno Institute for Urban Leadership—the name of IVCF's Urban Project in Fresno, California—articulates this well when it envisions Fresno as "a city full of partnerships which fosters the physical, spiritual, economic, and social transformation of our poorest urban neighborhoods, and a renewal of faith for the church."[10]

The heart of Urban Projects lies with its directors, who largely shape the vision and then carry that vision out in their respective cities. While some continue to serve on staff at college campuses alongside their Urban Project responsibilities, others have gone full-time in developing urban partnerships in their respective cities. White calls the latter *specialists* or *champions*.[11] The list of Urban Project specialists includes John Hochevar in Chicago, Kevin Blue in Los Angeles, Barb Weidman in Philadelphia, Marshall Benbow in Greensboro, North Carolina, Jen Vettrus in Milwaukee, Gerry Chappeau in St. Louis, Kim Koi in Orlando, and Josh Harper in the San Francisco Bay Area. Serving as cultural brokers between college campuses and the city, Urban Project directors negotiate with urban agency leaders in their respective cities and place university students accordingly. Under the oversight of both the Urban Project directors and the leaders of partner agencies, students engage in transformational ministry.

The length of time that students participate in an Urban Project differs from weekend *dips* to week-long *plunges* to two-week *immersions* to five-to-eight-week summer *dives* or *internships*. Although there is a place for each of these, the kingdom vision of *shalom* among the participants predictably comes into sharper and more sustained focus through the summer internships, when friendships between students, urban workers, and community residents have more time to develop.[12]

How do these urban projects get started? What do they look like? What roles do Urban Project directors and urban agency leaders play in the partnership? What are the benefits for both entities as well as for the communities they serve together? The answers to these questions reveal the contours of an urban-suburban partnership model that provides basic guidelines for other parachurch organizations seeking to partner with urban ministries for the sake of the kingdom.

How do Urban Projects get started? Directors initiate a partnership in one of two ways: relational or thematic.[13] Redirecting an existing relationship toward partnering together defines the relational approach. For example, Josh Harper in the Bay Area has utilized his personal connections with New Hope Covenant, an urban church in East Oakland of which he and his family are members. Referring back to the first Dos and Don'ts couplets for both urban and suburban entities in chapter 5, Harper has simply applied the *Do* of beginning a partnership with an existing relationship. He has been conducting internships at New Hope Covenant Church every year since 2004.

Discerning a missional theme around which an Urban Project is formed defines the other approach to initiate a partnership. For example, as an IVCF staff worker in the mid-1980s at Occidental College in Southern California, McNeil felt led to explore multiculturalism, so she partnered with the Harambee Center and sent a group of student interns to work together with Harambee's ethnically diverse staff.[14] Located at that time in an area that "had the highest daytime crime rate in Southern California," Harambee became an instrument of hope, as it facilitated reconciliation between African-American, Latino-American, and Anglo-American communities.[15] Another example of a theme-based beginning is the Broetje Orchard Project in eastern Washington State, which developed around the theme of justice for migrant farm workers. In 2005 Angela and Matt Rajnus, Urban Project directors in Walla Walla, Washington, initiated a partnership with Jubilee Youth Ranch, a ministry for at-risk youth, and placed students there not only to help with Jubilee's ministry to youth but also to interact with, minister to, and learn from migrant workers in Broejte Orchards.[16] Other examples of theme- or need-based Urban Projects include the Katrina response groups that joined relief agencies in New Orleans and joint house-building efforts in several cities with Habitat for Humanity.

After these Urban Projects get started, whether relationally or thematically, they begin to take shape according to their context, and no two look the same. Upholding the value of indigenous ministry, IVCF/USA has not imposed a strict standardization on Urban Projects. In fact, White points out that "there is a reason that my title is 'coordinator' and not 'director.' IV intentionally didn't make any official rules for Urban Projects that might stifle indigenous development."[17] So these projects look different depending on context—the Urban Project in Tampa, Florida, looks different from the one in Tacoma, Washington, which looks different from the one in Los Angeles, and so on. They also look different according to what type of urban agency gets involved. Some Urban Projects partner with churches, such as the one formed with Lawndale Community Church in Chicago. Others team up with classic service agencies such as the Salvation Army in Greensboro, North Carolina, and Esperanza Health Center in Philadelphia. Still others associate with community organizing groups such as the Jubilee Christian Development Corporation in St. Louis. Many Urban Projects also partner with secular organizations such as Campfire, a community-based youth program in West Oakland, California. Furthermore, each Urban Project partners with multiple churches and organizations in each of their respective locations; so the dynamic mixture of college students with churches, faith-based agencies, or secular organizations in any given location ensures a different look from project to project.

Having emphasized the factors that make each Urban Project distinct, it is also important to say that they do share a set of core practices, including teaching, study, worship, and a certain agreed-upon number of hours serving with the partner organizaton. Moreover, they "nearly all share a common commitment to teaching certain values, such as exploring issues of justice, poverty, racism, racial

reconciliation, violence, lifestyle, biblical community, and the ministry of the urban church."[18]

How do the roles of the Urban Project staff and the urban agency
leaders play out in a partnership? The answer here also differs from
area to area. For many, the delineation of responsibilities as to how to
care for, teach, and mobilize students is stipulated in a Memorandum
of Understanding (MOU), which is an agreement between an Urban
Project and the urban church or agency. MOUs differ from each other,
some being more formal and more detailed than others. White says that
every Urban Project is expected to have an MOU for each partnership,
but enforcement is loose (no MOU police are dispatched!).[19]

The stipulations of many of these MOUs include defining the roles
that both sides of the partnership play. (For an example of an MOU,
see appendix 1.) Generally speaking, the supervisory responsibilities
are divided according to the respective vision and goals of the two partners. For IVCF/USA, the vision of Urban Projects has to do with "the
development of transformational leaders for the new global city,"[20]
so the Urban Project staff workers take on the primary responsibility
of teaching the core values of the kingdom, directing their activities
toward leadership development, and reviewing the project for long-
term impact. For the urban agency, the vision has more to do with the
transformation of the community in which it ministers; so its leaders
take on the primary responsibility of assigning tasks and providing
opportunities for the students to serve according to the needs in the
community at any given time. As these visions overlap, Urban Project
leaders and urban agency leaders work out appropriate ways to share
in the guidance and supervision of the students. For example, Harper
notes that even though it is InterVarsity's primary responsibility to
instill a theology of the city in the students, "it is a rare and beautiful
partner that will provide a solid theological backdrop for why they are
doing what they do, to clarify their vision frequently and to process
with the students about what they are learning."[21]

What have been the benefits for both entities as they experience
ministry partnership together? Let us begin with urban partners and
their constituents. In light of his study of the Chicago Urban Project, Rick Richardson discusses the reasons agencies and communities welcome interns in terms of human, cultural, and social capital.
He first cites volunteer personnel—the human capital. "Overall," he
writes, "the primary reason for community people hosting InterVarsity students was the free skilled labor."[22] As IVCF/USA essentially

provides skilled, culturally sensitive, committed Christian students, urban agencies—which seem chronically lacking in personnel to accomplish their goals—are more than happy to host a group of unpaid interns who have a genuine desire to help in any way. An interesting distinction to Urban Project partnerships is that money does not factor in for the most part. Urban partners do not pay for the interns, and unlike other urban-suburban partnerships, IVCF/USA does not give financially. Such a nonmonetary-based partnership enables the participants to do ministry together unencumbered by many financial complexities.

Second to human capital gain, Richardson also cites "cultural identity-bridging and status linking capital,"[23] which refers to a less measurable gain that comes with being associated with college students—in the case of the Chicago Urban Project, with students from Northwestern University. By virtue of developing working and personal relationships with Northwestern students, urban agency staff and community participants become more aware of the cultural diversity that exists across the urban-suburban divide as well as become more prepared to interact with the world outside of their communities. Translating the language of this type of capital into plain English: authentic relationships, which form with the college students, broaden the cultural and social horizons of both urban partners and IVCF participants.

In Oakland, California, for example, Harper describes the impact of the Urban Project partnership on hardened men in a recovery program conducted by City Team in Oakland. Among other outreaches, City Team runs a residential recovery program for men fighting off drug and alcohol addictions. Fifteen to twenty-five men can live at the City Team facility—a former hotel in downtown Oakland—at any given time. Beyond the expected approaches to rehab—Bible study, counseling, community life, and education—City Team also has the men in residence serve the homeless in its soup kitchen (recovery through service). The Bay Area Urban Project, or BayUP, partners with City Team on a yearly basis and places interns in the facility to live with, get to know, and serve the homeless with the men. Harper looks back in amazement at how quickly deep relationships form between the residents and the student interns. "When it's time for the interns to leave," he says, "some of these street-wise, street-hardened men shed tears."[24] The interns become emotional too, indicating the relational connection that has formed between these ministry partners who have crossed the urban-suburban divide. Even after graduating from City Team's program, some of the men have maintained healthy contact with former interns, and many former interns continue to volunteer at City Team.

Such reciprocity segues conveniently to the benefits from the partnership to IVCF/USA itself, which are significant. In short, Urban Projects have been nothing short of prophetic. In other words, they have helped the organization remember God's heart for justice, transformation, and reconciliation and thus reshape itself in conformity to God's purposes in the world. McNeil largely credits Urban Projects, which she describes as "learning laboratories that tie the message of diversity and . . . reconciliation back to the college campus," for helping IVCF/USA to become more diversified and to develop into an increasingly more effective instrument of reconciliation.[25] For White, Urban Projects have served as a call back to IVCF's historical DNA. As a campus ministry, he says, the vision of IVCF will always be the development of transformational leaders, but Urban Projects have helped tremendously in reminding them of the integral place the city has in its overall vision.[26] Alec Hill, president of IVCF/USA, says it succinctly when he celebrates, "Thank the Lord for Urban Projects. Students are being transformed. Campuses are being renewed as they return from such life-altering experiences. And world changers are being developed."[27]

As for the student participants in Urban Projects, the fruit has been invaluable. Hill continues their praises and writes, "These experiences have deeply impacted our students. Their lives have been changed."[28] He cites statistics from a survey of eighty Urban Project alumni that demonstrate the depth of this change:

- 10 percent—purchased homes in at-risk neighborhoods
- 11 percent—committed themselves wholeheartedly to Jesus for the first time
- 18 percent—became involved with economic development
- 20 percent—began ministering to gang kids or at-risk youth
- 25 percent—joined a church of a different ethnicity
- 25 percent—rented an apartment in at-risk neighborhoods
- 45 percent—began mentoring younger leaders in their church
- 45 percent—increased their giving
- 50 percent—began tutoring in an urban neighborhood

- 68 percent—increased their prayer life
- 73 percent—crossed ethnic divides to seek racial reconciliation[29]

These statistics go beyond the anecdotal; they quantify inward changes that have resulted in outward active lives for the gospel; they quantify discipleship that has occurred through Urban Projects. White, who conducted the survey to which President Hill refers, writes, "It becomes abundantly clear that Urban Projects are effective tools for the development of measurable, proactive patterns of discipleship behavior."[30]

IVCF/USA's Urban Projects model the reason, the method, and the fruit of urban-suburban partnerships for parachurch organizations. It is when alumni and students alike go beyond the parameters of Urban Projects in the service of the city that fruit for all involved is clearly demonstrated. For example, when Urban Project alumni, staff, and students in Fresno, California, began in the early 1990s to move together into Lowell—the poorest neighborhood in the city—it was so they could serve the community year-round in ongoing partnerships with organizations such as World Impact, Evangel Home, Hope Now for Youth, and Habitat for Humanity. This relocation eventually led to what is now the Fresno Institute for Urban Leadership, where "students and community leaders live [together] year round and pursue leadership development, biblical community, and urban ministry."[31] These year-long communal arrangements of IVCF staff, alumni, and students in ongoing partnerships with urban agencies have begun to form in other cities as well; in addition to Fresno, what White calls "Urban Project extensions" have also formed in Philadelphia, Tampa, and Orlando.

Perhaps a snapshot of a relationship between a student and a person to whom an urban agency was ministering would bring the various pieces of this partnership model together. Mike Downey, a senior engineering student at the University of California–Berkeley, applied for an internship with BayUP (the Urban Project in the San Francisco Bay Area) in the summer of 2006. BayUP accepted his application and assigned him and three others to City Team, an urban mission agency in nearby Oakland with which BayUP has partnered since 2004. The students lived at the City Team facility for the duration of their five-week internship, along with the forty or so people who use City Team's shelter. City Team staff assigned Downey and his fellow interns to various tasks, including providing tutoring through the Learning Center, where those in City Team's recovery program receive assistance in basic educational skills in order to better their chances to reenter the working world. There were fifteen men in the program when Downey was there.

Because of Downey's lifelong penchant for math (with a fresh engineering degree to prove it), he spent much of his time tutoring the residents in basic arithmetic, especially a resident named Joe Juarez (aka "Big Joe"). "He was reluctant to work on any of the math in the Learning Center packets," remembers Downey, "because he had always had such difficulty with it."[32] As the two men began to develop a relationship of trust, communication, and shared faith in Christ, Juarez confided in Downey that ever since he was put in the "dumdum math class" (as he put it) in elementary school, he totally lost confidence in his educational abilities, even developing an irrational fear of math. Predictably, Juarez ended up dropping out of school.

Twenty years later, however, down and out but trying to recover with City Team's help, Juarez gave math another chance because of his growing friendship with Downey. Says Downey, "When I began working with him, he believed that he would never be able to learn anything related to math."[33] But the one-on-one approach and creative learning methods in the context of prayer, encouragement, and friendship yielded remarkable results. Juarez not only began to understand math for the first time, he became excited about it. He looked forward with eagerness to his time with Downey, who opened a whole new world to him. He even began using his free time to work on math problems. At the 2006 City Team graduation, Juarez singled out Downey and thanked him for helping him regain his self-confidence—an important trait to possess when reentering the working world.

Downey was also changed by his internship, crediting his friendship with Juarez as having the biggest impact on his understanding of the struggle these men undergo—men whom society in general, and the educational system in particular, have failed. For Downey, the whole experience at City Team, especially his friendship with Big Joe, has changed his life plans. "I now hope to live in the heart of the city, raising a family there instead of suburbia like I had previously imagined, and be part of the ministry of City Team or something like City Team."[34] The relationship between Downey and Juarez—with the ingredients of gospel, prayer, trust, communication, encouragement, and math—in the context of a partnership between BayUP and City Team demonstrates the two-way transformation that can occur when urban and suburban people dare to come together for the sake of the kingdom.

Another Parachurch in Partnership: Justice for All

IVCF/USA Urban Projects offer one model among university students. Other campus ministries have similar models, such as the Here's Life Inner City program of Campus Crusade for Christ International[35] and Bart Campolo's Mission Year.[36] Wheaton College's Human Needs, Global Resources (HNGR) program also provides a unique student placement program that places qualified undergraduates in organizations that work in needy areas around the world. But do such partnerships exist beyond the university? It is true that university students tend to be more willing to take risks or do something radical, thus making it easier to relegate incarnational urban partnerships as only fit for edgy, intellectual, Birkenstock-wearing, bohemian types. But how about those well beyond the college scene? Are there nonuniversity Christian organizations that have gotten involved in the city in partnership with urban agencies? As a matter of fact, yes.

Justice for All (JFA), a nonprofit organization based in Rock Valley, Iowa, readily comes to mind. Rock Valley is more rural than suburban, but as an organization, JFA also draws volunteers and resources from nearby suburban churches and individuals. According to its website, "JFA is a ministry based on the services of Christians from many different denominations who are willing to share their time, resources and skills for the benefit of the poor and underprivileged."[37] JFA began in 1980 when several members of Trinity Christian Reformed Church of Rock Valley heard John Perkins speak at Dordt College in nearby Sioux Center, Iowa. As Pat Vander Pol, JFA's ministry coordinator, tells it,

> Pastor Dan De Groot invited him to stay for a few extra days [as] members of our church visited with him. A short time later five men from our church, including Pastor Dan, went to Voice of Calvary Ministries in Jackson, MS [a ministry that was founded by Perkins] and visited with him there. As they explored together ways that our church could help Rev. Perkins and his staff carry out their mission, he challenged them to send some church members to Jackson, members with construction skills who can help VOCM renovate buildings that it could

use to carry out its mission. So in 1981, thirteen volunteers went to serve at VOCM. These buildings became the ministry's health clinic, thrift store and volunteer center.[38]

This firsthand experience with Perkins in the early 1980s gave birth to JFA, which inevitably invited other churches to become involved. Under De Groot's leadership, JFA has continued since that first trip to Jackson in 1981 to send volunteers to VOCM and now many other organizations, including the John Perkins Foundation for Reconciliation and Development also in Jackson, Salama Urban Ministries in Nashville, and Harvest Hands Ministries in Juarez, Mexico. True to its original inspiration, JFA articulates its vision today, over twenty-five years later, as seeking "to promote biblical justice and reconciliation, by encouraging and equipping volunteers, empowering the poor, and partnering with other ministries that share a commitment to Christian community development."[39]

JFA operates in two distinct ways: first, by collecting goods ranging from house furniture to church pews to farm equipment to clothing (JFA's Warehouse Ministry), and then by distributing them to ministries around the world as their partner agencies have need. Vander Pol reports in her 2006–2007 summary that forty-five semi-truck–size loads were sent out over the previous year to nine local, ten national, and three international ministries.[40] Of these ministries, nine of them are decidedly in the urban context.

The second way JFA operates is by its Work Projects Ministry, which coordinates volunteers from Rock Valley and surrounding communities to lend their time, skills, and love to JFA's ministry partners around the world. It is this second way that goes deeper into the heart of this book—namely, the joining together of urban and suburban Christians to experience and model reconciliation across racial and socioeconomic divides for both personal and social transformation. As JFA volunteers submit to the vision and leadership of their urban partners, they have lent a hand to many organizations. For example:

Volunteers worked with Harvest Hands Ministry in Juarez, Mexico, in 2006 to install plumbing and heating for the girls' dormitory building of the *Resplandor de Vida* orphanage.

Volunteers worked with the John Perkins Foundation in Jackson, Mississippi, to dig, pour, and lay the foundation for an addition to a home for the Zechariah 8 Project.

Volunteers worked with Phillips Medical Services, also in Jackson, to assist in the clinic for the needy.

These are only a few of the many ways in which over 150 rural and suburban Iowan Christians in a span of one year gave of their time and skills in partnership with urban sisters and brothers around the world.[41]

Beyond the projects, however, Vander Pol points most gratefully to the enduring relationships that have formed as a result of these partnerships. She reflects,

> A lot of work has been accomplished over the years, but by far the most important thing . . . is the friendships and understanding that have come about between people of totally different cultures and the bond of Christ's unity which has become so precious to so many people. The paint will fade and the bricks will tumble, but the gifts of love for one another and Christ-like compassion are eternal and will be celebrated together with all God's people for all eternity.[42]

C. J. Jones, community development coordinator of VOCM, concurs: "The work that JFA has done for all these places for all these years has got to be worth a million dollars, but the relationships that have been built over the years are priceless."[43] As an example of this kind of relational bond in Christ, Vander Pol celebrates the fact that fifteen people from Jackson and a handful of others from other partner ministries around the country traveled from afar to attend the funeral of her father, a faithful JFA volunteer until his death in September 2007.[44]

Through these relationships, richer and deeper discipleship in Christ has occurred for all involved. "Without the experience of being welcomed into a community like VOCM," writes Vander Pol, "our understanding of God's kingdom would never have been complete." She sums up the partnership experience this way: "Learning from one another, building relationships, studying God's Word from a different life experience and perspective, and praying together—these are what really matter."[45]

Parachurch organizations like JFA demonstrate that meaningful urban-suburban partnership is not the sole domain of radical Christian student groups. From IVCF/USA Urban Projects to Justice for All, college students and professional and working-class people alike have caught the vision of the kingdom of God and are acting upon it among the underserved and underprivileged in the world. As a result, transformation happens in all and through all.

Reflection Questions

1. What do you suppose motivates college students to participate in IVCF/USA Urban Projects?

2. Meaningful long-term partnerships are not just for radical student groups. What unique characteristics do suburban-based parachurch organizations like Justice for All have that enable Christians of all ages to partner with urban ministries?

3. Discuss both the challenges and the rewards of partnership for urban and suburban agencies.

4. What message do you suppose gets across to community residents when urban and suburban Christians come together to minister in the community?

11

Beyond Profit

Businesses in Partnership

Urban-suburban partnerships between churches and parachurch organizations seem logical enough, but ones that involve secular businesses
might be a leap for some. But consider the way in which Memphis-
based Diversified Conveyors Incorporated (DCI) conducts business as
both profit-making and kingdom-building. In a matter of a few years,
DCI has become one of the leading builders of conveyor systems for
major carrier companies such as UPS, DHL, and FedEx Ground. It
is licensed in forty-seven states and also does business in the United
Kingdom. DCI employs thirty-five people in the Memphis office and
has field representatives numbering in the hundreds at times. Established in 2000 by Tom and Beth Phillips, DCI has grown remarkably
in its operations as well as in its profits. From all angles, it has become
a successful business.

Its financial success, however, is only the beginning of DCI's story.
It turns out that there is much more to this company than simple
profit making. To begin with, it has a missions committee. You read
correctly: a corporate, profit-making business with a missions committee! Comprised of three employees—Keith Barger (account manager), David Devins (project manager), and Randy Ward (engineer)—

the committee regularly meets together and prayerfully decides on ministries with which DCI should partner.

Whether it is offering financial support, encouragement, expertise, labor, or all of the above, DCI is in active partnership with many organizations, both local and abroad. The list of Memphis-based organizations DCI supports includes Ministry of the Heart, a prison ministry providing Bible studies, prayer support, and encouragement for prisoners; and Economic Opportunities, a postprison ministry that helps those recently released from prison transition back into the working world. On the international scene, it partners with organizations doing ministry in the so-called 10/40 Window such as Opportunity International and African Children's Outreach. Tom Phillips says that the partnerships are becoming numerous and complex enough that DCI is considering hiring a missions coordinator.[1] Furthermore, DCI conducts an annual missions banquet for the purpose not only of informing DCI employees of the many worthy ministries the company supports, but also to show appreciation via good food, recognition, and celebration for the faithful work of the men and women who run these ministries. One leader of an inner-city organization confided in Phillips after the 2006 banquet, "For the twenty-seven years that I've been doing this, I've felt like a beggar [referring to fund- and support-raising]. This is the first time a supporter has fed *me* and thanked *me!*"[2]

From the beginning, Tom and Beth Phillips envisioned DCI as a *beyond-profit company*, intent from the outset to reflect the power and love of the gospel. "Any good that we do is in response to God's goodness," Tom asserts. "We don't do it to earn our salvation but rather in response to the gift of salvation given to us. Because of what Christ has done for us, how can we not bless others?"[3] Such a conviction flies in the face of the *more money, more power, more comfort, and more security* spirit that seems to drive much of the corporate world. The founders of DCI knew at the start that they wanted it to be a giving company, involved in hands-on ministry to the underprivileged and under-resourced.

It was unclear, however, what form this involvement would take locally until they met the people of Advance Memphis, a Christian nonprofit organization that serves the Cleaborn and Foote community, or zip code 38126. Cleaborn-Foote has the dubious honor of being the poorest urban sector of the state of Tennessee and the third most impoverished zip code in the nation. The relationship formed between DCI and Advance Memphis represents a partnership between a business and an urban agency that we hope will serve both as an inspiration and a concrete model for others.

The Advance Memphis–Diversified Conveyers Inc. Partnership

Advance Memphis has its own story to tell. Founded in 1999 by businessman Steve Nash, Advance Memphis seeks "to serve adults in the Cleaborn and Foote community by helping residents acquire knowledge, resources, and skills to be economically self-sufficient through the gospel of Jesus Christ."[4] In Cleaborn-Foote, "nearly half the residents are high-school dropouts, the unemployment rate is 14.5 percent, and only 4 percent of residents own their homes."[5] Drugs, crime, violence, teen pregnancies, households run by single working mothers, welfare dependence, and joblessness create a cloud of hopelessness and despair that hangs over the community. In this context, Advance Memphis offers financial literacy courses, a savings program, GED tutoring, job placement services, and community improvement opportunities. It envisions empowered adults who attain a significant level of socioeconomic self-sufficiency. In this way Advance Memphis is essentially a nonprofit that helps families profit and in turn contribute to the good of the whole community for the glory of God.

Advance Memphis is the culmination of Nash's involvement with various urban agencies, including STREETS Ministries, a community-based youth organization through which he developed the Cycle with a Mission program. Cycle with a Mission brought urban and suburban youth together to bike across town to do service projects on a monthly basis. Nash and his wife, Donna, also served on the board of Neighborhood Housing Opportunity, a program of the Memphis Leadership Foundation to help people own homes. These hands-on experiences, along with the biblical teaching he had heard through the years from holistic ministry advocates who came to Memphis, culminated in the birth of Advance Memphis.[6]

Because of Nash's business background, it makes sense that Advance Memphis relied heavily on partners in the corporate world to achieve its goals. "Business partners are key to our success!" exclaims its website. "You are the ones who are sourcing qualified applicants, working with us to meet your retention targets, and investing resources."[7] With Advance's desire to partner with businesses and DCI's desire to partner with worthy ministries, it was only a matter of time until the two Memphis entities crossed paths.

Phillips and Nash tell the beginning of the partnership similarly: Nash's good friend Ken Bennett, founding director of STREETS Ministry in Memphis, also happened to be a fellow member of Independent Presbyterian Church with Phillips. One day Phillips mentioned to Bennett the need for janitorial services at DCI's facility. Bennett responded by telling him about Advance Memphis and that one of the participants of Advance's jobs program, Janice Hopson, needed a job. Phillips hired Hopson, and unbeknownst to anyone at that point, an enduring partnership began.

Soon more people whom Advance helped in one way or another began working at DCI, including Derrick "DD" Osborne, who was hired as a kind of draftsman-in-training in 2003 and has since become a full-time project engineer for the company. In addition to employing residents of the Cleaborn-Foote community through Advance, DCI has done this indirectly through Cornerstone Manufacturing, a limited liability company owned by Phillips, which has also hired qualified graduates of Advance's training programs. Moreover, DCI has established two types of scholarships in 2003 that Advance administers. One scholarship provides recipients an opportunity to enroll in one of the local vocational training schools, and the second enables them to go to college to earn an undergraduate degree. In addition to outsourcing from Advance and providing these two kinds of educational scholarships, DCI also occasionally requests project proposals from Advance and other organizations that the missions committee can consider supporting. In 2005 DCI presented Advance a certificate of support that reads, "Based on our mutual desire to see God glorified through the spreading of the Gospel of Christ and your organization's commitment to justice through service to the poor and oppressed in Memphis, we are pleased to offer to you DCI's prayerful and financial support."[8] We display here the words of the certificate merely to reflect the official nature of the partnership; it is not an informal arrangement but rather an integral part in the life of both DCI as a company and Advance Memphis as an urban nonprofit organization.

As we have argued throughout the book, true partnership benefits both parties. For Advance, DCI has become one of the primary places to which it outsources its training graduates. If program and financial support are the tangibles, then encouragement, prayer, and friendships between DCI employees, Advance staff, and Cleaborn-Foote residents are the intangible rewards of the partnership. For example, Nash speaks of Hubert McManus, controller at DCI, as his brother and partner in Christ. They get together regularly to pray and study the Bible. McManus and Phillips recently attended Advance's open house; and Nash and other Advance staff, along with a contingent from Cleaborn-Foote, recently attended DCI's missions banquet. Rendi Hopper, accounting manager at DCI, regularly gets together with Betty Massey from Cleaborn-Foote for mutual learning and friendship. And the list of interactions across the urban-suburban divide goes on between these two entities. These are merely samples of the intangible rewards of spiritual and moral encouragement that Advance Memphis reaps from the partnership. Nash sums it up: "DCI has been invaluable to us in so many ways."[9]

As for the benefits to DCI, the qualified graduates of Advance's programs whom DCI hires are not charity cases or liabilities but real contributors to DCI's multifaceted operation. To have a local source of trained personnel to join the employee roster is a significant benefit for the company. But beyond that, there is much joy shared among the employees, from the president on down, simply knowing that DCI plays an important role in providing real hope to people in the form of jobs. "Anytime we give our service to the world, the benefits exceed what we can give," says Phillips.[10] Furthermore, because of DCI's beyond-profit philosophy, a beyond-profit ethos of compassion and justice rooted in the gospel is cultivated among the employees. While not all DCI employees are Christians (nor are they required to be), Christ is lifted up in the workplace as DCI employees come to work not simply to earn a paycheck but also to participate in the eternal profits of loving God and loving our neighbor as ourselves.

The life of DD Osborne exemplifies the fruit of this partnership. The fifth of eight children, Osborne grew up in the Cleaborn-Foote neighborhood, raised by a single, working mother. Despite being surrounded by the negativity of drugs, violence, financial hardship, and hopelessness, Osborne managed to stay out of trouble. He always knew there was more to life than that, and upon meeting Bennett at STREETS Ministry when he was in the seventh grade, that *more to life* began to be defined in terms of faith in Jesus Christ. Osborne describes STREETS "as a place where us kids wanted to be. It was a positive environment; it was safe. People there let us play and be kids; they supported us, loved us, taught us. So when they told me about God, I listened."[11]

With the exception of a brief period during his junior year in high school, he stayed active with STREETS. Then upon graduating from high school (which was a feat in and of itself given the dropout rate among Cleaborn-Foote youth), Bennett encouraged Osborne to join the STREETS staff, which Osborne eventually did. During the six years that he served on staff, he had several duties that included running the recreational facility, driving kids to-and-fro in the ministry van, and facilitating the computer lab. In these roles, Osborne demonstrated love to the kids, as former staff did unto him years earlier. He says of the decision to work with STREETS, "I'm sure glad I did. I am where I am today because of my involvement with them."[12]

His STREETS connection led him to Advance Memphis, which led him to DCI where he is now a full-time project engineer. Advance made the call to DCI about hiring Osborne, and an interview was set up. Advance prepared him for the interview, and when the time came, Osborne made enough of an impression that DCI hired him in March 2003. "To be honest," says Osborne, "I didn't know what I was actually hired for when they first took me on."[13] He just started going to work and began learning from DCI engineers, slowly but surely developing into a draftsman. Then as the first recipient of the DCI college scholarship fund, Osborne went back to school while working full-time at DCI and eventually earned a bachelor's degree in liberal studies with concentrations in business and manufacturing engineering technology from the University of Memphis.

"Everybody loves DD here at DCI," says Phillips. "He is a success story from Cleaborn-Foote, but besides that, he is a great employee."[14] Osborne returns the compliment: "Some of the most encouraging words have come from Mr. Phillips: 'You're not the best engineer I have yet, but you're going to be.' I know I'm not competing with anyone for a position, but words like that make you want to continue to work hard and learn more."[15] He goes on to say, "I have bonded with my entire DCI family. That's what we are here at DCI."[16]

Osborne has become a friend, mentor, and model for others in the neighborhood. For example, Leon Cash, five years Osborne's junior, is an Advance Memphis graduate and is receiving the same opportunities at DCI that Osborne was given. Having grown up in the same neighborhood and now employed together at DCI, Osborne has been an invaluable friend and accountability partner to Cash.

Through their similar backgrounds, they are able to learn from and encourage each other both professionally and spiritually.

Besides serving on the board of Advance Memphis until recently, Osborne has also referred others to Advance's services. For example, he tells the story of Geoffrey Bailey, a young man from the neighborhood whom Osborne had met while at STREETS. He had lost touch with Bailey after leaving STREETS, and when they reconnected, Bailey was down-and-out. Osborne helped him get back on his feet and hooked him up with Advance, where Bailey eventually enrolled in the Jobs for Life program. Through Advance, Bailey revived the hope that his life could amount to more than what his circumstances dictated, not just because of the jobs training but more importantly because of Christ, whom he encountered while at Advance. He cleaned himself up, stopped taking drugs, and applied himself in the program. Upon graduation in 2006, Bailey got a full-time job at National Guard Products, where he continues to work. Bailey testifies, "Advance Memphis helped me find a full-time job with benefits. I really enjoyed the biblical teachings I received as I attended the class."[17]

Osborne was helped through STREETS, Advance Memphis, and DCI, and he has in turn helped others like Cash and Bailey through the same partnership. The hope of the gospel depends on such multiplication of kingdom fruit. It also depends on God's people working together, even across the urban-suburban divide, as Advance Memphis and DCI have demonstrated. Through this partnership, God has touched not only many residents of Cleaborn-Foote but also Nash, the staff at Advance Memphis, Tom and Beth Phillips, and many employees of DCI. If there is a common denominator between all involved through this partnership, it is the sense of God's manifold blessing upon all.

Business Partnerships in Chicago

What DCI and Advance Memphis have accomplished as a partnership in a short period of time is remarkable. Equally remarkable are several businesses that have partnered with Lawndale Community Church (LCC) in Chicago. Malnati's Pizzeria sits on the corner of Ogden and Cermak, a stone's throw from the church. Marc Malnati, son of Lou Malnati, a highly successful restaurateur of twenty-five family-owned Chicagoland pizzerias, established another one in Lawndale in 1995 in partnership with LCC. The only sit-down restaurant of its kind in North Lawndale, the establishment is an anomaly in the neighborhood and, from a business standpoint, not a wise investment. But Malnati's motivation was not simply to add to his list of profit-making restaurants; rather, it was to help rejuvenate the neighborhood by providing excellent food at affordable prices and, more importantly, to reinvest all the profits back into the community. As expected, Malnati's Pizzeria in Lawndale has not made a profit, but as *Chicago Sun Times* reporter Mark Konkol writes, "[This restaurant's] financial failure is a success story," referring to the fact that this particular Malnati's trains and employs residents of Hope House, LCC's home for recovering drug addicts and ex-offenders trying to reenter the working world.[18] Malnati's Pizzeria in Lawndale models a beyond-profit business that, in partnership with LCC, is giving back to the community.

Another beyond-profit business, J & E Duff Masonry, has also partnered with LCC in significant ways. Owned and run by father and son tandem Dick and Richard Lauber, J & E Duff has donated literally a million dollars worth of building material and labor in the service of LCC and other urban ministries. Most of the brickwork for LCC's facilities was done by J & E. It also donated a truck to help with the many transporting needs of LCC's housing ministry. With LCC's help, J & E Duff has employed many from the Lawndale neighborhood. The company has also been a regular supporter of the Christian Community Development Association.

Yet another beyond-profit business, Bigelow Homes, has partnered with LCC and many other urban agencies to help build affordable, entry-level homes. Owner Perry Bigelow, who was *Builder Magazine*'s "Builder of the Year" in 2005, designed an energy-efficient, affordable home—with the environment, the poor, and a sense of community in mind. From a financial standpoint, the design went against what would normally make a profit in the homebuilding industry, but that did not stop Bigelow from partnering with LCC on several fronts. First, Bigelow Homes went alongside the Community Development Corporation of LCC in its Harambee program, which was a seven-year project enabling nine families to build their own homes in Lawndale. Four of these families were single-parent households. It was an empowering program as these busy families worked tirelessly under Bigelow's direction to design and build simple, energy-efficient homes for themselves. Another project that brought together Bigelow Homes, LCC, and many other churches was Ezra Community Homes, a development project that built one hundred affordable homes in North Lawndale. Bigelow was the principle planner and builder of the project, which was part of the United Power for Action and Justice—an Industrial Areas Foundation group in Chicago.

Bigelow Homes, J & E Duff Masonry, and Malnati's Pizzeria in Chicago model businesses that are successful in ways far more valuable than economic gain as they have joined in partnership with the holistic ministries of an urban church.

Business Executives for Mission

One other type of business partnership deserves mention—namely, when business executives partner with each other for the sake of the city. Though different from the model of a business directly partnering with an urban agency, a collaboration of businesspeople who seek the welfare of the city is yet another way in which the corporate world has meaningfully intersected with the world of the urban poor.

Take, for example, the Foundation for Community Empowerment (FCE) in Dallas, Texas. Established in 1995, the FCE "marshals people, data, ideas, and resources to lift up South Dallas and make Dallas a whole city. In whole cities, people have equal economic opportunities, are equally self-sufficient, and participate equally in political and civic life—regardless of what neighborhood they live in or how much money they have."[19]

J. McDonald "Don" Williams, retired chairman and CEO of commercial real estate giant Trammel Crow Company, established FCE in order "to develop an asset-based, comprehensive renewal initiative in the low-income neighborhoods of Southern Dallas."[20] Compelled by his Christian faith, Williams not only had the vision to help the under-resourced in Dallas's poorest section—the South Dallas–Fair Park area—he also had the connections to fulfill that vision. *Dallas Observer News* reporter Robert Wilonsky describes Williams as "a powerful man with connections to powerful people who . . . woke up one day and realized he needed to direct some of that power toward the powerless in this city."[21]

FCE came into being precisely to manage that redistribution of power in the service of the poor, and even though it is not legally faith-based, FCE undoubtedly derives its vision, inspiration, and energy from God, in whom Williams has placed his uncompromising faith. As its website says, "Individually and collectively we work from a moral and ethical impulse to live out the call that is central to the world's great religions—to be of service to our neighbors who suffer material, emotional, and spiritual deprivation." This open spirit of goodwill has enabled FCE to collaborate with a wide range of partners. The website continues, "We welcome partnerships with faith-based organizations as well as secular ones, and we challenge all people of faith to take seriously their obligation to embrace and help the forgotten and the despised."[22]

From the outset, FCE has supported authentic community-based leaders and organizations in an empowerment mode. At the same time, it has been committed to comprehensive change that is based on well-researched data on the community, and it has focused on multilevel partnerships. "What we do is we bridge [people]. . . . I've got some degree of credibility in the business community and the philanthropic community and, in some levels, in the political community, and it takes all of those in appropriate partnerships with community leaders and organizations to effect real changes. . . . Our interest is in large-scale system change, and I have become convinced that it is through empowering the neighborhood. . . . You've got to have grassroots relationships, and you've got to have relationships with the power structures. Otherwise, things don't change."[23]

In this light, FCE has partnered with the Dallas Independent School District (ISD), the National Center for Educational Accountability, and Texas Instruments to form Dallas Achieves, an ambitious program whose goal is for "every Dallas ISD student to graduate and to be college- and career-ready."[24] This transformational effort is guided by the sixty-five-member Dallas Achieves Commission, cochaired by Williams (along with Pettis Norman, CEO of PNI Industries, and Arcilia Acosta, CEO of Carcon Industries & Construction) and composed of leaders from every segment of the Dallas community.[25] Despite a public education system historically torn by acrimony and divisiveness, often occurring along racial and ethnic lines, the racially and ethnically diverse commission unanimously adopted a slate of more than one hundred recommendations based on intensive research into the practices of the nation's most successful urban school districts. Those recommendations were adopted wholesale by the Dallas school district's board of trustees and are being energetically implemented by the district's administration with continued oversight by the Dallas Achieves Commission.

FCE also was instrumental in creating Frazier Revitalization Incorporated (FRI), a separate nonprofit organization dedicated to redeveloping the Frazier neighborhood of southern Dallas in accordance with a plan that embodies the vision of community residents. In Frazier, where the poverty rate and other measures of distress surpass those that existed in the Lower Ninth Ward of New Orleans before Hurricane Katrina, two-thirds of the residents have fled since the 1970s. Yet FCE, working in partnership with those who remain, has enlisted a host of collaborators in a revitalization effort that includes the City of Dallas, the Dallas Housing Authority, the Dallas Area Rapid Transit, corporations, banks, medical and cultural institutions, and developers.

These partnerships have formed between the rich and poor and between black, white, and brown, igniting transformation in the community. In the past, promises of change in the Frazier neighborhood came up empty, and the residents had little hope to go on and little trust in those who came with big plans. But the progress being made through Frazier Revitalization Inc. has people hoping again. Wilonsky reports:

> For the first time in decades, there is real progress in Frazier. The bulldozers are churning; the bricklayers are spreading mortar; the carpenters are hammering nails. And FRI is about to close on a deal that would turn a piece of land across the street from the Shearith Israel cemetery on Dolphin Road, where a small church now sits, into a 150-unit assisted-living center, the first of its kind in the neighborhood.[26]

"It amazes me how this has happened," says Nat Tate, director of FRI, echoing the sentiment throughout the Frazier neighborhood.[27] Indeed, amazing things happen when powerful businesspeople like Williams—ignited by faith in Christ—join forces with corporations, foundations, developers, researchers, and grassroots organizations.

Another partnership for a city involving business executives deserves our attention. In 1999 automobile dealer Don Palmer, former state legislator Steve Stoughton, and NBC affiliate anchorperson Tom Cochrun put their heads and hearts together to form the Faith Leadership Series (FLS) in Indianapolis. The Faith Leadership Series sought to foster relationships between interdenominational church leaders from both the city and the suburbs, with the hope that as they found common ground in Christ, they would begin working together for community transformation. With help from the Central Indiana Community Foundation, FLS brought these leaders together on a monthly basis for half a day in order to cultivate fellowship as well as to hear outside practitioners discuss issues such as poverty, public education, racism, and community organizing. Relationships formed and issues were tackled head-on.

In order for this greater sense of *koinonia* across the denominational and urban-suburban divides to go to the next level, Palmer eventually partnered with Marty Moore of the Moore Foundation and formed the Indianapolis Christian Community Foundation (ICCF), which eventually became what is now the Barnabas Fund. The Faith Leadership Series ran its course after six years, but the Barnabas Fund continues what was begun there.

Barnabas was founded in 2002 (as ICCF) in conjunction with the Central Indiana Community Foundation in order to give small grants to organizations working in the neighborhoods of Martindale-Brightwood, King Park, and Haughville—three of the poorest sections in Indianapolis. For the first several years the board of then-ICCF—consisting of individual businesspersons, retirees, and representatives of various local foundations—came together quarterly to listen to ten-minute presentations from organizations and make on-the-spot decisions. They also did occasional site visits.

But according to Chuck Wills, former chairperson of ICCF, the way in which they operated seemed in retrospect unintentionally top-down and nonrelational.[28] Something had to change or ICCF would be just another source of funding for organizations. So in 2004, amid leadership changes, ICCF became the Barnabas Fund. Named after Barnabas, which means "son of encouragement" (Acts 4:36), the leaders of the Barnabas Fund wanted to continue dispersing financial resources to worthy endeavors but only as a part of the larger work of the gospel. They desired, in line with the original vision of the Faith Leadership Series, to make as their primary goal the development of relational, mutually encouraging partnerships through which transformational ministries would flow.

With Wills as former chairperson and Peggy Monson as current chairperson, Barnabas has restructured itself to meet quarterly as before, but now every other meeting consists of a site visit. Instead of meeting in an isolated conference room four times a year, they bus or carpool together to a site for two of those meetings, not necessarily to check up on a project, but rather to get to know the staff of an organization or to meet people whom the organization serves. This seemingly minor adjustment among Barnabas's board members has enlivened their meetings, brought new meaning to the work, and formed friendships across the urban-suburban divide. Now they speak from the heart about partner organizations, such as Rebuilding the Wall, a housing rehabilitation ministry run by Chris and Mary Provence that comes alongside the residents of inner-city Indianapolis to restore the neighborhood and fight against unjust gentrification. They also speak from the heart about the Shepherd Community Center, a poverty-fighting ministry in the near-eastside of Indianapolis that works primarily with children and families.[29]

Wills also shows heartfelt appreciation for the fruit of Barnabas's involvement with a group called Outreach Incorporated, a nonprofit organization that seeks to help homeless youth get off the streets and become productive members of society. Because of a long-standing relationship and engagement with Outreach and staff, Barnabas desired to promote ongoing sustainability within this organization and recognized that the best way to achieve this was to minister to its founder, Eric Howard, who was experiencing compassion fatigue after ten years of relentless, demanding ministry. Given Barnabas's renewed vision of relationship-based partnerships and in light of a study conducted by urban ministry consultant Amy Sherman, the Barnabas board members agreed that some kind of sabbatical plan would serve both Howard and the organization as a whole. As Barnabas learned more about the value of sabbaticals for ministry leaders, a Barnabas board member joined a few other key people from Outreach, the Mary E. Ober Foundation and Dei Ministries, in creating a sabbatical plan, which included putting an interim director in place while Howard was away. It also included a component of organizational renewal through leadership training by J. D. Levy and Associates, a reputable organizational consultancy firm. Funded by Barnabas, the plan was implemented in June 2007. Howard met with Danny Wright, a spiritual director; John Samples served as Outreach's interim director; and board members, caseworkers, and all of its other staff members received regular, professional leadership training for a period of three months. At the end of the sabbatical, Howard returned to his post personally rejuvenated and met by a staff eager to resume ministry as a team with Howard at the helm. Outreach was empowered all the way around, from the board to the director to its personnel on the ground, resulting in more effective ministry to the people Outreach services: the homeless and at-risk youth in Indianapolis.

One recent indicator of its effectiveness is that the Barnabas Fund has drawn the attention of the Lily Foundation, which gave a substantial grant for Outreach's ministry. As a result, the ministry now also works closely with Indianapolis public high schools. GOAL (Graduation, Occupation, Address, and Lifestyle) is a program of Outreach that coordinates with educational institutions such as Manual and Broad Ripple high schools to enable students in difficult situations to earn their diplomas. One graduate, Aaron Loften, who entered college in the summer of 2007, said at his graduation, "Outreach . . . helped me get my head together. Without them, I guarantee you I wouldn't be starting college next Monday."[30] Outreach's increased ministry effectiveness and resources are directly linked to the sabbatical plan made possible by its ministry partners of the Barnabas Fund.

Whether it is individual businesses like DCI partnering with agencies like Advance Memphis, or a group of businesspersons who come together for the sake of the city, these amazing models from the corporate world testify to the possibilities of community transformation when Christian businesspeople think beyond profit and commit to the vision of the kingdom of God, where no divides exist between the rich and the poor or between black, white, and brown.

| Reflection Questions

1. What can other companies learn from the practices of DCI in order to position themselves to partner with urban ministries?

2. What can business executives learn from the examples of the people involved with FCE in Dallas and the Barnabas Fund in Indianapolis in order to get involved in community transformation?

3. Discuss how these businesses bear witness to Christ in the corporate world by virtue of their community involvement.

12

Hall of Faith

Ordinary Saints in Partnership

It would be remiss to overlook the simple, uncomplicated type of partnership that involves faithful suburban individuals. Urban-suburban partnership certainly has a corporate side, as we have seen in the previous three chapters, but a partnership involving individuals who have dared to cross the racial, cultural, and socioeconomic divides (the urban-suburban divide) ultimately reveals its profoundly personal nature. Why and how suburban individuals engage in partnership with their urban sisters and brothers, and vice versa, demonstrates that a commitment to come together across a great chasm for the sake of the kingdom is finally a matter of the heart. We hope that concluding the section on proven urban-suburban efforts with the *hall of faith* model will serve as a reminder of this essential truth.

Many who have been captivated by the kingdom dream end up relocating to the city and thus become, for all intents and purposes, urban dwellers. As a transformational strategy, relocation seems ideal. Many, however, have been no less captivated by that same dream but have not necessarily felt the call to move into poor neighborhoods. As Barbara Elliott, director of the Houston-based Center for Renewal, explains, "Some street saints stay in the [suburban] neighborhoods they have come from and are effective because they know the people, the problems, and the dynamics there. Others have relocated from the suburbs into the inner city, taking their families with them, in order to be close to those they serve."[1] Albert Hsu addresses those who stay in the suburbs even as they have been changed by the kingdom vision: "We may be suburbanites, but we are also citizens of a larger, global, urban population. And as such, we must seek the welfare of the whole world."[2] This chapter focuses on those who have understood this truth—suburban people living out the kingdom dream via urban partnerships.

Ordinary Saints at CityLights

Elliott calls those so moved by the plight of the urban poor "street saints." She describes them as people who are:

> willing to go where there is pain and suffering and be a presence of healing and love. Street saints are walking into drug-infested neighborhoods to broker truces between gang members. They are scooping up heroin and crack addicts from our cities' streets and loving them back into wholeness. They are giving a hand to families in transition from welfare into work and productivity. They are coming into schools to put their arms around and mentor at-risk children.[3]

Meet street saints Pat Leidy, Ted Behr, and Frank Rottier—residents of suburban communities located twelve to twenty miles west of Philadelphia. These individuals have at least two things in common: First, they are all longtime members of Wayne Presbyterian Church (WPC) in Wayne, Pennsylvania. Second, they have partnered significantly on an individual basis with various urban agencies through the ministry of CityLights. As discussed in chapter 8, CityLights is a network of urban and suburban agencies and individuals founded by Carey Davis that seeks the welfare of the community of Southwest Philadelphia.[4] Through CityLights, these individuals have volunteered their time, effort, expertise, and friendship with a variety of urban organizations.

Frank Rottier has served as chairperson of the CityLights steering committee within WPC (a group that coordinates the church's involvement with CityLights) for the last five years, but for the past eighteen months he has focused primarily on the Philadelphia Training

Program—a nonprofit organization founded and directed by John McCullough that provides comprehensive skills training in construction for at-risk youth as they repair the homes of elderly people in the community. A retired business manager for Honeywell, Rottier volunteers at the training program twice a month, spending time and establishing rapport with the young people. In addition, he and fellow WPC member Peter Grim have recently worked with McCullough to develop program guidelines for the organization.

Pat Leidy, a stay-at-home mother and part-time librarian, has partnered primarily with Cornerstone Christian Academy, a kindergarten through eighth-grade school in the heart of the southwest neighborhood that was founded in 1988 by attorney James Sweet and sociologist-evangelist Tony Campolo. Leidy has served as a liaison for Cornerstone (and other organizations in the CityLights network), recruiting and coordinating volunteers from surrounding suburbs to help in the classroom as well as in the maintenance of the facility. For the last twelve years on a weekly basis, Leidy has driven into the heart of Southwest Philadelphia to Cornerstone as faithfully as if she were on the payroll. She calls, emails, and meets with volunteers and works strategically with Cornerstone staff to assign volunteers to appropriate tasks as the school has need. Besides serving as CityLights liaison, Leidy herself volunteers at Cornerstone, offering her help and friendship to teachers and staff.

Ted Behr is a retired marketing executive in the international pharmaceutical industry and a business instructor at Eastern University. His partnerships have formed on various fronts spanning fourteen years. For example, he has participated in financial investment training through Cornerstone Common Cents Investment Club, a program of CityLights that fosters urban and suburban people investing together for a more secure financial future; he has served as secretary-treasurer for the African-American Brotherhood, a Christian group that grew out of the Million Man March 1995 in order to affirm African-American culture and to recognize achievements in the black community; and he has helped in the intake of people using the services of the Southwest Community Development Corporation. One invaluable feat through a partnership, which Behr talks about with excitement, is the resurrection of the *Southwest Globe Times*.[5] Due to the increasing incapacity of owner Joseph Bartash, who had faithfully overseen the operations of the paper for fifty-eight years, the *Southwest Globe Times* ceased publication in 2003. The Southwest Philadelphia community felt the loss profoundly. Sensing the loss himself, Behr encouraged the Southwest Community Development Corporation and Wayne Presbyterian Church (through CityLights) to consider reviving the paper. The urban-suburban tandem took him up on it and partnered together to provide the financial resources and personnel to accomplish the task. Because of this partnership, with Behr's relentless enthusiasm as the driver, the *Southwest Globe Times* lives again as of July 15, 2005, as a source of community news, information, concerns, and upcoming events as well as carrying advertisements of neighborhood businesses to a circulation of ten thousand.

Why do these ordinary, suburban street saints engage in these partnerships that are not just occasional experiences to make them feel good about themselves but enduring commitments and lifestyles? These three CityLights volunteers speak both personally and collectively when they each in their own way affirm faith in Christ as the chief motivating factor, particularly as that faith compels them to love and serve others. Behr looks to the Great Commission in Matthew 28 as the jumping-off point to engage in mission, understanding "the world" of verse 20 as the Southwest Philadelphia community. He explains, "It is hard to conceive of a field more ripe unto harvest."[6] If Matthew 28 calls us to mission, then the parable of the sheep and the goats in Matthew 25:31–46 calls us to care sincerely and holistically for those who are disadvantaged and under-resourced. Behr understands this parable as primarily promoting and encouraging the positive works that groups and individuals are already doing in the community, rather than coming in from the suburbs as "knights in shining armor," bringing alien solutions to all of their problems. Behr asserts that supporting what is already going on in and through existing community organizations (partnering) is what suburbanites are called to do.[7] Rottier immediately confirms: "I totally agree with Ted. I don't have the Scriptures memorized, but he's right on. My eyes were opened through a study at church led by Carey [Davis] called 'Understanding Poverty,' where I learned the biblical view of the poor and our responsibility toward them. And what Ted is saying sounds exactly right."[8]

Leidy also claims her practical understanding of the faith as a motivating factor, recalling one particular National Day of Prayer. In observance of the day, Cornerstone teachers and students performed a ritual that demonstrated the power of God and the bond of Christian community. In the school yard was a wooden cross on which students and teachers pinned their prayer requests, until eventually the cross was covered. The sight of it—the cross bearing the weight of the world—evoked in Leidy and all present a profound sense of gratitude toward God and each other as singing and hugging broke out and tears were shed among the teachers and students. Leidy says that since that event she does what she does at Cornerstone and CityLights "because it lets me see God in action."[9] So faith in Christ, whether their own or their urban partners', motivates these individuals to engage the city on a long-term basis.

Second only to their faith, they point to the cross-cultural relationships that have formed as a powerful motivator. Leidy has developed many friendships with Cornerstone staff, but she beams when she talks about Deborah Lee, a teacher who became principal at Cornerstone. "Deborah and I hit it off immediately. I happened to be there when she needed help setting up for her third-grade poetry class way back when, and the relationship took off from there. I consider her my sister now."[10] Lee reciprocates: "I'm not sure how it happened. Pat and I established this magnetic bond to each other from the time we met. There's no other way to describe our relationship except that we're sisters."[11] The camaraderie that Leidy experiences from week to week with Lee and the rest of the Cornerstone staff and teachers is solidified a little more with an annual dinner at the Leidy residence in Wayne—a tradition that began in 2001.

Rottier speaks of his relationship with McCullough at the Philadelphia Training Program in similarly fond ways: "John and I have so many things in common, even though we grew up in completely different environments. He was suspicious of me at first—another white guy who wanted to help out. But we got to know each other at a CityLights retreat, and from then on we have worked together well and have grown in our friendship."[12]

Behr reflects upon his many personal relationships in the area, but he speaks for all three when he says, "It has been a privilege for me to come into contact with and to get to know so many fantastic saints in Southwest Philadelphia. I'm humbled by their commitment and sacrifice, and it has been tremendously uplifting for me when they call me 'friend.'"[13] They all acknowledge the challenge of the cross-cultural relationship as well, but their stick-to-itiveness has yielded immeasurable relational results. When asked about the personal fruit of the partnerships, it is these relationships, which cross the urban-suburban divide, that each of them reports with deep satisfaction.

Deeper discipleship also constitutes part of the personal fruit of these partnerships. Says Leidy: "I've learned so much about my own faith and beliefs—I've learned how to share it. I've always cared about people, but through my involvement with CityLights I've learned the reasons behind that care and the ways in which I can demonstrate it."[14] Behr cites John 15:13, where Jesus says, "No one has greater love than this, to lay down one's life for one's friends." But Behr confesses, "While I fall short of this obligation, I keep it before me as a goal."[15] Rottier celebrates the broadened perspective of life and faith as he has learned about the culture of poverty and God's heart for the poor through his involvement with CityLights. He has also deepened his conviction of the value of family as one of the keys to transformation. He says that seeing the struggles of people in the city as well as the suburbs has "reinforced and expanded my understanding of how critically important a stable, loving, God-fearing family is to a child, to the community, and to the nation."[16]

Yet another manifestation of personal fruit is the way in which such a commitment has produced social awareness in their own children. Leidy celebrates the fact that her now-grown children demonstrate Christian love and service in the world. In fact, one of her daughters works for a nonprofit organization in Washington, DC, that seeks to raise the standard of education among middle schoolers. Witnessing their mother form meaningful relationships with people in Southwest Philadelphia through the years and realizing her long-term commitment to the good of that community undoubtedly helped shape her children's view of God, mission, and the world.

These suburban street saints, however, have not gotten involved in urban partnerships primarily to better themselves and their families—although the personal by-products have proven invaluable. Beyond the personal fruit, community transformation has occurred and continues to occur through their faithful collaborative work. Cornerstone, for example, depends heavily on its volunteer corps that Leidy and others coordinate. Chris Petersen, director of development at Cornerstone, says, "Since we can't hire a full staff for certain positions that are normally part of a school, we call in volunteers to support in these areas." Petersen goes on to say that although working with volunteers has its challenges—dealing at times with untrained and inexperienced personnel and having to do the tedious work of establishing necessary guidelines for quality control—Cornerstone simply cannot serve the families of Southwest Philadelphia as effectively without them.[17] Principal Lee concurs: "Our volunteers come regularly like they're on the payroll! They're incredible, indispensable." She also adds that many parents affirm the volunteers, appreciating their love toward their children and their faithfulness to the school. Furthermore, Lee adds that all involved—from the parents to the children to the volunteers—get the opportunity to close the racial gap that exists between predominantly black Southwest Philadelphia and white suburbia.[18]

The Philadelphia Training Program has also benefited greatly from the volunteer help from Wayne Presbyterian Church, which includes the assistance of Rottier and Grim in both sharpening the training program's mission statement and establishing guidelines for its operations. McCullough says, "The guidelines have made it so much easier to make decisions about who is eligible to help and how to implement that help." Establishing guidelines is but one example of how WPC has helped the training program over a span of ten years. "They've supported us financially," says McCullough. "They've provided spiritual strength, and they've encouraged the staff and students all the way around." He is also very aware of the bridge building between city and suburban folks that occurs through the relationship. "Our students get to see the world beyond their own communities, just like the folks at Wayne get to see our world." He continues, "Twice a year we go out to Wayne and spend all day with the folks there. We eat together, talk, play, pray, and more. We always leave refreshed and encouraged, and I think they feel the same way."[19]

Behr's tireless work as editor of the *Southwest Globe Times* has done much to keep the people of the community connected and informed. Donna Henry, executive director of Southwest Community Development Corporation, has this to say about the vital role that the paper plays: "We would be out and about in the community hearing about what was going on, and the only way to share anything was to announce it at some meeting. Now, the *Globe Times* allows us and others to share important news and information with the entire community." The paper is also a source of encouragement, according to Henry: "There is enough bad news about Southwest Philadelphia in the larger media. I am asked regularly how I can go to work in a neighborhood that has so much crime and other social ills. The *Globe Times* is a way to remind people that 75,000 people live in Southwest and that there are many more good people than bad."[20]

Probably the most important thing that these three ordinary street saints from suburbia have demonstrated and the partnerships between CityLights and various urban organizations in Southwest Philadelphia have shown, is this: in a partnership that befits the kingdom, both urban and suburban parties benefit greatly, both personal and social transformation occurs, and God is glorified.

Other Members of the Hall of Faith

Leidy, Rottier, and Behr are but three of countless faithful individuals who live in the suburbs but who have partnered significantly with urban churches and organizations. At this point it would not be far-fetched in the least to invoke Hebrews 11:32, "And what more should I say? For time would fail me to tell of . . . ," because the number of individuals who have been captivated by the kingdom urban vision exceeds what we can include in this book. We thank God for that, and we pray that the number will only increase. Nevertheless, we want to provide a few more examples to inspire us all.

Phyllis VanderArk, wife of neurosurgeon Gary VanderArk, admonished her husband recently, "You can only be on fourteen boards." This good-natured reprimand attests to the breadth of humanitarian service in which her doctor-husband has gotten involved. From his suburban home in Denver, Colorado, he says, "We have spent the last forty years trying to bridge the gap between our comfortable suburban existence and our Christian responsibility to care for the poor."[21] This tension has inspired VanderArk to go beyond his profession (at which he has excelled) and to partner with many different urban organizations, including the John Perkins Foundation for Reconciliation and Development in Jackson, Mississippi. The partnership began in the early 1970s while VanderArk was serving as president of the Luke Society.

VanderArk tells the story this way: "During a board meeting in Cary, Mississippi, where the Luke Society had a clinic, John Perkins walked in and said, 'Wow, this is beautiful!' referring to the renovated facility. 'My name is John Perkins, and I need one of these in Mendenhall. Can you help us? We need a doctor too.'"[22] VanderArk says that this encounter was the beginning of an enduring partnership of financial support, prayer, ministry guidance, and mutual encouragement that has endured for over thirty years. When asked recently by

Blacktie-Colorado staff reporter Nancy Koontz, "Who is your hero?" VanderArk replied, "John Perkins of Jackson, Mississippi. . . . He's my best friend, my hero, and also one of my mentors."[23] In 1981, when Perkins went to Los Angeles to begin a work there, VanderArk served as chairman of the board of the John Perkins Foundation in Jackson. He continues to this day as an active member of the board (one of the fourteen!).

Within the medical profession, VanderArk has established different types of partnerships or networks that seek to help the medically underserved. For example, he catalyzed Doctor's Care, a program that has successfully recruited hundreds of physicians to serve "well over 1500 people per year and more than $30 million in free medical care services" in the last twenty years. He has also spearheaded the Colorado Coalition for the Medically Underserved, a movement that has put into motion a ten-year plan to ensure that eventually "all Coloradoans [will] have access to affordable, quality medical care."[24]

Another way VanderArk bridged the gap between suburbia and the underprivileged in the mid-1970s was partnering with Evangelical Concern (now called Volunteers in Action) to get suburban churches to sponsor refugee families from Southeast Asian countries and help these families resettle in the Denver area.[25] Out of these efforts, the Khmer Christian Reformed Church in nearby Aurora emerged in 1982. VanderArk has partnered with Pastor John Kim ever since to help in the growth and development of this local congregation. VanderArk models a well-to-do suburbanite who has gone the second and third mile for the advancement of the kingdom in the city.

Hall of faith inductees also include Sabra and Bill Reichardt of Syracuse, New York. Sabra, a retired educator, and Bill, owner of a dry-cleaning plant in Chicago, have partnered significantly with a number of organizations affiliated with the Christian Community Development Association (CCDA) as well as CCDA itself. The Reichardts have faithfully and generously supported CCDA and have participated every year in its annual conferences. As networkers, advisors, strategic thinkers, and financial supporters, they have been invaluable to the vision of CCDA and the many churches and organizations affiliated with it. For example, the Reichardts got involved with Hope House, a residential ministry of Lawndale Community Church in Chicago that strives to help men reenter society after prison. Hope House has a chapel called "The Dougout," which the Reichardts endowed in memory of their son Douglas. But their involvement with Hope House was not just financial; they also became involved in hands-on ministry alongside the staff and residents.

Beyond CCDA and its affiliates, the Reichardts, along with Marty and Sue Moore, also set up the Servant Leader Scholarship Award in 1998. The award annually recognizes over a hundred students at forty-seven colleges and universities across the nation. Then in 2001 Bill and Sabra established the Young Servant Leaders Award Program in Syracuse, which has enabled many students whose odds are against them to enter in or continue with their college education. For example, in 2007, seven students from Syracuse received this award—students who had overcome great challenges in order to pursue higher education. *Post-Standard* reporter Maureen Sieh covered the event at Ryder Park in Syracuse that honored the students. "There was a lot of positive energy at the park," she wrote, "as the students' advocates and mentors talked about the challenges they faced and how far they've come." As to why these students were chosen as recipients, Sieh wrote that Bill Reichardt, who was in attendance, "wanted to recognize young people who had overcome considerable odds and are giving back to their community." Reichardt said, "When you meet these young people overcoming odds, it gives you hope for what might become."[26]

There is also Howard Ahmanson Jr., who inherited millions of dollars from his father's fortune with Home Savings Bank. A second-generation multimillionaire, Ahmanson could ignore the less fortunate as he sits on top of the world in his home in Corona Del Mar, an affluent suburban community in Orange County, California. But instead, in 1979 he established Fieldstead and Company, Inc., "a private philanthropy working in national and international relief and development, education, the arts, family and children's concerns and religious freedom issues worldwide."[27] Through Fieldstead, Ahmanson's wealth has backed many organizations throughout the world.

The wide theological and political range of many of these organizations prevents easy categorization. Fieldstead has backed ministries ranging from the Oxford Centre for Mission Studies in the United Kingdom, which trains reflective holistic practitioners in the Two-Thirds World, to the Claremont Institute in Southern California, which seeks to restore the principles of America's founding according to the American conservative tradition. Supporters of these organizations usually find themselves on opposite sides of the theological and political fence. But Ahmanson reasons, "We're supposed to be compassionate and just; we just have to be smart about it. Rather than just give the poor money, like the welfare state, we need to empower them."[28] Translation: Fieldstead partners with any organization that cares for the poor in empowering ways.

It is the biblical call to compassion and justice that ultimately drives Fieldstead, not a political agenda. "We do this because we're supposed to [as Christians]," Ahmanson declares. "There's more to life than Newport Beach!" —referring to the lifestyle of the rich and famous that Newport Beach, California, represents.[29] The list of enduring partners of Fieldstead includes the John Perkins Foundation for Reconciliation and Development and the Christian Community Development Association. Ahmanson serves on the board of the former and as an advisor to the latter.

Beyond financial contributions and various board involvements, Ahmanson speaks of friendships that have developed through the years. He refers affectionately to John Perkins, not only as a partner in ministry (especially when Perkins was working in Pasadena) but also as a trusted friend. He speaks the same way about Vinay Samuel, the tireless pastor-activist from India who cofounded the Oxford Centre in the United Kingdom. (In 2007 Ahmanson and his wife, Roberta, flew to London to spend Christmas with Samuel and his wife, Colleen.) Ahmanson models an individual with considerable means who has managed his wealth in the service of the kingdom and who has not let his wealth get in the way of authentic relationships that cross the racial and socioeconomic divides.

But lest we think the urban-suburban *hall of faith* only includes people with extraordinary means, we conclude this chapter with an ordinary street saint in Oakland, California, named Barbara Franzen. Not that Franzen is without means; years of hard work and wise financial management have enabled her and her husband, Jeff, to live in a beautiful home overlooking the San Francisco Bay in the Oakland Hills, an affluent section of the city. But her ministry in the San Antonio district—one of East Oakland's most diverse and poorest neighborhoods—is not based on her financial support so much as on her enduring personal commitment to the youth and their families in this area. Driven by a desire to obey God and serve others in his name, Franzen has been ministering to the youth in a multitude of ways since 1987.[30]

Partnering with longtime friends Bill and Cathy Squires, Franzen began working with the youth who were being served by Harbor House, a community center in the San Antonio district that provides real hope to young people and their families via evangelistic, educational, and compassion and justice ministries. Franzen's work with the youth was holistic from the beginning as she shared the gospel by both word and deed. Many of the youth came to Christ as well as participated in a small jobs program that Franzen organized, encouraging her neighbors in Oakland Hills to hire them for odd jobs. One young person, Alan Mack, was hired as a facility manager by her husband, Jeff, who is part owner and managing general partner of 19th Avenue Storage in San Francisco.

As the ministry progressed and the youth turned into young adults, the need to provide a place of regular spiritual and social nourishment became increasingly acute. Many of them began making poor choices—developing drug and alcohol habits, and getting into trouble with the law—and many of the girls were getting pregnant. This disheartened Franzen and the others who worked faithfully with them. Franzen tried to connect many of the youth to First Covenant Church of Oakland, where she attended, and the Squires tried to do the same at nearby Berkeley Covenant Church. But the differences in culture and ethos between the residents of San Antonio and these suburban churches were so wide that their efforts proved in vain. This dilemma spurred Franzen, the Squires, and others to consider starting a church in the heart of San Antonio. Franzen recalls a vision she received while deep in prayer—she saw a tree that was firmly planted with branches reaching out far beyond itself. Then she heard the words, "I will bring back the lost." As she pondered the vision, Franzen developed a strong sense from God that a church needed to be planted for the sake of those in whom she and many others had invested their love and time. As she shared this vision with her colaborers in San Antonio, it became the impetus for the 1996 birth of what is now New Hope Covenant Church.

New Hope, however, could not be just another church on the block. In order to meet the needs of this neighborhood, this church had to be structured differently; it had to foster an authentic sense of Christ-centered community through deep, radical discipleship. Many people who shared the vision began to move into the neighborhood, including

Josh Horner, who served as New Hope's first overseer (before it was New Hope), and Dan Schmitz, who eventually took on the role of lead pastor. The infant fellowship structured itself after the cell-based model—emphasizing the fundamental importance of relationship building via small groups. Currently, Franzen mentors young leaders and helps in leading one of the cell groups that make up the church. New Hope members meet together in small groups, and until recently, only met together as a whole once a month. In these relationally based small groups, residents of the neighborhood, the relocaters, and those like Franzen who drive in from surrounding suburbs come together to worship God, grow together in discipleship, and participate in the transformation of the neighborhood.

And the neighborhood has indeed experienced tangible change. For example, in the late 1990s several members of New Hope got involved with the tenants of Oak Park Apartments, a dangerously run-down apartment complex less than a block from the church.[31] As the absentee landlord continued collecting rent while ignoring the tenants' pleas for help, Schmitz, Russell Jueng—a sociologist at San Francisco State University and a member of New Hope—and several others from the church who were also Oak Park tenants at the time filed a class action suit against the slumlord. Due in large part to their advocacy, the tenants won a million-dollar lawsuit in 2000. The East Bay Asian Local Development Corporation and the Affordable Housing Association have been working together ever since to dramatically improve living conditions for the Oak Park tenants.

Another example, though less dramatic but just as effective in bringing about gradual transformation, is the establishment of Little Sprouts Preschool in 2004. Under the direction of Cathy Squires, Barb Franzen, Shirley Wong, and Candace Martinez, Little Sprouts has not only been preparing the children of the neighborhood to succeed in school, it has also been ministering to them and their families in prayer, counseling, and many other ways that go well beyond the normal responsibilities of a preschool. Furthermore, many staff of Little Sprouts, past and present, including current director Thea Sit, were among those to whom Franzen and others ministered years before.

In summary, New Hope Covenant Church is a growing, holistic, cell-based church in the heart of inner-city Oakland that serves the people of San Antonio and beyond. And Franzen has been a significant part of its birth and development, which sprang from an enduring love for a group of inner-city youth. At the thirty-fifth anniversary celebration of Harbor House, Franzen was honored for her tireless work. The certificate awarded to her reads in part, "Thank you for decades of service to our ministry and our neighborhood. Thank you for helping us open doors to God's love to so many people. Your contribution has made a difference."

Why does an ordinary suburban saint get involved so deeply and vulnerably in the hard streets of east Oakland? "I used to be an entertainer in Chicago, engaging in all sorts of wild and crazy things," she responded. "If there was anything that God has been able to use from that lifestyle, it was that I've been less afraid to try the uncomfortable and even the dangerous."[32] She acknowledges gratefully that she could not have become the "urban missionary" that she is without the financial and moral support of her husband, Jeff. This speaks to the indispensable role of supporters who enable ordinary saints like Barb Franzen to commit to the work of urban transformation. She credits her adult missionary son Bret for leading her to Christ twenty-three years ago, and she has never really looked back, growing closer to God and interceding for those most vulnerable in society. "There's no use in doing any of this [referring to her faithful work in the inner city] if we're not getting closer to God ourselves. It is impossible to survive one hard story after another if we do not maintain our own intimacy with God."[33]

This chapter could not end on a better note, for partnerships that cross the difficult divides between races and socioeconomic classes are finally a matter of the heart—a heart touched by the God who longs to have a relationship with us and who calls us to radical mission together.

Reflection Questions

1. In light of the examples of street saints featured in this chapter, what motivates individual suburban Christians to engage in urban ministry?

2. Discuss both the challenges and the rewards of getting involved in partnership with urban ministries.

3. What benefits have come to whole communities as a result of urban-suburban partnership?

4. What would it take for you to consider partnering with an urban ministry?

Part 5

Almost Ready to Do It

Looking Ahead

If you have gotten this far, then the chances are good that you not only believe in the idea of urban-suburban partnership, but you also actually believe it can be done. Indeed it can! But we dare not charge ahead hastily and naïvely. We must be prepared as much as possible to get our heads, hearts, and hands ready for the adventure. Part 5 looks ahead to the actual implementation of this kind of partnership and suggests a way forward.

Part of effective preparation for just about any endeavor has to include rolling up your sleeves and just doing it. One does not learn, for example, how to drive a car by reading or even mastering the driver's manual. He or she must at some point get behind the wheel in order to learn both the written and unwritten rules of the road and to deal with both the exhilaration and the challenges of real traffic.

This *just do it* principle most definitely applies to partnering across the urban-suburban divide. At some point we have to put the manual down, get behind the wheel, and take the vehicle of urban-suburban partnership around the block. Pastor Bill Borror of Media

Presbyterian Church in suburban Philadelphia says, "The best way to disciple people in the way of Jesus Christ is to have them involved in hands-on ministry."[1] If we want to know how to do urban-suburban partnership, we finally just have to do it. Part 5 outlines the essential first steps to *just do it* well.

13

First Steps (or Just Do It!)

Based on the many experiences of urban ministry practitioners, eight basic steps emerge that we believe will give an urban-suburban partnership its best chance of succeeding.

1. Pray Like Nehemiah

Pray—but not just ordinary, ho-hum prayers to add to your morning devotions. Pray like Nehemiah, the cupbearer to the great King Artaxerxes in the Old Testament. Upon hearing the report regarding the ghetto that Jerusalem had become, this well-to-do, powerful man of God "sat down and wept, and mourned for days, fasting and praying before the God of heaven" (Neh. 1:4). He prayed for God's forgiveness, lamenting the grave sins of the people. "For the first time in his life," Christian development specialist Bob Lupton writes, Nehemiah "had cried out to Yahweh from the depths of his being, pleading for mercy, for hope, for restoration."[1] By praying this way, Nehemiah opened himself up to share in the divine burden, to take on God's heart for the devastated poor, and to participate in what God wanted to do about the fallen city.

In Christ, however, this burden transforms into inspiration, motivation, and a sense of opportunity to bring about God's kingdom in the world. Eventually, continues Lupton, Nehemiah's prayers "flowed spontaneously from a growing sense of excitement about the mission; [they became] requests more for divine wisdom than for relief from the stress."[2] Indeed the antidote to grief over the world's overwhelming poverty and injustice is to open oneself to participate in God's plan of transformation.

In doing so, it will not take long to realize that God's transforming work requires collaboration between members of the body of Christ—it will take partnership. Indeed, urban-suburban partnership begins with Nehemiah-like prayer or what Richard Foster calls "radical prayer," which he describes as communication with God that "refuses to let us stay on the fringes of life's great issues. It dares to believe that things can be different. Its aim is the total transformation of persons, institutions, and societies."[3] Radical, Nehemiah-like prayer produces a divine burden, which transforms into an opportunity to participate in God's mission, which leads to the great need to partner together for the sake of that mission.

2. Share the Vision

As the vision of God's compassion, justice, peace, and reconciliation captivates your heart, share it with others in your church, small group, organization, or company. It is essential to share it with others in your circle of influence so that it eventually becomes a corporate vision.

Robert White, a lay leader at First Baptist Church in Flushing, New York, read Craig L. Blomberg's *Neither Poverty nor Riches*, and it opened his eyes to the plight of the poor around the world.[4] Unable to keep such a life-changing perspective to himself, he started a small group, gathering people from the church to pray, study the Scriptures, and read *Neither Poverty nor Riches* carefully together. This began a renewal process in the group—its members increasingly wanting to see the church get more involved in compassion and justice ministries in the community and beyond. With the inspired group behind him, White approached their pastor, Rev. Gary Domiano, to discuss tangible ways in which the church could reach out holistically in the community. With the pastor's blessing, White contacted Evangelicals for Social Action (ESA), an organization with which the group became familiar during their study. He proceeded to plan a holistic ministry training day for the church with ESA's Word & Deed Network.

Beginning with Sunday morning worship and then continuing into the afternoon with a follow-up workshop, Word & Deed led the congregation in understanding the integration of evangelism with compassion and justice ministries and its importance to the church's community outreach.

If the turnout indicated how well White and others had shared the vision with the rest of the church, then they succeeded, because over eighty people participated in the afternoon workshop. White did not and could not keep the vision to himself; he shared it, and consequently the kingdom vision has become an aspiration for the larger church body. At the time of this writing, an in-house follow-up to the holistic ministry seminar has been planned, consisting of monthly workshops using the Word & Deed Holistic Ministry Starter Kit training materials.

If radical, Nehemiah-like prayer makes way for urban-suburban partnership, then sharing the kingdom vision with others and gathering those of like mind within your own institution virtually forces the issue of partnership; for how can a church or mission agency or company take on by itself the monsters of poverty, drugs, violence, and hopelessness that exist in the inner city? The desire to participate in God's mission together with brothers and sisters beyond the confines of one's own walls will lead to the necessity of ministry partnership.

3. Make Meaningful Contact with a Potential Partner

It is now time to make that telephone call, send that email, set up that appointment. Inspired by prayer and backed up by those of like mind, it is time to make meaningful contact with a potential partner. By *meaningful* we simply mean that the contact should be purposeful, intentional, and guided by the desire to explore the possibilities of working together for the kingdom. Where is God calling your group, and who is working there? Or go the other way: Who do you know who works among the poor, and where do they serve? Either order of inquiry should lead to a number of possible partnership candidates.

If you will recall, the first *Do* in the "Dos and Don'ts for Both Urban and Suburban Groups" (chapter 5) encouraged those wishing to enter into partnership to begin with an agency with which they already have some kind of connection. This eliminates the need for introductions, and it enables people to proceed with the idea of partnership almost immediately. Who do you know? Based on what you know of this person or the organization of which he or she is a part, do you sense compatibility in vision and practice? If so, make the call.

Consider the following conversation between a suburban church leader—let's call her Sally—and an urban ministry leader—how about Irving? After the preliminary *hellos* and *how are yous* (remember, they already know each other), their first conversation can go something like this:

> SALLY: Irv, God has been speaking to our church about serving the underprivileged in the city, and as we've been praying fervently about it, we get the overwhelming sense that partnership with an agency like yours, which is already doing great things, is the way to go.
>
> IRVING: I'm glad you think we're doing great things! The truth is, we could always use help. What do you have in mind?
>
> SALLY: You tell us. Consider us at your service. We want to support you in any way we can and come alongside to help you do what you do. I know you work with at-risk youth, the very people group we long to serve.
>
> IRVING: Great. We run an after-school program Monday through Friday and a sports program on Saturdays. Without volunteers these programs don't work very well. So I can foresee recruiting some folks from First Church to help out.
>
> SALLY: Yes! I knew this could work. Given how ready some people are, I think we can start immediately.
>
> IRVING: Well . . . I'm tempted to sign on the dotted line, Sally. But you know, partnership is harder than it sounds. Don't you think your people and my people *should get to know each other a little better*?

4. Plan Together Relationship-Building Activities

Irving's last comment points to the fourth significant step of urban-suburban partnership: plan together a series of relationship-building activities. Ongoing conversations between urban and suburban leaders, not unlike the one between Sally and Irving, should lead to some intentional planning to bring the two groups together, not primarily for the purpose of ministry so much as for the purpose of getting to know each other.

Steve Munz, associate pastor at City Line Church in suburban Wynnewood, Pennsylvania, and Zack Ritvalsky, pastor of Sweet Union Baptist Church in West Philadelphia, became friends while studying together at Westminster Theological Seminary. The burden for the city increased among the members at City Line, and when it was time to consider partnering with a city church, Munz contacted Ritvalsky. Their ongoing conversations uncovered their mutual desire to develop a partnership that is relationally based. So a series of events were put in motion over a span of one year: a number of pulpit swaps, encouragement of members to join the other church's small groups, joint worship services, and a summer picnic with accompanying recreational activities.

Such events do much to develop personal relationships, while never losing sight of the mutual goal eventually to come together for community transformational ministry. This book has suggested from the beginning that personal relationships serve as an indispensable basis upon which urban-suburban partnership can authentically form and flourish. If partnership is based on something less than a relationship rooted in Christ and in each other, then it falls short of the kingdom of God. Or as Leadership Professor Daniel Rickett puts it, "Partnership is nothing if it is not personal."[5]

5. Plan Together Cross-Cultural Learning Activities

Plan together activities that create cross-cultural learning opportunities. This step could have been absorbed within step 4 because in building relationships across the urban-suburban divide, you also learn by osmosis one another's respective cultures. But this aspect of partnership holds enough significance that it deserves to stand alone. Step 5 takes relationship-building to the next level, calling participants across the divide to learn each other's different values, worldviews, and communication patterns (while also affirming the shared convictions that unite them). It is precisely these kinds of differences that have created the gap between urban and suburban worlds, and we must do the hard, relational work of understanding them if ministry partnership across the great divide is going to work. As budding partners tackle these differences head-on, they pave the way for a truly intercultural relationship.

Cross-cultural learning activities range from introductory to advanced levels. When Carey Davis of CityLights took a group of members from suburban Wayne Presbyterian Church to various city neighborhoods in Philadelphia for an art tour, she introduced an aspect of urban culture, opening the door for fellow suburbanites to learn and appreciate urban culture as they marveled at amazing murals, which reflected neighborhood renewal efforts. Going the other way, John McCullough of the Philadelphia Training Center regularly brings groups of young people from Southwest Philadelphia to spend the day with church members in suburban Wayne, thereby opening the door for urban youth to develop a more positive view of white suburban culture as they develop real relationships with the people there.

But the entry level of cultural learning must eventually graduate to a more advanced level as urban-suburban partners confront the very real differences that exist between them. It seems easier on the surface to avoid the differences in order to protect the peace, but it would be a precarious peace. Some even go into denial and claim color blindness on the grounds that we are all one in Christ. Affirming our Christian unity, however, should not preclude taking cultural differences seriously. Experienced practitioners of multiculturalism strongly advise against "color blindness." "My prayer," pleads David Anderson, pastor of a multicultural church in North Carolina, "is that the church, whether Anglo, African, or Afghan, would refuse to be color-blind."[6] Those attempting to cross the urban-suburban divide must find ways not to deny differences but to face them.

This *facing up* can take many forms—such as the reconciliation meetings during the early days of Voice of Calvary in Jackson, Mississippi, where black-white issues of leadership and power were regularly aired.[7] Or it can happen by establishing regular personal and professional accountability check-ups, such as the daily calls and monthly face-to-face meetings between John Perkins and Wayne Gordon, which they have been doing for over twenty years. These veterans of reconciliation ministries have modeled what it takes to maintain an effective intercultural relationship. It does not happen as a result of avoiding cultural differences; it happens rather by tackling them head-on with honesty, grace, and love. Activities that work toward that end tremendously increase the chances for success in a partnership that crosses the urban-suburban divide.

6. Form a Cross-Cultural Ministry Team

Form a team that is made up of those dedicated to community ministry from both urban and suburban entities. There are two obvious moves to this particular step. First, not everyone in both organizations can or should be directly involved in the partnership; so some kind of selection process should take place within both urban and suburban groups to determine who among them will commit to being a part of the urban-suburban ministry team. This means that both urban and suburban entities separately need to form a committee or a task force or, at the very least, assign a contact person whose primary duty is to contribute to the nurture and mobilization of the multicultural ministry team. Both the urban group and the suburban group should also establish a system of reporting to their respective pastoral or organizational leadership. For example, when the Berkeley Covenant Church (BCC) in Berkeley, California, joined the efforts of nearby Mary Magdalene Catholic Church in a homeless ministry, the pastor recruited several willing members to coordinate the effort on BCC's end. These members worked with the coordinators at Mary Magdalene several times a month and then gave a report at the monthly local mission meeting at BCC with the pastor present.[8]

The second move in this step involves making sure that the team being formed reflects a fair representation of both urban and suburban presence. Otherwise the partnership suffers a one-sidedness in ethos, group dynamics, and decision making. A fair representation, on the other hand, makes a number of important affirmations:

1. It affirms that which binds them—a shared commitment to participate in God's transforming work in the community.
2. It demonstrates their willingness to define the partnership in terms of trust, equality, and interdependence across cultural and class barriers.
3. It affirms shared power in program development and in the decision-making process.

The importance of forming a ministry team of this kind cannot be stressed enough for an effective urban-suburban partnership. In order to develop such a team, the players must commit to meeting regularly—preferably weekly, but if that proves impossible, then monthly can work if regular email or telephone communication and informal meetings can happen in between. The meetings themselves should at least contain spiritual, relational, and strategic elements—keeping their purpose grounded in Christ, maintaining healthy relations with each other, and strategizing together to reach the community.

Moreover, it is especially important that team members be aware of default postures with which urban and suburban team players come to the table. Whereas urban partners often tend toward acquiescence and dependence, suburban partners tend toward assuming leadership positions and thus inadvertently establishing a pattern of dominance. To counter this, we recommend that the leader or facilitator of the team come from the urban side.[9] As a *leader among equals*, the urban facilitator runs the meeting with at least the following objectives: (1) helping the team to remain focused upon God and God's mission, perhaps beginning with a Scripture meditation that the facilitator either does herself or himself or assigns to another team member; (2) giving opportunity for healthy relationship building, perhaps allotting time for personal check-in with one another—thus practicing the art of listening and caring for one another; and (3) facilitating the team in making program decisions that help the ministry achieve its goals of community transformation.

7. Plan a Small, Doable Community Project

Plan a community project together, but start small, thereby increasing the chances that the partnership will experience success. Missionary strategist Bob Moffitt calls these "seed projects," which are "short, small, simple ministry activities" that have a larger impact than their smallness might suggest.[10] By beginning with something modest, the ministry team can do real ministry together while also testing the dynamics of the diverse team in action. And as the team experiences success in small projects, it can graduate to larger projects.

This is not to shortchange the power of small efforts, for they have had great impact in many communities all over the world. Futurist Tom Sine's body of work, from *The Mustard Seed Conspiracy* to *The*

New Conspirators, has done much to help the church understand the power of the biblical *mustard seed* to bring about kingdom change.[11] "Jesus lets us in on an astonishing secret," writes Sine. "God has chosen to change the world through the lowly, the unassuming and the imperceptible." But together in the hands of God, these small works serve as the conduit through which God's kingdom breaks in "to redeem a new global community from every tongue, tribe and nation."[12]

So we dare not underestimate small endeavors. We should in fact start there with a simple, doable project such as organizing a community cleanup, coordinating visits to a local nursing home, starting an after-school tutoring program, or organizing a mini basketball tournament that brings neighborhood youth together. And while implementing these types of seed projects, we should remember that in Christ they add up to become a subversive movement that changes the world from the bottom up.

Careful planning is also essential. Deciding what to tackle by way of a seed project must be done prayerfully and carefully. "Even though a seed project is simple and small," counsels Moffitt, "its success . . . requires planning."[13] Community development wisdom advises beginning with a need that the community residents have identified. Simple community surveys have proven indispensable in listening to local residents.[14] Another indispensable source of understanding the needs of the community is the very team members *from* that community. Assuming that the venue for holistic community outreach is the urban context in which some of the team members grew up or currently live, they will most likely know what the needs are. Their input, therefore, on the focus of the seed project must carry greater weight than the ideas of suburban partners.

8. Establish an Accountability System

Establish together a system wherein the partners keep themselves accountable to the values of the kingdom of God: justice, reconciliation, and transformation. As kingdom people, we are committed to countering the world's system of classism and racism and, as this book has been championing all along, to working together across the *isms* to change our communities. Being products of our culture, however, we also default to the very patterns we seek to challenge—patterns that advantage the rich over the poor and create unjust realities such as *white privilege* over *nonwhite underprivilege*. And then completely unaware, with these worldly patterns in place, we attempt to do kingdom ministry. We must establish together a system of kingdom accountability that safeguards against these patterns in order to maximize the values of justice and reconciliation for the sake of transformation. As Rickett asserts, "Partners with clear systems of accountability are better equipped to handle the inevitable mistakes and misunderstandings that occur in intercultural partnerships."[15]

An accountability system in an urban-suburban ministry partnership has to do with managing relationships across classes and cultures as well as clarifying roles and responsibilities in achieving the partners' shared goals. Regarding the first issue, the partners should together create a list of bold questions (similar to Rickett's "Dependency Checklist" and "Accountability Checklist")[16] that they ask themselves on a regular basis. These include:

- Do you detect any signs of inequality among us?
- Have you been offended recently by any of the team members?
- Has anything been said or done insensitively?

The list should also contain questions seeking positive feedback, such as:

- Have you learned anything from each other regarding urban or suburban culture?
- How has this partnership contributed to your cultural enrichment?
- How has it contributed to your spiritual walk?

Committing to ask these types of questions of each other on a regular basis keeps the lines of honest communication open, thus strengthening the ties that bind the partnership across the urban-suburban divide.

Accountability is not complete, however, without systemizing roles and responsibilities and then monitoring each other's performance in light of the assigned tasks. A typical Memorandum of Understanding between an InterVarsity Urban Project and its urban partner provides a good example (see appendix 1). Although MOUs are custom-drafted according to context and therefore differ significantly from each other, they share basic elements that establish ministry accountability. These elements include:

- Clearly stated objectives of both the urban and suburban organizations: What does each side of the partnership want, and how does each expect the partnership to help achieve their respective objectives?
- Designated leadership roles: How is leadership going to be shared? When does the urban partner take the lead and the suburban partner follow, and vice versa?
- Agreed-upon financial management: Who keeps the books? How will funds be handled, and how does the team decide this?
- An evaluation structure: How will the team evaluate the fruit of the partnership?

In written form, IVCF/USA Urban Projects call these "Memoranda of Understanding"; other organizations call them working agreements, and still others call them covenants. Regardless of what they are called, they serve as essential guidelines for keeping the partnership on track with regard to its ministry goals.

One other point that needs to be made regarding ministry accountability is the importance of documentation. Regular project status and financial reports should be a part of the accountability system. If the community ministry that the partnership is managing is merely a part of the larger ministry of the organizations involved, documentation can simply be included in the larger monthly, quarterly, or annual reports of the organization or church. Whether reports are separate or incorporated in larger reports, the point is that records should be kept, which establishes real accountability with each other.[17]

So, (1) pray like Nehemiah, (2) share the vision, (3) make meaningful contact with a potential partner, (4) plan relationship-building activities, (5) plan cross-cultural learning activities, (6) form a cross-cultural ministry team, (7) plan a small, doable community project, and (8) establish an accountability system. Although we have neatly organized these eight *first steps*, we guarantee that urban-suburban partnership will be messier than this. These steps should be viewed as essential but not sequential. The complex human elements of any relationship—our creative personalities, our different emotional makeup, unexpected life events, busy schedules, and so on—ensure a ministry adventure that is exciting, challenging, sometimes frustrating, and never boring. But in order for these initial steps to be successful in developing an effective urban partnership, which crosses the urban-suburban divide for the sake of the kingdom, they need to be wrapped in biblical faithfulness. Insofar as the partners commit to the biblical kingdom qualities of equality, dignity, respect, trust, and love, these steps will lead to mutual empowerment and community transformation. Upholding then both the wild card of human experience and the uncompromising commitment to the biblical kingdom, consider yourself ready to link arms and hearts across the urban-suburban divide in order to participate in the mission of the kingdom of God. "Rise," Jesus said to his disciples after they received encouragement and instruction. "Let us be on our way" (John 14:31). It is time. Just do it.

Reflection Questions

1. As you think about your own context, whether you are in a church, a small group, or an organization, how realistic are these first steps?

2. What are possible hindrances to taking these concrete steps toward urban-suburban partnership?

3. Spend time together in silence and then pray as Nehemiah and let the adventure begin.

Conclusion

We Can Do It!

We know what to do. This book demonstrates that some urban-suburban partnerships are already transforming countless numbers of broken people and renewing devastated neighborhoods throughout the land. The right kind of urban-suburban partnership is crucial to this wonderful transformation. Suburban churches are working with urban ministries. Business leaders, national organizations, and faithful individuals are linking arms with holistic urban ministries. Broken, despairing persons are both coming to personal faith in Jesus and experiencing life-changing transformation in all aspects of their lives. Thank God for what is already happening.

But we have the resources to do so much more. Only a tiny fraction of today's suburban churches, parachurch organizations, Christian business leaders, and individuals are currently partnering with urban ministries. Their numbers could—should—double, quadruple, and quadruple again. We undoubtedly have the economic resources. Do we have the will and the courage to obey?

Think of the impact if the current seven hundred local holistic ministries affiliated with the Christian Community Development Association were enabled to grow to programs with ten million dollar budgets because they developed partnerships with suburban churches, organizations, businesses, and people. Think of the impact if the number of such ministries ballooned to seven thousand. Whole sections of our most desperate urban neighborhoods would blossom and flourish. Countless children and young people would enjoy hope for the future. Suburban partners across the land would experience unexpected joy as they walked hand-in-hand with urban sisters and brothers.

If even 20 percent of North American churches embraced this vision of holistic urban-suburban partnerships, we could do all this and more. In the next two decades a vast expansion of wise, effective urban-suburban partnerships could transform thousands of hurting neighborhoods, offer a compelling witness to the gospel's power to a watching world, and bring great joy to our Lord.

We can do it!

Appendix 1

Memorandum of Understanding

Following is an example of an InterVarsity Christian Fellowship (IVCF) Memorandum of Understanding:

Memorandum of Understanding
BETWEEN
InterVarsity Urban Projects
AND
Leadership Foundations of America Affiliates

InterVarsity Christian Fellowship runs short-term, urban experiential service and learning projects ("Urban Projects" or "UPs") in twenty-six cities across the U.S. involving more than 1,000 students annually in urban ministry. Leadership Foundations of America (LFA) Affiliates exist in an equivalent number of cities, and there is a remarkable degree of overlap. LFA Affiliates have grassroots, community connections and experience; InterVarsity UPs have a consistent stream of emerging leaders who are socially conscious and committed to Christ.

In cities that contain both an InterVarsity UP and an LFA Affiliate we seek to achieve a healthy working relationship resulting in mutual benefits based on agreements such as these:

The Directors of InterVarsity UPs and LFA Affiliates agree to initiate contact with each other in cities where both ministries exist, to imagine potential points of partnership.

The Directors of InterVarsity UPs and LFA Affiliates agree to invest in a real relationship of mutual understanding and respect, with the potential of leading to friendship.

In cities that develop partnerships that allow for the placement of IVCF Urban Projects interns at an LFA Affiliate, Directors agree to meet at least once *prior* to the beginning of a UP, at least once *during* a project and at least once postproject to agree on goals, check signals, and evaluate.

UP Directors will clearly state their expectations and hopes for the kind of experience they want their students to have. UP Directors agree to consider the input of LFA Directors in shaping the design of an urban project.

LFA Directors agree to invest time in UP interns/volunteers, including:

  detailing policies and procedures to the interns, the "whys" and "hows" of things

  stating expectations and responsibilities clearly, giving actual tasks and direction

  debriefing their experiences and helping them interpret what they see

  appropriate risk management

  being flexible to accommodate the interns' other UP-related commitments and schedule

  educating UP students as to the mission of the LFA affiliate

LFA Directors agree to state their concerns about hosting UP interns/volunteers in terms of their impact on the agency, neighborhood, or community and work with the UP Director to address those concerns.

UP Directors agree to prepare their students for service at the LFA Affiliate, including anticipating potential problems, screening potential problem students, creating lines of accountability, etc.

LFA and UP Directors agree to define clear pathways for students for future involvement in the LFA Affiliate, either as volunteers or staff, as appropriate.

UP and LFA Directors agree to positively represent one another's ministries in the broader community, serving on one another's boards as appropriate, supporting one another's events, advocating for each other's financial viability.

This Memorandum of Understanding acknowledges that there are many variables and differences between LFA Affiliates in different cities, and differences between IVCF Urban Projects from city to city. The above points represent the general target goals of a relationship in any given city, and that Directors in each city will hammer out more specific objectives that reflect the realities of that city.

Appendix 2

Resources for Kingdom Partnership

Consider the following testimony:

> I was a promising young fundamentalist back in the early 1980s. Zealous to save desperate souls from the sinking ship called planet Earth, I went off to a Christian college to prepare for the task of getting as many people into the Jesus lifeboat as I could. As far as I knew, this defined the church's mission. But then I read Ron Sider's *Rich Christians in an Age of Hunger*, along with a handful of other prophetic books. . . . Talk about getting beat up—the multi-punch combination of these books knocked me off my feet, and my understanding of mission has never been the same. . . .
>
> I got up from the floor a bit wobbly, but with a strange new clarity about God's heart for the poor. I staggered like a drunkard, but with a strong resolve not to order my life according to the false promises of the American Dream.
>
> With my understanding of compassion and justice violently realigned, I headed off to complete a graduate course in Central America. Amidst the in-your-face poverty endured by so many people whom I had the privilege to meet, the God of the poor and oppressed spoke to me in a most profound and life-changing way. I returned home persuaded that if the gospel did not address human need in the here

and now, then the good news was no good at all. I refer to that time in my life as my "born again *again*" experience.[1]

Such testimonies, which are not all that uncommon among those in urban ministry today, point to an internal process, a journey toward kingdom sensitivity, a deepening of discipleship that realigns the way in which one lives according to God's kingdom purposes in the world.

In practical terms, this kingdom sensitivity develops as we master certain theological, cultural, and relational skills. More specifically, we first need to sharpen our awareness of God's mission, particularly the place of the poor in that mission, which will lead to a commitment to holistic ministry. Second, we need to understand, appreciate, and harness the diversity with which God has made humankind—in all of its color, ethnicities, and cultures—and thus, spearhead ministries of reconciliation and multiculturalism. And third, we need to develop just, incarnational relationships between the rich and the poor according to God's economy, sharing decision-making and society-shaping power in order to bring about true transformation together. Successful and effective urban-suburban partnerships totally depend on these kingdom sensitivity skills; without them, our attempts to partner across the urban-suburban divide are doomed from the start.

Theologizing with Holistic Eyes

First then, kingdom sensitivity develops as we cultivate a missional understanding of God—a view that sees mission as central to who God is. For many of us this may sound too basic to even have to mention, but the way many seminaries teach theology quite apart from missional considerations and the way many churches relegate mission efforts to exotic places show us that the idea of the *Missio Dei*—the mission of God—does not occupy the central place that it ought to have. Kingdom sensitivity begins with a firm grasp of the *Missio Dei*.

This naturally begins with the way in which we read Scripture, the primary source of our knowledge of God. Several study Bibles come to mind that are designed to help readers understand the biblical story with missional eyes. World Vision's *Faith in Action Study Bible* provides mission-oriented commentary alongside the biblical text. Corresponding articles contained in *Faith in Action*, from people such as Mother Teresa, John Stott, Bill Pannell, Ajith Fernando, Christine Pohl, Joni Eareckson Tada, Dolphus Weary, and Hwa Yung reinforce the biblical call to holistic action with insights based on experience. For churches in particular, World Vision has teamed up with Outreach, Inc. and Zondervan Publishers to expand this study Bible into the *Faith in Action Campaign Kit*, which includes a DVD, a CD-ROM, a manual, and many other tools to help local congregations become Faith-in-Action churches. (The bibliography provides full publication information for all resources recommended in this appendix.)

The *Word in Life Study Bible*, a joint project of InterVarsity Christian Fellowship and Thomas Nelson Publishers, provides similar guidance for Bible readers who want to know how to translate biblical knowledge into meaningful action in the world. The mission-mindedness of those involved in creating *Word in Life* enlivens the pages of Scripture for mission. The editorial roster includes former IVCF president Steve Hayner, IVCF's longtime champion of urban ministries Pete Hammond, lawyer Sue Cotten, and renowned urban leader Ray Bakke. Themes such as work, economics, ethics, ethnicity, and the city motivate readers to think missionally as they study the Scriptures.

Alongside these mission-oriented study Bibles are some must-read books that enable a missional understanding of the whole of Scripture from Genesis to Revelation. They include Christopher J. H. Wright's *The Mission of God: Unlocking the Bible's Grand Narrative* and Arthur F. Glasser's *Announcing the Kingdom: The Story of God's Mission in the Bible*. Wright introduces his book by describing a kind of identity crisis for a course he taught at London's All Nations Christian College. He reflects: "The more I taught the course, the more [I told] the students that I would like to rename it from 'The Biblical Basis of Mission' to 'The Missional Basis of the Bible.'" Why? "I wanted them to see not just that the Bible contains a number of texts which happen to provide a rationale for missionary endeavor but that *the whole Bible is itself a missional phenomenon*."[2] Glasser says it more succinctly, opening chapter 1 with, "The whole Bible, both Old and New Testaments, is a missionary book."[3]

If kingdom sensitivity begins with a missional reading of Scripture, then a holistic perspective that grows from it takes kingdom sensitivity to the next level. As our eyes refocus upon the biblical story of the *Missio Dei*, we begin to see that God's mission encompasses the whole created order, from humanity to the physical earth and everything in between. Such comprehensive scope is in part what it means to be holistic. It also means that God's mission to redeem humanity involves the whole person—body, soul, and social situation. Insofar as God's people take on God's mission, they engage in holistic ministry, demonstrating concern for the earth, practicing works of evangelism, and working for compassion and justice for all, especially the poor.

Transformation, the journal of the Oxford Centre for Mission Studies in the United Kingdom, has provided the widest range of reflections on holistic mission since 1984, both thematically and globally. We recommend not only that you subscribe to this journal but also that you find the back issues, which are replete with articles that have significantly shaped the holistic missionary movement around the world. For more popular periodicals, Prism magazine of the Evangelicals for Social Action features regular stories and insights on holistic ministry, while Sojourners magazine offers a broader, ecumenical perspective on the integration of faith, justice, and peace.

As for books, three classics come to mind: Waldron Scott's Bring Forth Justice, Stephen Mott's Biblical Ethics and Social Change, and the late Orlando Costas's The Integrity of Mission. These time-tested volumes ground holistic ministry firmly in biblical theology and consequently have remained the standard for integrating mission, disciple making, and social justice. Melba Maggay's Transforming Society has also proven helpful in providing biblically based models of holistic social change. Another invaluable resource of more recent vintage is Mission as Transformation, edited by Vinay Samuel and Chris Sugden, which compiles statements and articles that have shaped the global holistic missionary movement since the mid-1970s.

Other books that provide tools to read the Bible with holistic eyes include Thomas D. Hanks's God So Loved the Third World, Elsa Tamez's The Scandalous Message of James, and Miguel De La Torre's Reading the Bible from the Margins. The power of these volumes lies in their ability to expose presuppositions that we often bring to the biblical text. "I know that for me personally," reflects Hanks, "after eighteen years teaching in a Latin American context, the Bible is a new book."[4] Tamez points out that while European and North American theologians, beginning with Martin Luther, have historically had a difficult time with the epistle of James, a Latin American reading finds it hopeful from the start, as the letter at once lifts up the poor and judges the oppressive rich.[5] Likewise, some of the chapter titles of De La Torre's book, such as "Unmasking the Biblical Justification of Racism and Classism" and "Unmasking the Biblical Justification of

Sexism," reveal the book's penchant for making readers uncomfortable. Although some may find parts of these books offensive, they are essential reading to help us identify our own social and cultural blind spots. Everyone brings presuppositions to the Bible, but when these presuppositions are detrimental to other people, we commit a grave misreading that requires kingdom correction. These books can serve as part of the remedy.

Moving from biblical, holistic theology to biblical, holistic, *urban* theology, we could cite many books. But our short list includes Robert Lupton's *Renewing the City*, Harvie Conn and Manuel Ortiz's *Urban Ministry*, Mark Gornik's *To Live in Peace*, and Ray Bakke's *Theology as Big as the City*. Bakke's overview of Scripture through urban lenses transforms biblical material into fuel for those ministering in the city. Lupton's rereading of the book of Nehemiah with community development in mind connects the ancient rebuilding of Jerusalem to current efforts in rebuilding impoverished neighborhoods today. Conn and Ortiz do the whole urban ministry movement a favor with their comprehensive, five-hundred-page treatise on urban ministry, including an invaluable section on biblical perspectives of the city. And Gornik mines the riches of his experience living and ministering in Sandtown, a poor section of Baltimore, developing a biblically based incarnational theology of urban ministry for the benefit of practitioners around the world.

Works on urban ministry that lean more on the practical side include *Restoring At-Risk Communities*, a multiauthor volume edited by John Perkins that serves as the official handbook of the Christian Community Development Association. Translating urban theology into curriculum workbook form, Janell Williams Paris and Margot Owen Eyring's *Urban Disciples: A Beginner's Guide to Serving God in the City* has been a proven resource for small groups in churches, colleges, and mission agencies.

As if we have not already overloaded you, a viable holistic ministry library must ultimately include Ron Sider, Heidi Unruh, and Phil Olson's *Churches That Make a Difference (CTMAD)*, which documents the experiences of holistic churches mainly in the Philadelphia area and offers replicable principles for all churches seeking to engage their communities holistically. As an outgrowth of this book, Word & Deed Network has developed a "Holistic Ministry Starter Kit," which includes a CD-ROM and a workbook—both titled "Becoming a Church That Makes a Difference." Alongside these *CTMAD* resources, Amy Sherman's *Restorers of Hope*, Tim Keller's *Ministries of Mercy*, and Rick Rusaw and Eric Swanson's *The Externally Focused Church* tremendously strengthen anyone's holistic ministry library. Replete with stories, principles, tools, models, and case studies, these books provide practical steps to engage the world by both word and deed.

The point is, reading the Bible missionally, holistically, and with the city in mind, and consuming a steady diet of the right books will create a solid theological center from which kingdom sensitivity can flow.

Understanding and Harnessing Racial and Cultural Diversity

A second skill that needs to be developed in order to cultivate kingdom sensitivity has to do with understanding racial and cultural diversity as well as harnessing it for reconciliation and multicultural ministry. It is politically correct these days to appreciate, celebrate, and even mandate cultural diversity in our institutions. While some recoil at this trend and write books like Georgiana Preskar's *Diversity Addiction: The Cause and the Cure*,[6] others work hard to diversify the workplace as dictated by what is trendy. God's people, however, must go beyond the diversity that is defined by political correctness and take it to the next level if they desire to partner effectively across the urban-suburban divide. In other words, the church must gain an understanding of diversity according to nothing less than God's Word and then harness that understanding to partner together for justice and reconciliation in the world.

Understanding cultural diversity according to the Bible naturally entails having a grasp of what the Scriptures teach about it. Study Bibles have appeared in recent years to help access the Scriptures in a culturally sensitive way, such as *Aspire: The New Women of Color Study Bible*, which is an expansion of its predecessor, *Women of Color Study Bible*. Although *Aspire* speaks primarily to African-American women, it opens up the possibility of diverse readings to empower both genders and all people of color. Similarly, *The Original African-American Heritage Study Bible* (*OAAH*) has a wider audience than its name implies. It states its purpose "to interpret the Bible as it relates specifically to persons of African descent and thereby to foster an appreciation of the multiculturalism inherent in the Bible."[7] Under the direction of notables such as Cain Hope Felder, James W. Peebles, and Maggie S. Peebles, the *OAAH Study Bible* offers not only commentary on the biblical text itself, it also contains articles such as "Recovering Multiculturalism in Scripture" and "The Ancient Black Christians." At the time of this writing, an editorial team consisting of Curtiss DeYoung, Wilda Gafney, Leticia Guardiola-Saenz, George Tinker, and Frank Yamada are busy working on *The People's Bible*, with the objective of providing guidance for multicultural readings of Scripture and thus promoting ministries of racial reconciliation.

In addition to these study Bibles, recent books on scriptural teachings on race and multiethnicity include Daniel Hays's *From Every People and Nation: A Biblical Theology of Race*, Steven McKenzie's *All God's Children: A Biblical Critique of Racism*, Curtiss DeYoung's *Coming Together: The Bible's Message in an Age of Diversity*, and Melba Maggay's *Jew to the Jew, Greek to the Greek*. Hays rightly points out the unfortunate dearth of exegetical treatments on race and multiethnicity and hopes his book will help fill the void. McKenzie's and DeYoung's volumes demonstrate both the Bible's denunciation of the evil of racism and its call to diversity and reconciliation. Maggay's slim volume interprets selected biblical texts and makes the case not only that the many cultures flow out of the creativity of God, but also that cultures will retain their identity at the *eschaton*. She writes, "The end of Revelation talks of how the glory and honor of the nations—all the immense richness, splendor, and variegated color of it—shall be brought into the New Jerusalem."[8]

Several essential nontheological resources to support and enrich our biblical understanding of race and culture include Ronald Takaki's *A Different Mirror: A Multicultural History of America*. Takaki claims that America's history has been multicultural from the beginning, starting with the encounter between Native Americans and Europeans, and thus exposes the irony of the "emerging conversation" surrounding multiculturalism.[9] It is only "emerging" because the European shapers and movers of the American experiment have effectively defined her history in terms of the white experience. But addressing fellow nonwhite Americans, Takaki asks rhetorically, "What happens . . . when someone with the authority of a teacher describes our society and you are not in it?"[10] Takaki underscores the importance of recovering the country's multicultural roots in order to inform today's conversation about multiculturalism. Another nontheological must-read is Michael Emerson and Christian Smith's sociological tour de force *Divided by Faith*, which demonstrates—via a nationwide survey, hundreds of interviews, and historical analysis—the continuing problem of racism in America and how churches perpetuate it. They begin with their thesis, describing the book as "a story of how well-intentioned people, their values, and their institutions actually recreate racial divisions and inequalities they ostensibly oppose."[11] As convicting and depressing as it is, this book has inspired denominations, churches, and Christian organizations to take race seriously for the sake of the kingdom. Another nontheological work (though written by a clergyman) that deserves our attention is Joseph Barndt's *Understanding & Dismantling Racism: The Twentieth Century Challenge to White America*. Former director of an antiracism training organization in Chicago called Crossroads Ministry, Barndt shares a wealth of knowledge regarding racism in America—its history, definition, and ongoing challenge as well as ways to dismantle it.

A fuller understanding of race and culture, as provided by the aforementioned resources, necessarily leads to deeper thinking about ministries of reconciliation and multiculturalism. Several resources come to mind that provide theologically informed principles and models, including Dennis Okholm's edited work *The Gospel in Black and White: Theological Resources for Racial Reconciliation* and Curtiss DeYoung's *Reconciliation: Our Greatest Challenge, Our Only Hope*. Both of these volumes primarily address the enduring rift between Euro- and African-American communities, which, as Emerson and Smith have established, needs the most attention given the great division between white America and black America.[12] Both Okholm's and DeYoung's volumes give clear, solid, biblical-theological treatments of reconciliation, combining critical thinking and personal narrative. While the former is the work of one author, the latter brings together insights from a number of reflective practitioners including Eugene Rivers, Cheryl Sanders, Craig Keener, and others.

Although the black-white divide represents the widest rift in America, it does not tell the whole story of racism and the need for reconciliation. Broader treatments of the Bible's call for reconciliation include Robert Schreiter's *Reconciliation: Mission & Ministry in a Changing Social Order* and Miroslav Volf's *Exclusion and Embrace*. The thinness of Schreiter's volume can deceive you into thinking that it does not have much to offer, but in fact it exudes a rich biblical understanding of reconciliation and implications for ministry in a war-torn world. Volf's not-so-thin volume provides similar offerings, urging Christians to confess the sin of exclusion and replace it with the biblical metaphor of embrace. The power of his argument not only comes from sophisticated theology but more forcefully from his own struggle as a Croat-American living out the call to embrace Serbs, who at the time of the writing of his book, were implementing a campaign of ethnic cleansing of Croats and Bosnians in his homeland of former Yugoslavia.

Understanding racial and cultural diversity and hearing the biblical call for reconciliation must lead to practical action, and this moves us to the need to harness racial and cultural diversity and bind ourselves together by the ties of the gospel in order to testify to the peace and justice of the kingdom. Harnessing diversity entails at least two active pursuits: (1) genuine reconciliation, and (2) genuine multiculturalism.

Excellent resources that translate reconciliation theology into a practical pursuit have already been cited extensively in this book, such as Spencer Perkins and Chris Rice's *More Than Equals*, Raleigh Washington and Glen Kehrein's *Breaking Down Walls*, Brenda Salter McNeil and Rick Richardson's *The Heart of Racial Justice*, and Edward Gilbreath's *Reconciliation Blues: A Black Evangelical's Inside View of White Christianity*. These have in common the real experiences of ministry partnerships across the black-white divide and the principles that they have gleaned from the experience. Norman Anthony Peart's *Separate No More: Understanding and Developing Racial Reconciliation in Your Church* augments the list by providing a resource specifically for local congregations as he shares from his own experience as the pastor of a multiracial church in North Carolina. Part 3 of his book offers models of reconciliation as well as practical steps to achieve what Peart has coined "inHimtegration—when a church makes intentional choices to mix, accept, represent, and manifest racial and ethnic differences" in the unity of Christ.[13] McNeil and Richardson's book also contains, as appendix 2, "Reconciliation Generation Bible Studies" designed for small groups or personal study.

Books that move beyond the black-white divide and provide practical guidance to multicultural ministry include Elizabeth Conde Frazier, S. Steve Kang, and Gary A. Parrett's *A Many Colored Kingdom: Multicultural Dynamics for Spiritual Formation*. Written by Christian educators, this book links multiculturalism to the vision of God's kingdom and then suggests practical ways to teach the faith multiculturally in both church and institutions of higher learning. Other practical books on cultural diversity include David Anderson's *Multicultural Ministry* and Michael Emerson, Curtiss DeYoung, George Yancey, and Karen Chai Kim's *United by Faith*, which serves as a hopeful sequel to Emerson and Smith's *Divided by Faith*. Whereas *Divided* demonstrates the problem of the church perpetuating racism, *United* makes a case that multicultural congregations can show the way for the rest of society to dismantle racism. Anderson agrees and begins his book with an analogy of an orchestra: "I'd like to paint a picture and give practical insights on how to bring the sections of God's orchestra together so that the world can hear a sound unlike they have ever heard before."[14] Anderson's volume contains practical tools such as a racial reconciliation survey, which he used to obtain data for the book but which can also be easily adapted for use in any church. It also contains a six-session racial reconciliation curriculum that churches will find useful. Keeping with the orchestra analogy, Anderson continues, "The white church, black church, Asian church, Latino church—the whole church must come together under the skillful conducting of the Lord Jesus Christ. The biblical score has been written and arranged. God is calling his players to perform their parts in harmony with Spirit-empowered precision."[15]

One resource that effectively incorporates reconciliation and multiculturalism into the bigger vision of cultural transformation is *Christianity Today*'s "Intersect Culture" DVD with an accompanying six-session curriculum. Users of this tool will hear from a variety of cultural perspectives throughout the DVD, while session 4 deals specifically with racial reconciliation.

There are other resources on race, reconciliation, and multiculturalism. We have merely highlighted a sampling of them in order to guide both our understanding and harnessing of cultural diversity—a skill set that kingdom sensitivity demands and upon which effective urban-suburban partnership depends.

Developing Just, Incarnational Ministry Relationships

Kingdom sensitivity requires one other skill: developing just, incarnational ministry relationships between the rich and the poor. In a world where the gap between the rich and the poor continues to widen, the kingdom demands that its citizens show an alternate way;

it demands that the church overcome classism—a prejudice based upon socioeconomic class by which resourced people dominate under-resourced people—and practice the incarnation with and for the poor for community transformation.

In order to understand the importance of this skill, we must first grasp the Bible's teachings regarding the poor. Beyond the study Bibles mentioned previously, in which the issue of poverty is part of the missional and multicultural readings of Scripture, there is also the book *For They Shall Be Fed: Scripture Readings and Prayers for a Just World*, edited by Ron Sider. This book "brings together in one place passages from the Scriptures pertaining to hunger, justice, and the poor." Furthermore, it includes inspiring prayers for a needy world from such people as Billy Graham, Tony Campolo, and Vonette Bright.[16]

Several important, explicitly biblical theological classics also come to mind, such as Sider's *Rich Christians in an Age of Hunger*, especially part 2 on biblical perspectives on the poor and possessions, and Orlando Costas's *Christ Outside the Gate*. These remain the biblical standards for reflective evangelicals in understanding God's heart for the poor and how that truth informs the way the church should engage the world in radical, holistic mission in solidarity with the poor. The fact that these books are still in print today attests to their enduring value. Another important volume of more recent vintage is Craig Blomberg's *Neither Poverty nor Riches*, which provides a thorough survey of the Bible's teaching on wealth and poverty.

In terms of a theology of wealth and poverty, the church is indebted to many scholars in the non-Western world. Jayakumar Christian's *God of the Empty Handed* sits on top of the list as it tackles the giant issue of global poverty. Defining poverty primarily in terms of powerlessness, Christian makes the case that the church's ministry to the poor entails the restoration of God-given power to shape their own lives and their communities. Benigno Beltran's *Christology of the Inarticulate* documents the remarkable way in which the poor—in his case, the thirty thousand poor who once lived on Manila's infamous thirty-story high garbage dump called Smokey Mountain—express their devotion to the Christ of the poor. Beltran's book serves as a voice for the voiceless—a voice that profoundly changed his own life. He writes, "I thank [the poor] for making me less the theologian I thought I was and more the human being I dream of becoming."[17] Virginia Fabella and R. S. Sugitharajah's *Dictionary of Third World Theologies* surveys the many different theologies that have emerged out of impoverished communities, and Vinay Samuel and Chris Sugden's *Sharing Jesus in the Two-Thirds World* brings together reflections from evangelical theologians around the world, including Rene Padilla, David Lim, and Kwame Bediako, concerning faithful gospel witness amid religious pluralism, strife, and poverty.

Bryant Myers's tandem of *Walking with the Poor* and *Working with the Poor* combines a theology of poverty and the practice of transformational development. While *Walking* provides a theological understanding of poverty as well as principles of poverty alleviation via transformational development, *Working* provides stories and models from practitioners around the world, including Joy Alvarez, Sarone Ole Sena, and Corina Villacorta. A U.S.-based resource that translates theology into workbook form is Deanna Carlson's *The Welfare of My Neighbor* and accompanying *Workbook and Supplemental Guide* put together by Amy Sherman. The genius of Sherman's workbook lies in its user-friendly format, offering chapters like "Sixty Six Ways to Love Your Neighbor Off of Welfare" and "Christ-Centered Welfare-to-Work Ministries," which gives an annotated listing of organizations working with and for the poor. It is somewhat dated (published in 1999), but it continues to be a goldmine of practical insights and networking opportunities.

Developing the biblical, theological, and practical conviction of God's heart for the poor leads to deeper thinking about what has become known among missionaries and development practitioners as "incarnational ministry." As the phrase suggests, incarnational ministry is a model of Christian service that is based upon the miracle of Christmas—the God-become-human event. As God chose to become one of us in order to convey the living message of redemption, so too missionaries have "incarnated" into cultures other than their own in order to establish real presence and to form just relationships between the rich and the poor in order to bear witness to the Good News of the kingdom. Urban ministry practitioners call this "relocation"—one of the three Rs of community development, the other two being "redistribution" and "reconciliation." The CCDA handbook, *Restoring At-Risk Communities*, explains the virtues of relocation and states, "Relocation transforms 'you, them, and theirs' to 'we, us, and ours.' Effective ministries plant and build communities of believers that have a personal stake in the development of their neighborhoods."[18]

Sherwood Lingenfelter and Marvin Mayers's *Ministering Cross-Culturally* and the late Paul Hiebert and Eloise Hiebert Meneses's *Incarnational Ministry* have proven helpful in better understanding the incarnational approach. As cultural anthropologists committed to sensitive and effective world evangelization, these authors provide practical principles for understanding other cultures and for developing authentic relationships across cultures. Although they write primarily with missionaries in mind (in the traditional sense of the word), their insights apply directly to what is needed to bridge the gap between urban and suburban cultures.

Several journeys of incarnational ministry attest to the effectiveness of this approach to bearing witness to the gospel in impoverished communities. New Zealander Viv Grigg's *Companion to the Poor: Christ in the Urban Slums* tells his story of living in Damayan Lagi, a squatter community in the megacity of Manila. Grigg's story inspired the formation of several mission organizations, such as Servants Among Asia's Poor and the U.S.-based Servant Partners. Missionaries who work with these organizations assume an incarnational approach wherever they are sent. Jean Thomas's *At Home with the Poor* tells the story of him and his wife, Joy, living and ministering in Fond-des-Blancs, Haiti. Jean and Joy met at the Voice of Calvary Ministries in Jackson, Mississippi, where they internalized the three Rs of community development and then implemented them in one of the poorest parts of one of the poorest nations in the world—Haiti. The fact that Jean is Haitian makes up one of the unique aspects of their story because their call to incarnational ministry has involved a return home. "I knew the minute I arrived in Fond-des-Blancs that I was home," he writes, "home where the Lord wanted me—*at home with the poor*."[19]

In the United States, Wayne Gordon's relocation into the innercity of Chicago's Westside and the remarkable model of church-based holistic ministry that emerged from it are documented in his autobiographical *Real Hope in Chicago*, while Robert Lupton's *Theirs Is the Kingdom* tells his compelling story of moving into inner-city Atlanta and learning with and from the poor about how to participate in kingdom transformation. Shane Claiborne's *The Irresistible Revolution* chronicles the story of The Simple Way, a way of life and service among the poor in inner-city Philadelphia that has spearheaded what is being called today "the new monasticism." While students at Eastern University a Christian liberal arts school in suburban St.

Davids, Pennsylvania—Claiborne and others went to Calcutta and
spent a summer with the famous nun of *agape* love, Mother Teresa.
There they learned simple ways to love the poorest of the poor, while
assuming poverty themselves. Upon their return to the U.S., they took
residence in Kensington, a poor section in the heart of Philadelphia,
and defined their lives this way: "To love God. To love people. To
follow Jesus." The Simple Way is but one expression of this new
revolutionary monasticism.

Scott A. Bessenecker's *The New Friars: The Emerging Movement
Serving the World's Poor* brings together many of these stories, including Grigg's, Claiborne's, and many others, and distills replicable
and doable principles of an incarnational lifestyle for all who desire
to live out the gospel among the poor. Appendix A, "How to Join
the New Friars," gives descriptions of various organizations to which
we can look for guidance as well as practical suggestions for simple
living. An even more practical book is Jimmy and Janet Dorrell's
Plunge2Poverty, which provides a 42-hour poverty simulation program
wherein middle-class participants experience a short but intense concentrated time of being without. The book's many testimonies from
"poverty simulation graduates" inspire readers, and its step-by-step
instructions serve as a manual for churches and small groups to take
a guided plunge into poverty. The hope, of course, is to better prepare
people to enter into a more long-term, experience-based incarnational
lifestyle and ministry for the sake of the poor.

Adopting a simpler lifestyle than our consumerist society encourages is a necessary part of developing just, incarnational relationships
among the poor. Richard Foster's classic *The Freedom of Simplicity*
lays the biblical and historical foundation for this countercultural life
posture, while Christine Sine's *Godspace* shows the way of becoming
in tune with God's rhythms and thus doing mission as an outflow of an
authentic spiritual life. A Canadian-based magazine called *Geez: Holy
Mischief in an Age of Fast Faith* offers creative insights and practical
suggestions to defy the winds of consumerism and to restore meaning
into our lives by living more simply and serving the poor. Similarly,
a PBS video series called *Affluenza* and *Escape from Affluenza* has
been used by churches, small groups, and nonprofit organizations to
help them understand the inseparable connection between what they
aspire to do in service to others and their own lifestyles.

Allowing God's heart for the world's poor to grip us and then
motivate us to take on an incarnational presence among them makes

up a skill set that creates kingdom sensitivity, and the aforementioned resources can help us develop this. Just like understanding biblical mission from a holistic perspective and understanding and harnessing racial and cultural diversity, effective *border crossing* over the urban-suburban divide also depends on our ability to develop just, incarnational relationships between the rich and the poor.

It may sound to some that we are calling people to enroll in three years of seminary training in holistic, multicultural, and incarnational ministry. It certainly would not hurt to do that, and indeed, there are seminaries, graduate programs, and institutes that specialize in these emphases.[20] For the busy practitioner, however, enrolling in such a program may not be realistic. In that case, we hope this chapter can serve as a guide for self-study that can better prepare you for the adventure of crossing the urban-suburban divide in partnership together for the sake of the kingdom.

Notes

Introduction

1. Scott Oostdyk, in an interview by Laurie Carter, "Urban-Suburban Church Partnerships—Lessons from a Church Leader," *Workbook and Supplemental Guide: Applying the Principles Found in the Welfare of My Neighbor*, ed. Amy L. Sherman (Washington, DC: Family Research Council, 1999), 53.

2. Martin Luther King Jr., address at a workshop on civil disobedience at Southern Christian Leadership Conference staff retreat, November 29, 1967, Martin Luther King Jr. Papers, 1950–1968, Martin Luther King Jr. Center for Nonviolent Social Change, Inc., Atlanta, Georgia.

3. Stewart Burns, *To the Mountaintop: Martin Luther King Jr.'s Sacred Mission to Save America: 1955–1968* (New York: HarperSanFrancisco, 2004), 324.

4. Dennis Farney, "River of Despair," *Wall Street Journal*, October 19, 1989.

Chapter 1 Location and Beyond

1. Thomas J. DiFilippo, *The History and Development of Upper Darby Township*, 2nd ed. (Upper Darby, PA: Upper Darby Historical Society, 1992), 125.

2. Thomas J. DiFilippo, telephone conversation with Al Tizon, July 27, 2006. DiFilippo, however, does not believe that white residents are fleeing from people of color; they are simply moving to better places because they can.

3. Nicholas Lemann, *The Promised Land: The Great Black Migration and How It Changed America* (New York: Alfred A. Knopf, 1991), 6, 70.

4. Ronald Takaki, *A Different Mirror: A History of Multicultural America* (New York: Back Bay Books, 1993), 312–13.

5. Dudley Kirk and Earl Huyck, "Overseas Migration from Europe Since World War II," *American Sociological Review* 19, no. 4 (August 1954): 447.

6. Albert Y. Hsu, *The Suburban Christian: Finding Spiritual Vitality in the Land of Plenty* (Downers Grove, IL: InterVarsity, 2006), 33–49.

7. Kenneth T. Jackson, *Crabgrass Frontier: The Suburbanization of the United States* (New York: Oxford University Press, 1985), 233.

8. Mark D. Bjelland, *Thinking Regionally: Justice, the Environment, and City Planning*, Crossroads Monograph Series no. 29 (Wynnewood, PA: Evangelicals for Social Action, 1999), 16.

9. Ibid., 30.

10. Robert D. Lupton, *Renewing the City: Reflections on Community Development and Urban Renewal* (Downers Grove, IL: InterVarsity, 2005), 126.

11. Hsu, *Suburban Christian*, 22.

12. Alexander von Hoffman, *House by House, Block by Block: The Rebirth of America's Urban Neighborhoods* (Oxford: Oxford University Press, 2003).

13. Paul S. Grogan and Tony Proscio, *Comeback Cities* (Boulder, CO: Westview, 2000), 3–9, 48–61.

14. David Claerbaut, *Urban Ministry in a New Millennium* (Waynesboro, GA: Authentic Media, 2005), 36; Robert D. Lupton, "Suburbanization of Poverty," Urban Perspectives (March 2008), www.fesministries.org/up/index.html (accessed March 18, 2008).

15. Hsu, *Suburban Christian*, 21–23.

16. Elvin K. Wyly and Daniel J. Hammel, "Islands of Decay in Seas of Renewal," *Housing Policy Debate* 10, no. 4 (1999): 711–71.

17. William Julius Wilson, *The Truly Disadvantaged* (Chicago: University of Chicago Press, 1987), 6–8.

18. Claerbaut, *Urban Ministry*, 37.

19. Ibid.

20. John C. Raines, "Preface," in *The Work of Latino Ministry: Hispanic Protestant Churches in Philadelphia*, a study commissioned by the Pew Charitable Trusts (February 1994), i.

21. Bjelland, *Thinking Regionally*, 18.

22. Hsu, *Suburban Christian*, 12–14.

23. Ibid., 178.

Part 2 Why We Do It

1. John H. Yoder, *The Original Revolution: Essays on Christian Pacifism* (Scottdale, PA: Herald Press, 1971), 28.

Chapter 2 The Call to Radical Community

1. Waldron Scott, *Bring Forth Justice* (Grand Rapids: Eerdmans, 1980), 55.

2. The following description of *ideal Israel* is based on the arrangement and interpretation of Old Testament material concerning equity by Stephen Mott and Ronald J. Sider, *Economic Justice: A Biblical Paradigm*, Crossroads Monograph Series no. 26 (Wynnewood, PA: Evangelicals for Social Action, 1999), 31–46. See also Christopher J. H. Wright, *An Eye for an Eye* (Downers Grove, IL: InterVarsity, 1983), 54–55.

3. Lowell Noble, *From Oppression to Jubilee Justice* (Jackson, MS: Urban Verses, 2007), 83–89.

4. Stephen C. Mott, *Biblical Ethics and Social Change* (New York: Oxford University Press, 1982), 59–64.

5. Mott and Sider, *Economic Justice*, 31. For their statement, "The contrast between early Israel and surrounding societies was striking," the authors credit Roland de Vaux, *Ancient Israel: Its Life and Institutions*, vol. 1, trans. John McHugh (London: Darton, Longman and Todd, 1961), 164.

6. Mott and Sider, *Economic Justice*, 41.

7. John Bright, *The Kingdom of God* (Nashville: Abingdon, 1953), 60–70.

8. Ibid., 67.

9. Thomas D. Hanks, *God So Loved the Third World* (Maryknoll, NY: Orbis, 1983), 97–104. Hanks strengthens the case for Jesus referring to the Jubilee Year in his inaugural speech by pointing out how Jesus inserted Isaiah 58:6, "to let the oppressed go free," into his rendering of Isaiah 61 (Luke 4:18).

10. Noble, *From Oppression to Jubilee Justice*, 24.

11. John H. Yoder, *Politics of Jesus* (Grand Rapids: Eerdmans, 1972), 34–39, 64–77.

12. Arthur G. Gish, *Living in Christian Community* (Scottdale, PA: Herald, 1979), 24.

13. Donald B. Kraybill, *The Upside Down Kingdom* (Scottdale, PA: Herald, 1978), 136.

14. Ibid.

15. Ronald J. Sider, *Rich Christians in an Age of Hunger: Moving from Affluence to Generosity*, 5th ed. (Dallas: Word, 2005), 76.

16. Ibid., 81–86.

17. Ibid., 82.

18. Ronald J. Sider, ed., *For They Shall Be Fed: Scripture Readings and Prayers for a Just World* (Dallas: Word, 1997), 101.

19. Ibid.

20. Craig L. Blomberg, *Neither Poverty nor Riches: A Biblical Theology of Possessions* (Downers Grove, IL: InterVarsity, 2001), 162.

21. See Craig S. Keener, *1–2 Corinthians* (Cambridge: Cambridge University Press, 2005), 203–4. The author makes a case for Paul taking advantage of the "friendly competition" between Corinth and Macedonia to motivate Corinthian Christians to give sacrificially toward the collection.

22. William F. Albright, *The Biblical Period from Abraham to Ezra* (New York: Harper and Row, 1949), 5.

23. Burton L. Goddard, "Hebrew, Hebrews," in *New International Dictionary of the Bible*, ed. J. D. Douglas and Merrill C. Tenney (Grand Rapids: Zondervan, 1987), 425.

24. J. Daniel Hays, *From Every People and Nation: A Biblical Theology of Race* (Downers Grove, IL: InterVarsity, 2003), 30–31.

Chapter 3 The Call to Spirit-Empowered, Holistic Mission

1. Walter Brueggemann, *Living Toward a Vision: Biblical Reflections on Shalom* (New York: United Church Press, 1982), 15–16. Brueggemann claims that no one biblical word captures the well-being of all of existence, but *shalom* comes close.

2. Bryant Myers, *Walking with the Poor: Principles and Practices of Transformational Development* (Maryknoll, NY: Orbis, 1999), 27.

3. Yoder, *Politics of Jesus*, 147–48.

4. Melba P. Maggay, *Transforming Society* (Oxford: Regnum, 1994), 16.

5. Myers, *Walking with the Poor*, 40.

6. J. Rodman Williams, "Baptism in the Holy Spirit," in *Dictionary of Pentecostal and Charismatic Movements*, ed. Stanley M. Burgess and Gary B. McGee (Grand Rapids: Zondervan, 1988), 42, 45.

7. Douglas Petersen, *Not by Might nor by Power* (Oxford: Regnum, 1996), 78.

8. Peter Kuzmic, "Pentecostals Respond to Marxism," in *Called and Empowered: Global Mission in Pentecostal Perspective*, ed. Murray W. Dempster, Byron Klaus, and Douglas Petersen (Peabody, MA: Hendrickson, 1991), 160.

9. For examples of a fuller treatment of this shift, see Rudolph Schnackenburg, *God's Rule and Kingdom*, trans. J. Holland-Smith and W. J. O'Hara (New York: Herder and Herder, 1965); Mortimer Arias, *Announcing the Reign of God: Evangelization and the Subversive Memory of Jesus* (Minneapolis: Fortress, 1984), 55–67.

10. Leslie Newbigin, *The Open Secret*, rev. ed. (Grand Rapids: Eerdmans, 1995), 40.

11. Arias, *Announcing the Reign of God*, xv, 12, 55–67.

12. The difference is indeed simply a matter of preference. For example, while ESA prefers "holistic," CCDA prefers "wholistic." Other words used by advocates of this kind of comprehensive mission include "integral," "transformational," and "word and deed." These are essentially interchangeable.

13. Hanks, *God So Loved*, 53; see also 43–60.

Part 3 How We Do (and Don't Do) It

1. John M. Perkins, "What Is Christian Community Development?" in *Restoring At-Risk Communities*, ed. John M. Perkins (Grand Rapids: Baker, 1995), 18.

2. Michael O. Emerson and Christian Smith, *Divided by Faith* (Oxford: Oxford University Press, 2000), 16–17.

3. Ibid., 135–36.

Chapter 4 Partnership Essentials

1. The findings of this consultation can be found in Vinay Samuel and Chris Sugden, eds., *Sharing Jesus in the Two-Thirds World: Evangelical Christologies from the Contexts of Poverty, Powerlessness, and Religious Pluralism*, papers of the First Conference of Evangelical Mission Theologians from the Two-Thirds World, Bangkok, Thailand, March 22–25, 1982 (Grand Rapids: Eerdmans, 1984).

2. For a more detailed account of the rift that planted the seed for INFEMIT, see Chris Sugden, "Evangelicals and Wholistic Evangelism," in *Proclaiming Christ in Christ's Way*, ed. Vinay Samuel and Albrecht Hauser (Oxford: Regnum, 1989), 29–51.

3. Ibid., 38.

4. Emerson and Smith, *Divided by Faith*, 7.

5. Robert J. Schreiter, *Reconciliation: Mission and Ministry in a Changing Social Order* (Maryknoll, NY: Orbis, 1992), 45.

6. Spencer Perkins and Chris Rice, *More Than Equals: Racial Healing for the Sake of the Gospel*, rev. ed. (Downers Grove, IL: InterVarsity, 2000), 20.

7. Racial Profiling Data Collection Resource Center of Northeastern University, "History of Racial Profiling Analysis," www.racialprofilinganalysis.neu.edu/back ground/history.php (accessed March 2, 2007).

8. "MSA National Condemns Recent Attack on Palestinian Students in Greensboro, North Carolina," www.msanational.org/news/6/91/ (accessed April 26, 2007).

9. Martin Luther King Jr., speech given at Western Michigan University, 1963, www.wmich.edu/library/archives/mlk/q-a.html (accessed February 17, 2007).

10. Perkins, ed., Restoring At-Risk Communities, 22.

11. Perkins and Rice, More Than Equals.

12. Raleigh Washington and Glen Kehrein, Breaking Down Walls: A Model for Reconciliation in an Age of Racial Strife (Chicago: Moody, 1993).

13. Melba P. Maggay, "Engaging Culture," Missiology 33, no. 1 (January 2005): 62.

14. Perkins and Rice, More Than Equals, 19.

15. Ibid.

16. Chris Rice, phone interview with Al Tizon, May 20, 2008.

17. Perkins and Rice, More Than Equals, 24, 241–42.

18. F. Albert Tizon, "Team-Building in a Cross-Cultural Context," in Leadership and Team-Building, ed. Roger Heuser (Matthews, NC: CMR, 1999), 254–55

19. Washington and Kehrein, Breaking Down Walls, 94–97.

20. Perkins and Rice, More Than Equals, 230; see also 227–37.

21. Ibid., 230.

22. "The Witness of Spencer Perkins," Reconcilers, Spring 1998, 9.

Chapter 5 Dos and Don'ts for Both Urban and Suburban Groups

1. Wayne L. Gordon, Real Hope in Chicago (Grand Rapids: Zondervan, 1995), 159–60.

2. Mother Teresa, cited in Shane Claiborne, The Irresistible Revolution (Grand Rapids: Zondervan, 2006), 89.

3. Brenda Salter McNeil and Rick Richardson, The Heart of Racial Justice (Downers Grove, IL: InterVarsity, 2004), 61, 63.

4. Ibid., 60–61.

5. Mark Labberton, The Dangerous Act of Worship: Living God's Call to Justice (Downers Grove, IL: InterVarsity, 2006), 14.

6. Heidi R. Unruh, "Six Qualities of Healthy Partnerships," unpublished manuscript presented at the Knoxville Compassion Coalition, September 27, 2004, 7.

7. Carey Davis, "Missional Renewal of the Church in a Culturally Diverse World," unpublished paper written for a DMin seminar on urban ministry, Palmer Theological Seminary, 2004.

8. Unruh, "Six Qualities," 7.

9. Gordon, Real Hope in Chicago, 156.

10. Perkins and Rice, More Than Equals, 210.

11. Ibid., 58.

12. Unruh, "Six Qualities," 7–8.

13. Carey Davis, personal interview by Al Tizon, Philadelphia, Pennsylvania, April 24, 2007.

14. Washington and Kehrein, Breaking Down Walls, 117 18.

15. Ibid., 117.

16. Oostdyk, cited in Carter, "Urban-Suburban Church Partnerships," 53–54.

17. "STEP (Strategies to Elevate People)," in *The Welfare of My Neighbor*, ed. Deanna Carlson (Washington DC: Family Research Council, 1999), 82.

18. Oostdyk, cited in Carter, "Urban-Suburban Church Partnerships," 53.

Chapter 6 Dos and Don'ts for Urban Partners

1. Claerbaut, *Urban Ministry*, 115.

2. Eugene Rivers, "No Cheap Reconciliation," *Reconcilers*, Summer 1997, 6.

3. Perkins and Rice, *More Than Equals*, 55.

4. Ibid., 139–40.

5. Ibid., 246.

6. Ibid., 130.

7. "Why YUBM," www.yubm.org/Why_YUBM.htm (accessed April 17, 2007).

8. Perkins and Rice, *More Than Equals*, 138.

9. National Hispanic Leadership Conference, "Apostolic Partnerships," www.nhclc.org/about/apos_partnerships.html (accessed April 7, 2007).

10. Samuel Rodriguez, cited in Tim Stafford, "The Call of Samuel," *Christianity Today*, September 2006, www.christianitytoday.com/ct/2006/september/31.82.html (accessed April 17, 2007).

11. Ibid.

12. Charles Kraft, *Anthropology for Christian Witness* (Maryknoll, NY: Orbis, 1996), 76–77.

13. Paulo Freire, *Pedagogy of the Oppressed* (New York: Continuum, 1970), 32–34, 122–66.

14. Wallace C. Smith, lecture on multiculturalism and racism, Current Issues in Urban Mission, Palmer Theological Seminary, Wynnewood, Pennsylvania, March 26, 2007.

15. Shane Claiborne, lecture given on incarnational ministry, Current Issues in Urban Mission, Palmer Theological Seminary, Wynnewood, Pennsylvania, April 16, 2007. To know more about The Simple Way, go to www.thesimpleway.org.

16. Hsu, *Suburban Christian*, 179–81.

17. Davis, personal interview.

18. Hsu, *Suburban Christian*, 13.

Chapter 7 Dos and Don'ts for Suburban Partners

1. Harvie Conn and Manuel Ortiz, *Urban Ministry: The Kingdom, the City, & the People of God* (Downers Grove, IL: InterVarsity, 2001), 168–69.

2. Ray Bakke, *The Urban Christian* (Downers Grove, IL: InterVarsity, 1987), 63.

3. Ruby Barcelona, "The Face of the Poor," *Patmos* 11, no. 2 (1995): 3.

4. Bob Lupton, Peggy Lupton, and Gloria Yancy, "Relocation: Living in the Community," in Perkins, ed., *Restoring At-Risk Communities*, 89.

5. Perkins and Rice, *More Than Equals*, 56, 194.

6. Perkins, ed., *Restoring At-Risk Communities*, 21–22. Since developing the three Rs, the Christian Community Development Association (CCDA) has added five more important principles: (1) leadership development, (2) listening to community,

(3) church-based, (4) holistic approach, and (5) empowerment. For a fuller discussion of all eight principles, see Wayne Gordon, "The Eight Components of Christian Community Development," CCDA website: www.ccda.org/?p=9 (accessed January 18, 2008).

7. See, for example, Ken Baker, "The Incarnational Model: Perception of Deception?" *Evangelical Missions Quarterly* 38, no. 1 (January 2002): 16–24; Harriet Hill, "Incarnational Ministry: A Critical Examination," *Evangelical Missions Quarterly* 26, no. 2 (April 1990): 196–201.

8. Lupton, Lupton, and Yancy, "Relocation," 75.

9. Ibid., 87.

10. Claiborne, *Irresistible Revolution*, 121–22.

11. Bernard T. Adeney, *Strange Virtues: Ethics in a Multicultural World* (Downers Grove, IL: InterVarsity, 1995), 51.

12. Melba P. Maggay, "Some Do's and Don'ts," in *Communicating Cross-Culturally: Towards a New Context for Missions in the Philippines*, ed. Melba P. Maggay (Quezon City: New Day, 1989), 27.

13. Davis, personal interview.

14. Ibid.

15. Ronnie Mapanoo, email correspondence with Al Tizon regarding the Church-to-Church Partnership in Community Transformation Program, February 12, 2007. Mapanoo served as LIGHT Ministries' Executive Director from 1998 to 2007.

16. DEACON Team/Action International Ministries, *Christian Community Development* (San Juan, Metro-Manila: ACTION, 1994), 26. Inspired by real events, the basketball project is used in this workbook as a case study of the importance of listening to community leaders as a principle of community development that is Christian.

17. Richard A. Swenson, *Margins* (Colorado Springs: NavPress, 1992), 35.

18. Hsu, *Suburban Christian*, 177–78.

19. One of the assignments for the course Current Issues in Urban Mission, which was offered in Spring 2007 at Palmer Theological Seminary, required the students to keep a journal. The quote comes from a journal entry of a male, African-American M.Div. student reflecting upon a class field trip to a poor Latino section of northeast Philadelphia.

20. Davis, personal interview.

Chapter 8 Partnership Fruit

1. John Piper, *The Dangerous Duty of Delight: The Glorified God and the Satisfied Soul* (Portland, OR: Multnomah, 2001), 13.

2. For a definitive article by Piper on Christian hedonism, go to www.desiringgod .org/ResourceLibrary/Articles/ByDate/2006/1797_We_Want_You_to_Be_a_Christian Hedonist (accessed June 8, 2007). Or for a full treatise on the subject, see John Piper, *Desiring God: Meditations of a Christian Hedonist*, 10th anniversary expanded ed. (Sisters, OR: Multnomah, 1996).

3. Ken Fong, cited in Glen Kinoshita, "On Earth as It Is in Heaven," *Prism*, March–April 2006, 10.

4. Adam Edgerly, cited in ibid., 11.

5. Fong, cited in ibid., 13, 37.

6. Ibid., 37.

7. Carey Davis, "CityLights: Considering the Value of an Urban-Suburban Partnership through the Lenses of Social Capital and *Koinonia*," DMin dissertation, Palmer Theological Seminary, 2007. Davis appropriately notes that "defining social capital is an imprecise exercise" (29). Our definition comes from a composite of the various sources with which Davis interacts in her dissertation.

8. Davis, personal interview.

9. Davis, "Considering the Value," 1.

10. Ibid., 53.

11. Carey Davis, telephone conversation with Al Tizon, May 22, 2007.

12. Unruh, "Six Qualities," 5.

13. Gordon, *Real Hope in Chicago*, 155–68. More of the partnership between Lawndale Community Church and Christ Church of Oakbrook will be discussed in chapter 9.

14. Al Tizon, "Ang Pagyabong ng Komunidad at ang Iglesia," in *Hasik-Unlad: An Experience in Community Development Training*, ed. Institute for Studies in Asian Church and Culture (Quezon City: ISACC, 1998), 83–85.

15. Kraft, *Anthropology for Christian Witness*, 69–96. Kraft identifies seven myopic qualities of a monocultural perspective: (1) ethnocentrism, (2) absolutism, (3) naïve realism, (4) superiority, (5) disrespect for other cultures, (6) faulty evaluation of other cultures, and (7) use of pejorative terms to describe other cultures.

16. Tom Sine, *Wild Hope: Crises Facing the Human Community on the Threshold of the 21st Century* (Dallas: Word, 1991), 262–63.

17. Edgerly, cited in Kinoshita, "On Earth as It Is in Heaven," 37.

18. Adam Edgerly, email correspondence with Al Tizon, June 20, 2007.

19. Roger S. Greenway, "Urban-Suburban Coalitions for Mission and Renewal," *Urban Mission* 2, no. 4 (March 1985): 3.

20. Unruh, "Six Qualities," 4.

21. Edgerly, cited in Kinoshita, "On Earth as It Is in Heaven," 38.

22. Mary Nelson, personal interview with Al Tizon at Bethel New Life, Chicago, Illinois, June 17, 2007.

Chapter 9 Leap of Faith

1. Gordon, *Real Hope in Chicago*.

2. Gordon describes this partnership in some detail in ibid., 156–63.

3. Cathleen Young, "Pastor, People Send Their Hopes Aloft," *Chicago Tribune*, November 24, 1983.

4. In addition to Gordon's words about Chiu in *Real Hope in Chicago*, see also Connie Sowa-Wachala, "Radiology Volunteer Gives from the Heart," *Chicago Tribune*, July 29, 1998.

5. Gordon, *Real Hope in Chicago*, 163.

6. Dan Meyer, email correspondence with Al Tizon, September 20, 2007.

7. Ibid.

8. Ibid.

9. Bill and Nan Barnhart, email correspondence with Al Tizon, September 26, 2007.

10. Meyer, email correspondence.

11. George W. Bush, in "President Bush Discusses Faith-Based Initiatives in Tennessee," www.whitehouse.gov/news/releases/2003/02/20030210-1.html (accessed September 12, 2007).

12. Michael McCormick Huentelman, email correspondence with Al Tizon, August 13, 2007.

13. Lina Thompson, email correspondence with Al Tizon, July 13, 2007.

14. Robert A. Romero, "White Center church gets 'divine makeover,' " www.king5.com/localnews/stories/NW_060907WABchurchmakeoverKS.30a80e78.html (accessed September 13, 2007).

15. Huentelman, email correspondence.

16. Timothy Cole, telephone conversation with Al Tizon, June 14, 2007.

17. Timothy Cole, "CVC 2007 Charity Profile," www.cvc.vipnet.org/cgi-bin/cvc-view.cgi?org_id=1a07116151827211800 (accessed September 17, 2007).

18. Urban-suburban church partnership is one level toward which WDN works. To see the other levels, go to www.worddcednetwork.org.

Chapter 10 Expanding to the City

1. For a general history of IVCF, see Keith Hunt and Gladys Hunt, *For Christ and the University: The Story of InterVarsity Christian Fellowship of the U.S.A./1940–1990* (Downers Grove, IL: InterVarsity, 1991).

2. Randy White, personal interview by Al Tizon, October 29, 2007. For an account of the Jesus Lane lot outreach, see Oliver R. Barclay, *Whatever Happened to the Jesus Lane Lot?* (Leicester, England: InterVarsity, 1977). See also Rick Richardson, "Reshaping Evangelicalism's Future Leaders: How Short Term Urban Service Experiences are Influencing the Theology, Social Change Strategies, Cultural Awareness, and Social Connections of a Group of Evangelical College Students," PhD dissertation, Trinity International University, 2007, 61–62.

3. Richardson, "Reshaping Evangelicalism's Future Leaders," 65–78.

4. For the full story, see Barbara Benjamin, *The Impossible Community: A Story of Hardship & Hope at Brooklyn College in New York* (Downers Grove, IL: InterVarsity, 1978).

5. Hammond's passionate work to raise awareness of urban issues includes spearheading IVCF urban conferences in Washington, DC (1980), San Francisco (1983), and Chicago (1986). He also codeveloped the urban ministry–informed *Life Study Bible* with Ray Bakke. At Hammond's retirement party, Paula Fuller, IVCF's director of multiethnic ministry, honored him by saying, "If it weren't for you, many of us wouldn't be in the room." "Pete Hammond Ends 41 Years with InterVarsity," www.intervarsity.org/news/pete-hammond-ends-41-years-- (accessed December 12, 2007).

6. Edward Gilbreath, *Reconciliation Blues: A Black Evangelical's Inside View of White Christianity* (Downers Grove, IL: InterVarsity, 2006), 62.

7. Brenda Salter McNeil, personal interview by Al Tizon, August 29, 2007.

8. Ibid.

9. InterVarsity Christian Fellowship, "Urban Projects," www.intervarsity.org/urban/ (accessed October 30, 2007).

10. Fresno Institute for Urban Leadership (FIFUL), "About FIFUL," www.fiful.org/about.htm (accessed October 28, 2007).

11. White, personal interview.

12. Ibid. Another metaphor that White uses extensively for these Urban Projects are "onramps" to global urban awareness. See Randy White, *Encounter God in the City: Onramps to Personal and Community Transformation* (Downers Grove, IL: InterVarsity, 2006).

13. Ibid.

14. McNeil, personal interview.

15. Harambee Center, "About," www.harambee.org/?page_id=2# (accessed October 31, 2007). John Perkins founded Harambee in 1982.

16. White, personal interview.

17. Ibid.

18. InterVarsity Christian Fellowship, "Urban Projects." Regarding both the content and method of teaching employed by many Urban Project directors, see Randy White, "Driver's Ed: Leader's Guide to Designing Urban Experiential Discipleship Events," www.ivpress.com/title/disc/3389supplement.pdf (accessed October 30, 2007), which is an online supplement to White, *Encounter God in the City*.

19. White, personal interview.

20. Ibid. White calls this idea the "North Star" of urban projects (i.e., the chief and ultimate end goal).

21. Josh Harper, personal interview with Al Tizon, October 30, 2007.

22. Richardson, "Reshaping Evangelicalism's Future Leaders," 306.

23. Ibid.

24. Josh Harper, personal interview.

25. Brenda Salter McNeil, email correspondence with Al Tizon, November 5, 2007.

26. White, personal interview.

27. Alec Hill, "From the President: Bay Area Urban Project," www.intervarsity.org/aboutus/president.php?id=2488 (accessed November 1, 2007).

28. Ibid.

29. Ibid. These statistical findings are based on an online survey of eighty-two alumni chosen by the Urban Project directors around the country. For more information on the methodology of the study, see Randy White, "National IVCF Urban Project Alumni Survey," unpublished manuscript, October 2002. See also Richardson, "Reshaping Evangelicalism's Future Leaders," which essentially asks the same research question, but because he used different methods, Richardson came up with different results. Both would agree, however, that Urban Projects have had a significant impact on college students.

30. White, "Urban Project Alumni Survey," 9.

31. "About FIFUL" (accessed November 2, 2007).

32. Mike Downey, email correspondence with Al Tizon, December 13, 2007.

33. Ibid.

34. Ibid.

35. For more information, see "Here's Life Inner City," www.hlic.org (accessed November 2, 2007).

36. For more information, go to www.missionyear.org (accessed December 12, 2007).

37. Justice for All, "About Us," www.jfa-nwiowa.org/AboutUs.dsp (accessed November 2, 2007).

38. Pat Vander Pol, email correspondence with Al Tizon, November 3, 2007.

39. Justice for All, "Home," www.jfa-nwiowa.org (accessed November 2, 2007).
40. Vander Pol, email correspondence.
41. Ibid.
42. Ibid.
43. C. J. Jones, cited in Vander Pol, email correspondence.
44. Vander Pol, email correspondence.
45. Ibid.

Chapter 11 Beyond Profit

1. Tom Phillips, telephone interview with Al Tizon, November 14, 2007.
2. Ibid.
3. Ibid.
4. Advance Memphis, "Hope for Memphis Urban Community," www.advance memphis.org (accessed November 8, 2007).
5. Marilyn Sadler, "The Poor Side of Town," *Memphis—The City Magazine*, September 2006, www.memphismagazine.com/gyrobase/Magazine/Content?image Index=6&oid=oid%3A20106 (accessed November 13, 2007).
6. Steve Nash, telephone interview with Al Tizon, November 13, 2007.
7. Advance Memphis, "Business Partners," www.advancememphis.org/index.php? page=business-partners (accessed November 15, 2007).
8. Nash, telephone interview.
9. Ibid.
10. Phillips, telephone interview.
11. Derrick Osborne, telephone interview with Al Tizon, November 20, 2007.
12. Ibid.
13. Ibid.
14. Phillips, telephone interview.
15. Osborne, telephone interview.
16. Ibid.
17. Geoffrey Bailey, "Success Stories," www.advancememphis.org/index.php? page=succeed (accessed November 20, 2007).
18. Mark J. Konkol, "Financial Failure Is Success Story," *Chicago Sun Times*, January 2, 2007.
19. The Foundation for Community Empowerment, "Analyze, Mobilize, Transform," www.fcedallas.org/Home/tabid/403/Default.aspx (accessed December 13, 2007).
20. FCE, "Board Chairman J. McDonald 'Don' Williams," www.fcedallas.org/Default.aspx?tabid=2054 (accessed December 14, 2007).
21. Robert Wilonsky, "Change Is Gonna Come," *Dallas Observer News*, August 17, 2006, www.dallasobserver.com/2006-08-17/news/change-is-gonna-come/full (accessed December 14, 2007).
22. FCE, "Our Beliefs," www.fcedallas.org/Home/ABOUTFCE/FromBeliefto Action/tabid/2022/Default.aspx (accessed December 18, 2007).
23. Wilonsky, "Change Is Gonna Come."
24. FCE, "Dallas Achieves," www.fcedallas.org/EducationSystemsChange/Dallas Achieves/tabid/2232/language/en-US/Default.aspx (accessed December 14, 2007).

25. Dallas Achieves Commission, www.dallasachieves.org/Default.aspx?tabid=317 (accessed December 14, 2007).

26. Wilonsky, "Change Is Gonna Come."

27. Ibid.

28. Chuck Wills, telephone interview with Al Tizon, November 29, 2007.

29. For more information about Rebuilding the Wall, Inc., go to www.rebuilding thewall.org. For more information about Shepherd Community Center, go to www .shepherdcommunity.org.

30. Aaron Loften, cited in Francesca Jarosz, "12 More Cross the Finish Line," *IndyStar*, www.outreachindiana.org/Portals/0/documents/Indy%20Star%20June %2010%202007.pdf (accessed December 4, 2007).

Chapter 12 Hall of Faith

1. Barbara J. Elliott, *Street Saints: Renewing America's Cities* (Philadelphia: Templeton Foundation, 2006), xx.

2. Hsu, *Suburban Christian*, 193.

3. Elliott, *Street Saints*, xix.

4. Refer to chapter 8, pp. 113–15, where we talk about CityLights in detail. See also Davis, "Considering the Value."

5. This newspaper is accessible online at www.southwestcdc.org/pdfs/SWGlobe Times.pdf.

6. Ted Behr, personal interview with Al Tizon, November 16 and 27, 2007.

7. Ibid.

8. Frank Rottier, personal interview with Al Tizon, November 16 and 27, 2007.

9. Pat Leidy, personal interview with Al Tizon, November 16 and 27, 2007.

10. Ibid.

11. Deborah Lee, telephone interview with Al Tizon, December 5, 2007.

12. Rottier, personal interview.

13. Behr, personal interview.

14. Leidy, personal interview.

15. Behr, personal interview.

16. Rottier, personal interview.

17. Chris Petersen, email correspondence with Al Tizon, November 27, 2007.

18. Lee, telephone interview.

19. John McCullough, telephone interview with Al Tizon, December 6, 2007.

20. Donna Henry, email correspondence with Al Tizon, November 27, 2007.

21. Gary VanderArk, telephone interview with Al Tizon, November 21, 2007.

22. As told by VanderArk, telephone interview.

23. Nancy Koontz, "Have You Met?" *Blacktie Colorado*, www.blacktie-colorado. com/haveyoumet/archive2.cfm?id=180 (accessed November 28, 2007).

24. Ibid.

25. VanderArk took part in the formation of Evangelical Concern in 1974, which had as its original goal to "solve all the problems of the inner city through resources in the suburbs."

26. Maureen Sieh, "Seven Youths Offer Lessons for Success," *Metro Voices,* blog. syracuse.com/metrovoices/2007/07/the_seven_students_honored_at.html (accessed November 27, 2007).

27. Discovery Institute, "Howard Ahmanson, Board of Directors," www.discovery .org/scripts/viewDB/index.php?command=view&id=23&isFellow=true (accessed December 5, 2007).

28. Howard Ahmanson Jr., telephone interview with Al Tizon, December 5, 2007.

29. Ibid.

30. Barbara Franzen, telephone interview with Al Tizon, December 2, 2007.

31. To read more about this story, see "Landlord Lawsuit Puts Gospel into Real-Life Context," www.covchurch.org/cov/news/item1505.html; and more recently, "Pastor Honored for Helping Tenants Defeat Slumlord," www.covchurch.org/cov/news/item5912 (accessed December 6, 2007).

32. Franzen, telephone interview.

33. Ibid.

Part 5 Almost Ready to Do It

1. Bill Borror, *What Is Holistic Ministry?* DVD, produced by Phil Olson (Wynnewood, PA: Evangelicals for Social Action, 2000).

Chapter 13 First Steps (or Just Do It!)

1. Lupton, *Renewing the City,* 19.

2. Ibid., 22.

3. Richard J. Foster, *Prayer: Finding the Heart's True Home* (New York: HarperSanFrancisco, 1992), 243.

4. Blomberg, *Neither Poverty nor Riches.*

5. Daniel Rickett, *Making Your Partnership Work: Finding Your Church's Unique Rhythm* (Enumclaw, WA: Winepress Publishing, 2002), 55.

6. David A. Anderson, *Multicultural Ministry* (Grand Rapids: Zondervan, 2004), 119.

7. Perkins and Rice, *More Than Equals,* 55–59

8. Al Tizon was serving as lead pastor of BCC at the time.

9. Refer to chapters 6 and 7, where several of the Dos and Don'ts deal with these issues.

10. Bob Moffitt, with Karla Tesch, *If Jesus Were Mayor* (Oxford, UK: Monarch, 2006), 275.

11. Tom Sine, *The Mustard Seed Conspiracy: You Can Make a Difference in Tomorrow's Troubled World* (Waco: Word, 1981); Tom Sine, *The New Conspirators: Creating the Future One Mustard Seed at a Time* (Downers Grove, IL: InterVarsity, 2008).

12. Tom Sine, *Mustard Seed Versus McWorld: Reinventing Life and Faith for the Future* (Grand Rapids: Baker, 1999), 22.

13. Moffitt, with Tesch, *If Jesus Were Mayor,* 286. See also 287–306, where the author provides an excellent seed project planning guide and a sample of how to use it.

14. There are many community surveys that ministry teams can use. For example, see survey questions found in Carl Dudley, *Community Ministry* (Bethesda, MD: Alban Institute, 2002), 195–96.

15. Daniel Rickett, *Building Strategic Relationships* (Pleasant Hill, CA: Pleasant Hill Media Center, 2000), 27.

16. Ibid., 25, 37.

17. For samples of partnership documentation, see Rickett, *Making Your Partnership Work*, 108–11.

Appendix 2

1. Al Tizon, "The Journey Continues," *Prism*, January–February 2008, 7.

2. Christopher J. H. Wright, *The Mission of God: Unlocking the Bible's Grand Narrative* (Downers Grove, IL: InterVarsity, 2006), 22.

3. Arthur F. Glasser, with Charles E. Van Engen, Dean S. Gilliland, and Shawn B. Redford, *Announcing the Kingdom: The Story of God's Mission in the Bible* (Grand Rapids: Baker, 2003), 17.

4. Hanks, *God So Loved*, xiii.

5. Elsa Tamez, *The Scandalous Message of James* (New York: Crossroad, 1990), 73–74.

6. Georgiana Preskar, *Diversity Addiction: The Cause and the Cure* (Bloomington, IN: AuthorHouse, 2007).

7. "Introduction," in *The Original African-American Heritage Study Bible* (Valley Forge, PA: Judson, 2007), v.

8. Melba P. Maggay, *Jew to the Jew, Greek to the Greek* (Quezon City: ISACC, 2001), 56.

9. Ronald Takaki, *A Different Mirror: A History of Multicultural America* (New York: Back Bay Books, 1993), 1–17.

10. Ibid., 16.

11. Emerson and Smith, *Divided by Faith*, 1.

12. Ibid., 11–17.

13. Norman Anthony Peart, *Separate No More* (Grand Rapids: Baker, 2000), 140.

14. Anderson, *Multicultural Ministry*, 14.

15. Ibid.

16. Sider, ed., *For They Shall Be Fed*, back cover. This book was originally published as *Cry Justice: The Bible on Hunger and Poverty* (New York and Ramsey, NJ: Paulist, 1980).

17. Benigno Beltran, *Christology of the Inarticulate* (Quezon City: Divine Word, 1987), ix.

18. Perkins, "What Is Community Development?" in Perkins, ed., *Restoring At-Risk Communities*, 22.

19. Jean L. Thomas with Lon Fendall, *At Home With the Poor* (Newberg, OR: Barclay, 2003), xiii.

20. A few of the institutions that are especially committed to preparing women and men for multicultural holistic ministry include the Oxford Centre for Mission Studies, www.ocms.ac.uk; the Sider Center for Ministry Public Policy at Palmer Theological Seminary, www.sidercenter.org/Display.asp?Page=siderhome; the Reconciliation Studies Program at Bethel University, http://cas.bethel.edu/dept/

anthropology/faculty/deyoung/reconciliation; the Center for Reconciliation at
Duke Divinity School, http://www.divinity.duke.edu/reconciliation/index.html;
the Chalmers Center at Covenant College, www.chalmers.org/site/index.php; the
John Perkins Center at Seattle Pacific University, www.spu.edu/depts/jperkins/
about_perkins.asp; and the CCDA Institute, www.ccda.org/?p=7.

Bibliography

Resources for Theologizing with Holistic Eyes

Study Bibles

Faith in Action Study Bible. Grand Rapids: Zondervan, 2005.
The Word in Life Study Bible. Nashville: Thomas Nelson, 1996.

Books

Bakke, Ray. *A Theology as Big as the City*. Downers Grove, IL: InterVarsity, 1997.

Conn, Harvie, and Manuel Ortiz. *Urban Ministry: The Kingdom, the City, & the People of God*. Downers Grove, IL: InterVarsity, 2001.

Costas, Orlando. *The Integrity of Mission*. San Francisco: Harper & Row, 1979.

De La Torre, Miguel. *Reading the Bible from the Margins*. Maryknoll, NY: Orbis, 2002.

Glasser, Arthur F. *Announcing the Kingdom: The Story of God's Mission in the Bible*. Grand Rapids: Baker, 2003.

Gornik, Mark. *To Live in Peace: Biblical Faith and the Changing Inner City*. Grand Rapids: Eerdmans, 2002.

Hanks, Thomas D. *God So Loved the Third World*. Maryknoll, NY: Orbis, 1983.

Keller, Timothy. *Ministries of Mercy: The Call of the Jericho Road.* Phillipsburg, NJ: P&R Publishing, 1997.

Lupton, Robert D. *Renewing the City: Reflections on Community Development and Urban Renewal.* Downers Grove, IL: InterVarsity, 2005.

Maggay, Melba P. *Transforming Society.* Oxford: Regnum, 1994.

Mott, Stephen C. *Biblical Ethics and Social Change.* New York: Oxford University Press, 1982.

Paris, Jenell Williams, and Margot Owen Eyring. *Urban Disciples: A Beginner's Guide to Serving God in the City.* Valley Forge, PA: Judson, 2000.

Perkins, John M., ed. *Restoring At-Risk Communities.* Grand Rapids: Baker, 1995.

Rusaw, Rick, and Eric Swanson. *The Externally Focused Church.* Loveland, CO: Group Publishing, 2004.

Samuel, Vinay, and Chris Sugden, eds. *Mission as Transformation.* Oxford: Regnum, 1999.

Scott, Waldron. *Bring Forth Justice.* Grand Rapids: Eerdmans, 1980.

Sherman, Amy L. *Restorers of Hope.* Wheaton: Crossway, 1997.

Sider, Ronald J., Heidi Rolland Unruh, and Philip N. Olson. *Churches That Make a Difference.* Grand Rapids: Baker, 2002.

Tamez, Elsa. *The Scandalous Message of James.* New York: Crossroad, 1990.

Wright, Christopher J. H. *The Mission of God: Unlocking the Bible's Grand Narrative.* Downers Grove, IL: InterVarsity, 2006.

Journals and Magazines

Prism: America's Alternative Evangelical Voice. Subscription information available at www.esa-online.org/Display.asp?Page=Prism.

Sojourners: Faith, Politics and Culture. Subscription information available at www.sojo.net.

Transformation: An International Journal of Holistic Mission Studies. Subscription information available at www.ocms.ac.uk/transformation.

Training Kits

Faith in Action Campaign Kit. Description and purchasing information available at www.putyourfaithinaction.org/Display. asp?page=FIAResources.

Holistic Ministry Starter Kit. Description and purchasing information available at www.esa-online.org/Display. asp?page=HolisticMinistryTools.

Selected Websites

Christian Community Development Association. www.ccda.org.

Christians Supporting Community Organizing. www.cscoweb. org.

Evangelicals for Social Action. www.esa-online.org.

Resources for Appreciating and Harnessing Cultural Diversity

Study Bibles

Aspire: The New Women of Color Study Bible. Grand Rapids: Zondervan, 2007.

The Original African-American Heritage Study Bible. Valley Forge, PA: Judson, 2007.

The People's Bible. New Revised Standard Version. Minneapolis: Fortress, forthcoming in 2008.

Books

Anderson, David A. *Multicultural Ministry: Finding Your Church's Unique Rhythm.* Grand Rapids: Zondervan, 2004.

Barndt, Joseph. *Understanding & Dismantling Racism: The Twentieth Century Challenge to White America.* Minneapolis: Fortress, 2007.

Conde-Frazier, Elizabeth, S. Steven Kang, and Gary A. Parrett. *A Many Colored Kingdom.* Grand Rapids: Baker Academic, 2004.

DeYoung, Curtiss P. *Coming Together: The Bible's Message in an Age of Diversity*. Valley Forge, PA: Judson, 1995.

———. *Reconciliation*. Valley Forge, PA: Judson, 1997.

Emerson, Michael O., and Christian Smith. *Divided by Faith*. Oxford: Oxford University Press, 2000.

Emerson, Michael O., Curtiss DeYoung, George Yancey, and Karen Chai Kim. *United by Faith*. Oxford: Oxford University Press, 2004.

Gilbreath, Edward. *Reconciliation Blues*. Downers Grove, IL: InterVarsity, 2006.

Hays, J. Daniel. *From Every People and Nation: A Biblical Theology of Race*. Downers Grove, IL: InterVarsity, 2003.

Maggay, Melba P. *Jew to the Jew, Greek to the Greek*. Quezon City, Philippines: ISACC, 2001.

McKenzie, Steven L. *All God's Children: A Biblical Critique of Racism*. Louisville: Westminster/John Knox, 1997.

McNeil, Brenda S., and Rick Richardson. *The Heart of Racial Justice*. Downers Grove, IL: InterVarsity, 2004.

Okholm, Dennis, ed. *The Gospel in Black and White: Theological Resources for Racial Reconciliation*. Downers Grove, IL: InterVarsity, 1997.

Peart, Norman A. *Separate No More*. Grand Rapids: Baker, 2000.

Perkins, Spencer, and Chris Rice. *More Than Equals: Racial Healing for the Sake of the Gospel*. Rev. ed. Downers Grove, IL: InterVarsity, 2000.

Schreiter, Robert J. *Reconciliation: Mission and Ministry in a Changing Social Order*. Maryknoll, NY: Orbis, 1992.

Takaki, Ronald. *A Different Mirror: A History of Multicultural America*. New York: Back Bay Books, 1993.

Volf, Miroslav. *Exclusion and Embrace*. Nashville: Abingdon, 1996.

Washington, Raleigh, and Glen Kehrein. *Breaking Down Walls: A Model for Reconciliation in an Age of Racial Strife*. Chicago: Moody, 1993.

Other Training Tools

"Intersect Culture" DVD. Available at www.christianvisionproject.
com/dvd-2006.html.

Selected Websites

Ethnic Harvest. www.ethnicharvest.org.
John Perkins Foundation for Development and Reconciliation. www.
jmpf.org.
Salter McNeil and Associates. www.saltermcneil.com.

Resources for Developing Just, Incarnational Relationships

Bible Helps

(See Study Bibles listed above.)
Sider, Ronald J., ed. *For They Shall Be Fed: Scripture Readings and Prayers for a Just World.* Dallas: Word, 1997.

Books

Beltran, Benigno. *Christology of the Inarticulate.* Quezon City, Philippines: Divine Word, 1987.

Bessenecker, Scott A. *The New Friars: The Emerging Movement Serving the World's Poor.* Downers Grove, IL: InterVarsity, 2006.

Blomberg, Craig. *Neither Poverty nor Riches: A Biblical Theology of Possessions.* Downers Grove, IL: InterVarsity Academic, 2001.

Christian, Jayakumar. *God of the Empty-Handed: Poverty, Power & the Kingdom of God.* Monrovia, CA: MARC, 1999.

Claiborne, Shane. *The Irresistible Revolution.* Grand Rapids: Zondervan, 2006.

Costas, Orlando. *Christ Outside the Gate: Mission Beyond Christendom.* Eugene, OR: Wipf and Stock, 2005.

Dorrell, Jimmy, and Janet Dorrell. *Plunge2Poverty.* Birmingham, AL: New Hope, 2007.

Fabella, Virginia, and R. S. Sugirtharajah, eds. *Dictionary of Third World Theologies*. Maryknoll, NY: Orbis, 2003.

Foster, Richard. *The Freedom of Simplicity*. Paperback ed. New York: HarperOne, 2005.

Gordon, Wayne. *Real Hope in Chicago*. Grand Rapids: Zondervan, 1995.

Grigg, Viv. *Companion to the Poor: Christ in the Urban Slums*. 2nd ed. Colorado Springs: Authentic and World Vision, 2004.

Hiebert, Paul G., and Eloise Hiebert Meneses. *Incarnational Ministry*. Grand Rapids: Baker Academic, 1995.

Lingenfelter, Sherwood, and Marvin K. Mayers. *Ministering Cross-Culturally*. 2nd ed. Grand Rapids: Baker Academic, 2003.

Lupton, Robert. *Theirs Is the Kingdom*. New York: HarperOne, 1989.

Myers, Bryant L. *Walking with the Poor: Principles and Practices of Transformational Development*. Maryknoll, NY: Orbis, 1999.

————, ed. *Working with the Poor*. Monrovia, CA: MARC, 1999.

Samuel, Vinay, and Chris Sugden, eds. *Sharing Jesus in the Two-Thirds World: Evangelical Christologies from the Contexts of Poverty, Powerlessness, and Religious Pluralism*. Papers of the First Conference of Evangelical Mission Theologians from the Two-Thirds World, Bangkok, Thailand, March 22–25, 1982. Grand Rapids: Eerdmans, 1984.

Sider, Ronald J. *Rich Christians in an Age of Hunger: Moving from Affluence to Generosity*. 5th ed. Dallas: Word, 2005.

Sine, Christine. *Godspace*. Newberg, OR: Barclay, 2006.

Thomas, Jean L., with Lon Fendall. *At Home with the Poor*. Newberg, OR: Barclay, 2003.

Magazine

Geez: Holy Mischief in an Age of Fast Faith. Subscription information available at www.geezmagazine.org.

Workbooks and Videos

"Affluenza" and "Escape from Affluenza" DVDs. Available at www.simpleliving.net/main/item.asp?itemid=934.

Carlson, Deanna. *The Welfare of My Neighbor.* Washington, DC: Family Research Council, 1999.

Sherman, Amy L., ed. *Workbook and Supplemental Guide.* Washington, DC: Family Research Council, 1999.

Selected Websites

Alternative for Simple Living. www.simpleliving.org.

Servant Partners. www.servantpartners.org.

Word Made Flesh. www.wordmadeflesh.org.

Ronald J. Sider is president of Evangelicals for Social Action and professor of theology, holistic ministry, and public policy at Palmer Theological Seminary. He is the author of the bestselling *Rich Christians in
an Age of Hunger* and *The Scandal of the Evangelical Conscience*.

John M. Perkins is cofounder of the Christian Community Development Association and director of the John M. Perkins Foundation for
Reconciliation and Development in Jackson, Mississippi. He is the
author of nine books, including *Let Justice Roll Down*.

Wayne L. Gordon is cofounder of the Christian Community Development Association and lead pastor of Lawndale Community Church
in inner-city Chicago where he has ministered for thirty years.

F. Albert Tizon is assistant professor of evangelism and holistic ministry at Palmer Theological Seminary and director of Network 9:35
of Evangelicals for Social Action. He is the author of *Transformation
after Lausanne: Radical Evangelical Mission in Global-Local Perspective* and numerous articles in publications such as *Prism* magazine,
Missionalia, *Radix*, and *Covenant Quarterly*.